A Lone Furrow

A retired police inspector, **Alan Stewart** specialised in poaching cases in the 1960s and 70s. Most of his service with Tayside Police from 1980 to 1993 was in CID in Perth and Drugs Branch at Force HQ. He was appointed Force Wildlife Crime Officer in 1993, a post he held until retirement in 2011. He lives in Perthshire with his wife Jan, two dogs and twenty domestic ducks. Alan Stewart was featured as one of BBC Scotland's Wildlife Detectives.

previous books by the author

Wildlife Detective (Argyll 2007)
The Thin Green Line (Argyll 2009)

A Lone
Furrow

**the continued fight
against wildlife crime**

ALAN STEWART

ARGYLL✣PUBLISHING

© Alan Stewart 2011

Argyll Publishing
Glendaruel
Argyll PA22 3AE
Scotland
www.argyllpublishing.co.uk

The rights of the author have been asserted by
him in accordance with the Copyright, Designs
and Patents Act 1988.

British Library Cataloguing-in-Publication Data.
A catalogue record for this book is available from the
British Library.

ISBN 978 1 906134 79 2

Printing & Binding Bell & Bain Ltd, Glasgow

For my grandchildren,
Hannah, Bridget, Martha, Freida and Sam,
who have given me a lot of pleasure, and continue to do so.

CONTENTS

Introduction

SCOTLAND has a stunning variety of wildlife, with many spectacular species such as the red deer, otter, pine marten, golden eagle, osprey, capercaillie and a host of waders and sea birds. The sight of any of these species thrills those who take to the Scottish countryside; their presence contributes millions of pounds to the economy through tourism; and their conservation and management keep thousands of people in extremely interesting and rewarding occupations. Scotland has other species that are less well-known, but maybe even more important in conservation terms. How many people have seen a white-tailed eagle, brown long-eared bats, a polecat or any of the rare orchids that grow in the wild? How many people know that Scotland has *half* of the world population of freshwater pearl mussels, a bi-valve threatened through illegal river engineering, water pollution or selfish individuals in search of the rare pearl sometimes found inside a mussel? How many people realise that when they chop down a tree or a bush in their garden in spring or early summer they must first of all check for nesting birds, or if they are involved in development or drainage work they may destroy the habitat of the endangered water vole?

Consider a swift, increasingly the rarest of our summer visitors to grace the summer skies with their shrill screams as they fly in almost Red Arrow formations through the sky in their search for flies and midges. The swift migrates here from Africa in May and generally nests in gaps under the gutters in old buildings; gaps which might be considered 'untidy' and cemented up, regardless of eggs or chicks being entombed.

Consider the peregrine, a bird which regularly nests on steep craggy places on grouse moors, but may be considered a threat to the maximum production of grouse for shooting. The incubating birds are sometimes shot off the nest, with the presence of a female with shattered wing feathers, a lone male at a nest site or a male with an immature female late in the season often silent signs to a seasoned observer of an earlier criminal act. On some estates peregrines fail to fledge chicks for more than a decade.

Consider a badger sett encroaching onto a field that a farmer is ploughing. He ploughs over the top of it rather than skirting round the edge, caving in part of the tunnel system in the process.

The investigation of all of these crimes is the responsibility of the police, but what sort of reaction can someone expect when such a crime is reported? Assuming that you have the knowledge to recognise a wildlife crime and report it to the police, does the police response indicate that they know what you are talking about. . .

'Hello, is that the police?'

'That's correct, can I help you?'

'Hopefully you can. I'd like to report a man in the River Tay with a glass-bottomed bucket and a long stick who I think is taking freshwater pearl mussels. He is on the other side of the river from the village of Stanley.'

Alternatively the caller might say, 'I'd like to report a man circling bottlenose dolphins in the Firth of Tay at Broughty Ferry and disturbing them.' The caller might report that 'a building that has a brown long-eared bat roost is about to be demolished,' or 'a pet shop is selling Hermann's tortoises and the shop worker said that the owner didn't have Article 10 certificates for them.' Not much more than a decade ago – in the mid nineteen-nineties – there is little question that the caller would have come off the phone annoyed, frustrated, and wondering who the hell *does* have the responsibility to deal with these offences.

The answer, of course, is that these crimes have always been the responsibility of the police. That said, it is only comparatively recently that a nucleus of officers from the eight Scottish police forces has gained the level of knowledge and expertise that ensures they deal confidently and competently with this highly specialised area of policing. In tandem, the level of experience in prosecuting wildlife crime is improving. The Crown Office and Procurator Fiscal Service now have specialist wildlife prosecutors, who train alongside police wildlife crime officers.

For my own part, I have been the full-time wildlife crime officer with Tayside Police, in a support staff role, since retiring in 1997 after over 31 years as a serving police officer. Prior to that I was force wildlife crime officer from 1993 until I retired, though my wildlife remit was carried out in addition to my responsibilities as inspector covering two sections of Perth and Kinross, the areas around the burghs of Crieff and Kinross. For those who know this area, the beat for which I was responsible stretched from the Fife/Tayside boundary on the M90 almost to Lochearnhead. Many of the cases in which I was involved in this earlier period are related in my first book, *Wildlife Detective* (Argyll Publishing 2006).

Some of the UK's wildlife crime officers have a background that helps gear them towards dealing effectively with this specialist and complex area of policing. A background of conservation, farming, biology, animal welfare, shooting or fishing helps, though is not essential. My own knowledge stems mainly from having an insatiable interest in anything to do with the countryside, particularly if it relates to animals and birds. As a youngster I used to keep caterpillars, tadpoles, frogs, newts, budgies, rabbits and dogs. I listed the birds that I had seen and watched, and verified their identification from *The Observer's Book of Birds*. I vividly remember my first sighting of an exquisite male hen harrier in 1966, ash grey, almost white, with the glint of the low March morning sun on its feathers, and with its distinctive black wing tips. I considered this to be an incredibly rare bird that I was honoured to have seen. I was with a gamekeeper at the time checking stoat traps on an estate owned by a titled lady near Dunblane, and he rushed away to the Land Rover for his gun. Thankfully by the time he returned the bird was gone.

Like many boys of my day I had a small egg collection consisting of a single egg of the more common birds, identifying them from *The Observers' Book of Birds' Eggs*. This was a great series of books and I still have part of it, including those for dogs, horses, trees and flowers and refer to them regularly, even though they've long been replaced by more expensive and detailed reference books. As a teenager I guddled trout in hill burns and set snares for hares (most of the rabbits had been exterminated by myxomatosis in the 1950s) at holes in netting fences between agricultural land and woodland. In later life I've worked on a farm, helped gamekeepers (which included some in the bad old days when most keepers paid scant regard to the law protecting birds of prey), regularly used a shotgun, rifle and fishing rod, and trained gundogs.

I suspect my background in many ways resembled that of the writer Alexander Maitland. As he recollected some of his childhood adventures in one of his books, *The Highland Year*, the following paragraph may be as relevant to me as he saw it was to him.

> Whatever feelings I have for the moors and hills owe a
> great deal to experiences like these. As a child I learned an
> awareness for the value of life, and the fact that there is
> beauty in every living thing, however humble. Even so I
> can't pretend that I have always treated nature with
> respect; but at least I've always known that I should. In
> this sense, I suppose, a man can be every bit as much an
> explorer when he gazes into the heart of a wild flower as
> he is when he is crossing the immeasurable wastes of ice or
> sand. . .

I put much of my background experience to good use in my early days in policing, regularly catching poachers of game, deer and salmon. There may be few, if any, serving or retired police officers who have dealt with more poaching cases (and I number these cases literally in the hundreds) especially during the first decade of my service from 1966.

In Tayside I expanded my role not just to include offences committed against our wildlife but to give advice on any offence to do with animal welfare or relating to dogs. Since these are investigations that are not part of a police officer's everyday work it is helpful for them if they can pick up the phone and ask for some guidance or direction. If their investigation is carried out more professionally as a result, then that satisfies the person reporting the incident and reflects positively on the police.

The interest of the public and their support for the way in which the police now deal with wildlife crime is always appreciated. In Tayside we took every opportunity through posters, leaflets and public presentations to take the message to town and country dwellers alike that we encourage the reporting of what they suspect to be wildlife crime. We enabled them to recognise the signs, to know how to preserve evidence (and, equally importantly, how not to destroy evidence), to make contact with the police as soon as possible, even from the site of the suspected crime, and ask where possible to speak to a wildlife crime officer.

Our pleas and publicity were augmented by the variety and professionalism of the many wonderful wildlife documentaries on television. These have raised awareness of wildlife crime tremendously, and in many cases have highlighted the struggle that some creatures endure daily just to survive, even without the added pressure of human interference. I have already met and congratulated Charlotte Uhlenbroek on her work. I would love to do likewise with David Attenborough, Kate Humble, Simon King, Gordon Buchanan, Chris Packham, Saba Douglas-Hamilton and many more wildlife experts. Every day I see evidence that the majority of people, through this vast network of information, are aware of and support our effort to reduce and to detect wildlife crime.

There have been major changes in the attitude to policing offences against our wildlife. As a rookie cop in the 60s I had the impression that we were working – in relation to complaints of game poaching at least – at the behest of landed gentry: the laird's lackey. No such allegations are justified in the twenty-first century, though they are still occasionally made by people who are either outside the circle of those who assist in police investigations, or unhelpful individuals who want to make mischief. The truth is that the few remaining landowners who think the law does not apply to them or their staff in their kingdom of thousands of heather-clad acres are now very much the target of police attention. We work in a much more cohesive way, alongside responsible partner organisations that support and educate their respective membership, and try to drag the remaining dinosaurs from criminality to conformity.

Despite the extensive training wildlife crime officers receive, and the experience both in policing methods and natural history I have gained over the years, I have still found the investigation of wildlife crime the most challenging and frustrating of all the criminal investigations I have encountered. This area of criminality remains the 'new kid on the block' and, despite the promulgation of its import-ance, seems only to have climbed to about the second rung of the ladder in comparison with the importance of other crimes and offences investigated by the police. While this is understandable, an analogy may be made between the job of a wildlife crime officer and that of a bygone image of a farm worker with his horse and single furrow plough trudging up and down a field making a very small difference relative to the massive amount of energy expended. He was alone with his thoughts and, until very recently, largely unsupported. By the time you have finished this book I'm sure you, the reader, will agree.

Chapter 1

Double D's Obsession
with Hare Coursing

THE COURSING of hares with dogs is one of the more common wildlife crimes in the east of Scotland. I have dealt with many hare coursing incidents under the older legislation, the Game (Scotland) Act 1832, where there was no power of arrest for the police, though bizarrely this was available to landowners and their 'servants'. In the more recent Protection of Wild Mammals (Scotland) Act 2002 the procedure is much more straightforward for police officers. Though by 2002 I was in a support staff role with none of my former police powers, I nevertheless had an active advisory part in just about every hare coursing incident that took place in Tayside. In addition, I linked in with my colleagues in just about every other police force as most of the criminals involved in coursing regularly crossed force boundaries and were invariably involved in other spheres of criminality.

In Tayside in 2005 we devised an operation, Operation Lepus, to deal more effectively with the handful of people who consider coursing their right. One of the first tactics was to convince landowners, farmers and gamekeepers that we would take reports of coursing seriously and investigate the incidents as we would with any other crime or offence.

As an immediate consequence, many more incidents were reported: incidents where in the past the farmer or gamekeeper might not have bothered to phone the police as they expected that little of worth would happen, and it would be a waste of their time. In policing terms wildlife crime might have a lower priority but every offence that is reported to the police deserves to be considered for investigation. For some wildlife crimes the investigation might be minimal because of the extremely unlikely chance of the person being detected, but hare coursing is not one of these crimes.

For a start, when the offence is reported, the people involved are normally still at the scene and they can be caught provided police are able to get there quickly enough (clearly, this is not always possible). It is those cases where the police officers don't catch the hare coursers in the act, or do catch them but don't take the right action, where I can help out. Here are classic examples, all relating to the same person from Dundee, a compulsive hare courser who we'll call Double D.

On a Thursday in early February 2006, Double D and a pal were arrested by two police officers after a report that they had been coursing. I discovered this on the following Saturday morning when I went in to the office to catch up on some paperwork. On learning from the Control Room that they had been released before their court appearance, I accessed and read the police report. I was not surprised that the fiscal had let Double D and his pal out before court as the evidence was paper-thin. Neither of the men had been interviewed under caution to establish why they were raking about fields with their lurchers, and no search of any sort seemed to have been carried out in the field for evidence – normally something that I would be asked to help out with. Though the fiscal had released the men, I decided to visit the scene and ask the arresting police officers if there was any further evidence before a decision was made whether or not to proceed with the case. I was determined to ensure that there would be further evidence to present.

I telephoned the farmer who had made the complaint and arranged for him to show me the fields in which he had seen Double D & Co, and the route they had taken. The ground being soft I was reasonably sure that we would be able to track them and I hoped the farmer would have time to come with me to corroborate anything that was found. As I neared his farm at Kirriemuir it started to snow quite heavily, the surrounding fields rapidly losing their everyday green, orange and brown colours under a dusting of snow. Buggeration! There was now no possibility of any tracking. Even though the spiteful snowfall lasted only fifteen minutes or so, and was no deeper than quarter of an inch, any tracks would be hidden. They were likely to have been faint in any case; now they would be invisible.

The farmer took me on the route that Double D and his pal had taken. He had seen them in four contiguous fields, with the dogs having chased a hare in two of them. The third field was newly ploughed and it would have been a dawdle tracking them had it not been for the snow. I was angry that the opportunity of gathering this evidence had been lost.

In the last field we visited the farmer told me that the men walked through it diagonally and were met by the police at the top of the field. Right in the centre of the field, on the diagonal line, I could see two carrion crows picking at something. I would have put money on it that it was the remains of a hare carcass.

As we approached, the frustrated corbies abandoned their mid-morning snack and, sure enough, it was the remains of a hare. Exactly on the route the farmer said the men had taken. More significantly from an evidential point of view, it was at the very point in the field where, once Double D popped his head over the skyline, he would have seen the police car at the top awaiting their arrival. My interpretation of the situation was that, unusual as it is with hare coursers, Double D was taking the hare home and had dropped it on seeing the police. The police would not have seen the hare, only the heads of the two men appearing over the horizon. I was frustrated that this valuable piece of evidence had been lost for want of a phone call to me at the time for some advice.

I took possession of the hare, though after the corbie's feast its evidential value was almost zero and hardly worth examination by a veterinary pathologist. A fox had also fed on the carcass at some stage since the hare's rib bones were eaten through, something a carrion crow can't do. We could not categorically link the hare to the two men without having followed their tracks but I felt that the finding of the hare on the route the farmer said the men took – a route that would also be corroborated by the two police officers in due course – constituted a link, albeit a small link, in the chain of evidence.

I photographed all of the fields and drew a map so that the court would have a better idea of the layout of the farm and the relevant fields. This would also allow witnesses in court to point to various places where some particular activity of evidential interest in the case had taken place. I also noted a statement from the farmer to the effect that he had seen hare coursing on previous occasions and that, from his previous experience, Double D and pal had definitely been engaged in this activity rather than just walking their dogs. Even without having been grilled by the officers, I felt that the two men had some explaining to do if they expected the court to believe that they were simply out exercising their dogs. No-one would seriously expect a pleasant walk in the countryside with dogs to include a perambulation through the middle of a newly ploughed field. Both men were from Dundee where are many grass fields or parks within or adjacent to the city. To have rejected them for a walk in a ploughed field, with the associated build up of sticky clay to footwear struck me as stretching the benefit of a sheriff's doubt a tad too far. I concluded the farmer's statement by asking him about the presence or absence of rabbits on the farm. Rabbits were scarce, and I was pleased that the farmer was aware that, at least during daytime, rabbits would not be found in the middle of any of the fields in question.

On the following Monday morning I made contact with the arresting officer, who gave me the bad news that the fiscal had dropped the case, *deserted simpliciter* being the legal term. I was damned if I was going to all this extra work for nothing and telephoned the fiscal to ask if the case could be resurrected. The reply was that the case was completely closed. Dead! I told him of the additional evidence and managed to get him to agree to allow us to submit a completely new case. This was great news – and in my experience a very unusual step for a fiscal to take. I was determined that every possible scrap of evidence would be included.

In the knowledge that their case (which should have been rock-solid) had been tossed out, Double D and his pal would meantime be laughing all the way to their next coursing outing. I would like to have seen their faces when a new copy complaint – or summons as it is sometimes called – was delivered to their respective doors.

Once he had recovered from the shock, and after an initial plea of not guilty, Double D changed his plea to guilty. A plea of not guilty by his co-accused was accepted by the court. The outing cost Double D a fine of £150, not the highest fine by any means but £150 more than he though he was going to have to fork out.

It's worth noting that when an investigator specialises in dealing with a particular type or series of crime the results are usually much better. When I was a detective sergeant in Perth there was a spate of overnight break-ins to houses in the Letham housing estate. It was summertime and security of windows was less than would be encountered in colder months. We suspected that it was someone who lived locally and who was taking advantage of his local knowledge of back gardens and rat-runs through the estate. Most of the break-ins were taking place while folk were asleep in bed and they could hardly believe that someone could have come, unheard, into their house during the night, rifled through their property and taken whatever they thought would bring them a quick return on its re-sale. Several of the likely suspects had been brought in and interviewed but we were as sure as we could be that they were not involved. Detective chief inspectors always monitor crime figures, and undetected domestic housebreakings were going through the roof. I was asked to deal with it and was allocated a task force of three uniformed police constables and a detective constable all working in plain clothes. As it turned out I did not get to pick the detective officer, though my choice would not have been any better – DC Shaun McKillop, now a Detective Chief Inspector – and we kicked off the operation.

I was directing but not participating in the operation at that stage, and I asked the officers to take a couple of days walking about the estate just speaking to people to see what information they could glean. This paid off in the form of information about crimes that were not necessarily linked to the series we were investigating but nevertheless proved a valuable spin-off. Part of the remit was to lower the incidence of crime and to increase detection rates. I asked the officers to act on the information they had received and they jailed a number of petty thieves for thefts and housebreakings, though they had mostly been daytime ones and not at all linked to the main nocturnal series.

By the beginning of the second week we had a break. One of the petty thieves arrested stated that if we could go lightly on him for the crime with which he was charged he could put us on to a man who was committing a lot of night-time crime in Letham to get money to buy drugs. This seemed a good deal to me and we went for it. At the end of the day if the petty thief was telling porkies he would still have the full force of the law coming down on him.

A search warrant was obtained for the houses occupied by the girlfriend and of the mother of the named man as he flitted between both. He was known to us as a person who was regularly involved in crimes of violence but he did not have a lengthy record for house-breaking. Two officers went to the mother's house, and I went with the two others to the girlfriend's house, the more likely place to find him.

The work of the specialist team paid off. Property from a number of the night-time break-ins was found in both houses and the man was arrested by us at his girlfriend's address. We had solved around 20 housebreakings and recovered a considerable proportion of the stolen property, the remainder of which had been sold and turned into drugs. As it turned out, drugs were the undoing of the man as several years later he died of an overdose. I have always been an advocate of short-term, focussed units. The achievements of this particular team vindicated my belief.

In another case of selective bargaining with criminals, my own house was broken into one night just before Christmas 1986, and a number of items stolen. I was surprised that when I calculated the value of the stolen items the total came to about £3000. I had a good idea that the person responsible came from a nearby housing estate and I was determined to find out who it had been. A uniformed sergeant at the time, I teamed up with a detective constable, Ian Cantwell, who had a vast number of informants. We visited a number of the likely local criminals but drew a blank.

A couple of weeks later, while I was in the public enquiry office at Perth Police Station a man suspected of shoplifting was brought in. He was desperate to speak to me and I went through to the cells after the paperwork was completed to hear what he had to say. He told me that he knew who had broken in to my house and that he would tell me if I could get him off with the shoplifting. It seemed quite a good deal; a substantial HB being cleared up in exchange for a petty theft by shoplifting. He gave me the name – a person in Falkirk with family links to the local housing estate – and I had him released. If the name was correct I would speak with the shop and ask them to drop the charge. If it was wrong he would still be charged with the shoplifting.

A fingerprint had been lifted from the bathroom window during the scenes of crime examination at my house. I passed the name given to me to identification branch and found that indeed he was the man for the housebreaking. It turned out not to be his fingerprint: it was a small part of his palm print. The man was arrested, pleaded guilty and was sentenced to six months imprisonment.

I was sure that there was a second person involved in the housebreaking and kept asking questions of a number of criminals, as did Ian Cantwell. Ian came up trumps first and managed to get the name of the resetter of much of my property. Some had been sold on but we did recover roughly half of what had been stolen, which was good news.

My next break came unexpectedly. I was charge bar sergeant again one day when a man was brought in for a theft. I was present when he was giving his name and address and I suspected that he was related to the person who broke into my house. I watched while he was emptying his pockets and saw that he had several pfennigs, part of the old German currency that was worth a hundredth of a deutsch-mark. We holidayed frequently in Germany and several deutschmarks and pfennigs had been stolen in the break-in. He glanced up at me momentarily as the pfennigs clinked on to the charge bar. I said to him, 'I know where you got those you little bugger.' Quick as a flash he retorted, 'I found them in a skip in Lochgilphead.' I gave him grudging credit for his quick-witted answer, which I suppose is the Scottish equivalent of finding a needle in a haystack.

He was interviewed about my housebreaking but denied having been involved. Nonetheless I was absolutely convinced he was the second person as I had established by this time he was the brother of the man who got the six months imprisonment.

In late March, most likely before Double D realised he had not in fact wriggled free of his Kirriemuir episode, he featured again. Because

I monitored hare coursing activity throughout Tayside, I was aware of the favourite farms certain individuals liked to visit for their coursing activities. Double D liked farms in the Kirriemuir and Glamis areas of Angus, and in the Abernyte area of Perthshire, all within a 15 minute drive of Dundee. I was also aware that he was one of the rare hare coursers who sometimes operated on his own.

On this particular occasion a man was seen walking through a field of winter wheat adjacent to the Perth to Dundee dual carriageway near Abernyte. He had two lurcher dogs with him which were off the lead and which eventually found and chased a hare. The two witnesses did not see whether or not the hare was caught as the dogs disappeared out of sight. They then saw the man and dogs reappear, this time with the dogs on leads, and walk towards a car parked near the dual carriageway. The witnesses managed to note the registration number of the car and while one called the police to pass in details, the other watched the man and dogs get into his car and drive half a mile to another farm, where within a short time he saw the man and dogs emerging from the car and the two dogs chasing yet another hare. The police attended the scene but the birds had flown.

This time the system worked and I was notified of the ongoing incident and of the registration number of the car involved. As is mostly the case in coursing, the car had been sold and was not registered to its current owner. This was another trait of Double D, to have a new car every week or so, none of which was ever registered to him. I felt we were a step ahead of him this time and I asked officers in Dundee to go to the area of Double D's house and await him returning.

Within a short time I received a call from the Dundee officers to the effect that they had stopped the car in Dundee and it was indeed Double D & dogs. In a way we were a bit unlucky in that the two witnesses had gone out before the police who had attended the incident called at their house to note statements. We had only a resume of what had happened so had not really enough evidence to arrest Double D at that point. We could have detained him, a facility which allows the police six hours to decide whether or not a person can be charged, but if there is insufficient evidence he must be released before the end of the six hours. We didn't know when the witnesses might return home so the instruction was for the Dundee officers to photograph and video the two dogs in case the court, in due course, might want to forfeit them. Double D had admitted being at the Abernyte farm, but stated he had simply been walking his dogs. His trousers were soaked up past the knees in a green slime, evidence that his 'walk' had not really been a good day out. We were losing nothing evidentially by allowing him to go.

I met the investigating officers later in the day at the farm. They, one of the witnesses and I managed to effectively track Double D's route through the field. He had first of all been walking, then had started running, presumably to try to keep up with his dogs once they were on to a hare. The tracks of one dog, running flat out and with all toes spaced widely, were followed along an access track into the field, which ran between some buildings and a deep ditch. The tracks of a hare could also be seen at one point where the earth on the access track was damp. It was in line with the dog's tracks but this did not necessarily prove that these were the tracks of the hare that was being chased. I suspected from the heel of the hare's back legs making a deep indentation into the earth that it was travelling fast. What I could say to the court now was that a large dog had been running flat out along that access track, and that a hare had been running fast along the same track. I could not say that the dog was chasing the hare, only that it was a possibility. The tracks of the second dog could not be seen and it may well by that time have tired and returned to Double D.

The access track led to the public road, a narrow country lane. I could not see any relevant marks entering any of the fields off the road and it may be that the chase continued along the road. The road was bounded by a deep and wide ditch and unless the hare took to the ditch it would have been easily caught as it would not be able to jink about and avoid the dog. The greater speed of the dog would have prevailed and it would have caught the hare. However there was no evidence at the roadside of the hare having been caught and I suspect it had launched itself into the green foetid water of the ditch and saved its skin.

At the second location pointed out to us by the witnesses we tracked Double D and his two dogs from where he parked the car. It was not long before the marks of the dogs disappeared from their initial obedient walking to heel, but the field into which the dogs ran was stubble and the tracks were lost. We had a good search but did not find any evidence of a hare being caught and killed. The searches at both locations had further value in that we established that the fields were full of hares, probably the magnet drawing Double D repeatedly to this area. The farm is in the Carse of Gowrie, flat and fertile land with clay soil. Because the land is flat it is literally segmented with drainage ditches: wide ditches full of green water of an uncertain depth. Our tracking of Double D took us to one of these ditches. By our reading of the signs his dogs had managed easily to jump the width of the ditch. Double D had almost managed. Almost is not good enough and we could see that he had been just a few inches short and had slithered into the water, hence the green slime on his trousers. Without seeing the bottom of the ditch this let us know that it was probably at least knee-deep. Overall he'd not had a good day, and it was getting worse!

Countering a likely defence argument that rabbits were the intended target, there were no signs of rabbits anywhere apart from some evidence of their coming from the wood at the other side of the public road into one of the fields at the second site. Rabbit droppings, closely nibbled winter cereal and some scrapes in the ground were evidence of their nocturnal visits before they returned over the road to their burrows in the wood for safety during the day.

So what did we have against Double D so far?

1. Two witnesses seeing a man coursing a hare with two dogs.

2. The same man getting into a car, with the registration number noted, which moved to a different farm where one of the witnesses saw the two dogs coursing a hare within a short time of the man and dogs coming out of the car.

3. The man being stopped in the same car in Dundee with two dogs and being identified as Double D.

4. A degree of corroboration of events from the tracking, though less-so at the second farm

Had these been the only cases we would probably only have gone for the first, corroborated, incident. But more was to follow.

The following week near the village of Glamis in Angus, a woman returning home one evening saw a man in a car on a narrow country road near her house. He was driving slowly and his machinations included reversing. When she reached home, acting on her suspicions she ran into the house for binoculars and watched the man who was by this time in a field of winter wheat accompanied by a large black lurcher dog. She watched the man walk down the side of the field nearest to her then turn and head into the centre of the field. A hare rose and the dog took off pursuing it determinedly back and forth across the field. The man was running to try to keep up with the dog, which eventually caught and killed the hare near the top of the field. The woman saw the man pat the dog on the head in return for its efforts, collect the hare, and put the hare and the dog into the car.

The woman had meantime phoned the farmer whose field this was and he and his son arrived on the scene just as the man was driving off. They attempted to block him by keeping to the middle of the road with their Land Rover but he came straight for them and they wisely made way for him to get past. They managed to get the registration number of the vehicle which turned out to be the same one Double D had been driving at his previous incident. The police attended but the man was long gone. They checked on the vehicle registration number but since it was still in the name of the previous owner their enquiry came to a dead end.

I learned of the incident the following day, and recognised Double D's car registration number. I went to the scene and, accompanied by the woman who had watched him, searched the field. We found little in the way of tracks as the field was so dry but did find the spot where the dog had caught and killed the hare. I photographed the small area of flattened crop and collected some of the hare's fur. This helped corroborate what the witness had seen. I then had Double D identified from a set of 12 photographs.

Double D was out again three evenings later. On this occasion a man and woman saw two dogs chasing a hare in the field at the other side of the road from their house near Kirriemuir. The dogs chased the hare for some time but disappeared after it into the next field where they couldn't see the outcome. They saw three men on the road and knew they were connected with the dogs, one having a lurcher on a lead. This man released the dog (or it escaped from him) and ran off down the field that the first two dogs had been in, hotly pursued by the man.

Just before this happened the man was passed by a car with one male occupant who, seeing the men on the road, thought that cattle had escaped and slowed down. It was not just any male occupant who happened to be driving the car but a man who recognised the person who was just about to take off after his dog. He had recognised him from a previous coursing incident the year before, one in relation to which he was charged and appeared in court. How unlucky can you be if you are just out for a quiet bit of coursing?

In the meantime the three wayward dogs were rounded up and they and the three men piled into a car and drove off. They were not about to escape that easily and were followed by one of the first witnesses, who had jumped into his car to pursue the 'Kirrie Three' in order to get their car registration number. The registration number was passed to the police but, like the incident from three days before, the police enquiry concluded when the vehicle was found still to be registered to its previous owner.

I picked up the investigation in the morning and telephoned the witnesses. I learned from one of the witnesses about the incident the previous year and asked him in which month that had taken place. When I checked, I found that Double D had been caught and charged with a hare coursing incident that month. This was something positive to work on. I then met up with an enthusiastic young officer from Kirriemuir and we visited the witnesses to obtain statements. We also showed to the witness of the incident of the preceding year a set of 12 photographs that naturally included Double D. There are no prizes for guessing who he picked out.

We then did some tracking in the field. Luckily this field was easy to track in, being yet another ploughed field. We could clearly follow the tracks of the two dogs back and forward the field then across a dyke into a grass field where even the Lone Ranger's pal Tonto would have had difficulty following the track. I was a bit surprised that we couldn't see the tracks of the hare in the ploughing but I had no doubt from the zig-zag marks of the dogs that they had been after a hare. We then followed the track of the dog that had run from the roadside and of the man who had chased after it. The dog had run half-way down the ploughed field, turned sharp left, over a broken dyke and into a winter barley field where it seemed to have been caught by the man. Man and dog then walked back up the winter barley directly to where their car had been reported as being parked. Tracking is nearly always time well spent.

We had no idea who the other two men may have been but I considered we had sufficient evidence for yet another charge against Double D. There was no direct evidence that it was his dog that had been chasing a hare but he was art and part involved in the coursing of a hare. I considered that it would be better that the charges were all taken together. The slight difficulty was that two had taken place in Perthshire and would go to Perth Sheriff Court, while the other two had taken place in the part of Angus covered by Forfar Sheriff Court and should go there. I made contact with the specialist wildlife fiscal and asked if she would take all the charges together at Perth. She agreed, and also concurred with my next suggestion that we should arrest Double D as part of a continuing series of offences and bring him before the court.

The continuing investigation and reporting of the case was delegated to the officers who were involved with the first pair of charges and they called regularly at Double D's door in Dundee to arrest him. He was either never at home or failed to answer the door, and after a week or so it would not be reasonable to arrest him unless he committed another coursing offence. Power of arrest diminishes with the passage of time. If a person is to be arrested some time after a crime or series of crimes then an arrest warrant should normally be applied for. The case was reported to the procurator fiscal and Double D would get a summons with the four new charges in due course.

These latest four incidents took place between 23 March and 4 April 2006. He inevitably entered a plea of not guilty and was due to go to trial in late October of that year. For whatever reason, after all the witnesses turning up at court on the October date, the trial was adjourned till January 2007. I thought we may have cured Double D of his addiction to hare coursing but he was identified by photograph yet again for another incident in December of 2006, this time using a greyhound and a spaniel, an unusual combination.

A few days before Double D's January trial, I was contacted by the procurator fiscal who was to be prosecuting it. She told me that a plea to the first charge had been offered and wondered if we should just settle for that. This is really the procurator fiscal's call but I was always glad when they discussed it with me before making a decision as there may be a particular reason that the police would want the full circumstances to be heard, the only way to do this being to run the trial. In this particular case I was aware that the mother of one of our witnesses had just died and that he would not have been able to give evidence in any event, which would mean that either one charge would have to be dropped or the case would need to be part-heard, with another date set to complete the evidence. I have never liked part-heard trials as the impetus seems to be lost and sentences always appear to be less appropriate to the crime charged than would normally have been expected. Further, if this charge were to be dropped, not only would it weaken the case but this was the only charge in which we could prove that a hare had been caught.

I considered the options and asked the fiscal before she agreed to a guilty plea to the first charge only, to try again for a guilty plea to a second charge. If that failed I would have no gripe with a plea to one out of the four charges. This was not to be and when she phoned me back later it was to tell me that we were unfortunately only getting the offer that had originally been on the table. Though I was disappointed I was pleased for the eight civilian witnesses that they would now not have to appear in court, an experience that is at worst traumatic, at best tedious.

On the Monday morning of the case I went to the court to listen in to what the fiscal, the defence and the sheriff had to say. By good luck Double D's case was first to be heard so I didn't have too long to wait. The fiscal presented a summary of the circumstances to the court and handed a list of previous convictions to the sheriff. Double D has a considerable – and varied – record, including two convictions under the Game (Scotland) Act, analogous convictions for the purposes of this case. The fiscal was quizzed by the sheriff on the nature of these convictions but had no knowledge other than that offences under the Act relate to trespassing on land in unlawful search or pursuit of game, pretty much the same as in this case.

The defence solicitor told the court that in the charge to which his client pleaded guilty the hare being chased by the dogs had not been caught. He explained that the hare was never likely to have been caught as the dogs were not fit enough and they just enjoyed the chase. He then said that his client had since sold the dogs. These mitigating excuses probably impressed the accused though it's unlikely that anyone else in the court – particularly the sheriff, who hears this twaddle day in and day out – believed a word. The excuses got even better. The defence contended that the Protection of Wild Mammals Act 2002 was really about banning fox hunting and that hare coursing was at the lower end of the scale. Furthermore, he was led to believe that the authorities turned a blind eye to hare coursing! Considering the publicity I had given to the media on Operation Lepus, for anyone in Tayside seriously to believe this they must have been on the moon all of the previous year.

The sheriff did not believe the stories and commented to the defence, 'I hope you are not inferring that I should turn a blind eye to this.' 'No, M'Lord,' the defence solicitor replied, 'I am merely passing on the information I have been given.' He may as well have added, 'to keep my client happy.' The sheriff addressed Double D and asked him to stand. He told Double D that with the penalties made available by the Scottish Parliament (6 months imprisonment and/or a Level 5 fine – £5,000) it was clear that Parliament considered hare coursing to be a serious matter and that he would deal with it accordingly. He fined Double D £400, the highest fine for hare coursing up to that time during the course of Operation Lepus and a satisfying conviction considering that Double D was unemployed and unable to pay a fine much in excess of that amount. I doubted that it would have been any higher had he pleaded guilty to two or even four charges.

In this particular case no account could be taken of Double D's earlier conviction, when he was fined £150. The reason for this is that he had not yet been convicted when the four incidents relating to this case had taken place. The earlier conviction *was* able to be taken into account when his outstanding case for the December incident with the greyhound and spaniel came to court, though the conviction for the case with the £400 fine could not be taken into account, the reason again being that this case was still pending when he was charged with the latest offence. I was glad that I attended the court and heard the defence solicitor's excuses. I was able to ensure that in double D's *next* case the fiscal could tell the court at the outset that the charge was a result of an operation specifically to respond to regular complaints by farmers, gamekeepers and landowners about the scourge of hare coursing.

Double D pleaded guilty to coursing with the unlikely mix of dogs, though this time was only fined £250. Though this seems a light fine, bear in mind that the sheriff was only aware of his £150 fine; and not the case where he was fined £400. Nevertheless within the space of a year Double D accumulated fines of £800 for hare coursing and still had another case pending. Some people just never learn.

Chapter 2

Poaching All Hours

I'M ALWAYS amazed how far some people will travel to carry out a bit of poaching. We have a number of poachers resident in Tayside but we still get plagued by many others coming through from the west of Scotland. There are regular visitors: an individual from Carluke and a group from Greenock and Port Glasgow. I have no doubt that they venture into Tayside far more often than we realise and may frequently head home with a cargo of game in their vehicles. Like many wildlife criminals, they are involved in other criminality including drug dealing and crimes of violence.

Mr Carluke is an early morning person who concentrates on taking roe deer with his dogs. He knows west Perthshire well and apparently gets to know the lie of the land by offering his services as a pigeon shooter. This is a remarkable achievement considering he is not a shotgun certificate holder.

From his knowledge of the area Mr Carluke becomes aware of which fields are favoured by roe deer. Roe does need extra feeding in late winter and early spring to sustain the pair of foetal fawns growing inside them, and to obtain this they continue feeding out in grass or winter cereal crops until well after daylight. This was well demonstrated during the long winter of 2009/2010. I live 6 miles outside Perth and most mornings, in early March and just before 7.00 am, with snow almost cleared off fields that had been under a white blanket most of the time since mid-December, I could count over 40 roe in fields juxtaposed to an A class road. The deer were hungry, and empty rumens made them take more risks than would a mammal normally wary of humans. Mr Carluke takes advantage of this knowledge and concentrates most of his deer poaching in the early mornings from

February till May. Invariably he will be taking pregnant does with his dogs; they are the ones that will be taking advantage of that extra bite of food, they will be carrying extra weight in the form of twin fawns and will be more easily caught.

Mr Carluke has evaded capture so far but has been seen several times in the early mornings by gamekeepers, who now appreciate what he is up to and have my telephone number to hand. A gamekeeper told me he spoke to him one morning and saw a dead roe deer in the back of his vehicle. He said he warned him that he better not have been poaching deer on his land, which he probably had. Hopefully the keeper's response will be more practical if he encounters him again. There are some data protection issues with the police giving out vehicle registration numbers but provided we give out a vehicle registration number in the interests of the detection of crime to specific people who may be likely to encounter the vehicle, with the clear instruction that the action they are to take is to call the police when they see it, we have not contravened the Data Protection Act.

The Act rightly limits the privileged information that the police can access and can share with others but I have never found it to seriously impinge on the detection of crime. Nowadays the police have to be more accountable for their actions and must obtain the proper authority to access information but this safeguards the public as well as the officers.

I'm well aware that the Mr Carluke is still visiting west Perthshire to take roe deer but I'm sure the day is not far off when we will catch him. It is unusual for a person to pursue a series of illegal activities overlong without his luck running out.

The Greenock and Port Glasgow mob were after deer as well. The first I knew about them was when a gamekeeper, Jock McDonald, spotted their lamp shining into a field near his house in the early hours of the morning, jumped out of bed, quickly dressed, and took off in his car to investigate. He found the offending vehicle with the lamp and followed it to see what was happening. As sometimes happens in remote areas he had no reception on his mobile phone to contact the police and hung back to watch. A few minutes later Jock saw the vehicle, a long wheelbase Land Rover, driving towards him at speed.

He took to the verge to let is pass and turned to pursue it. As he followed the Land Rover a roe deer was thrown from the back on to the roadway. Jock gave up the chase at that point and collected the roe deer as evidence. By the time he did this he had lost the Land Rover and gave up in disgust.

Jock contacted me in the morning and I went to see the roe deer. There were the usual marks on the haunch of the deer where it had first been gripped by a dog to take it down, then the marks on the throat where the dog had killed – or tried to kill – the deer. What was unusual in this case was there was also another mark on the deer that seemed to be from a bullet. The wound was far too serious to have been caused by a .22 rim fire bullet. It looked more like a wound from a slightly larger calibre, perhaps a .22 Hornet and was in a non-fatal place so would only have injured the deer. It looked like the deer had been shot and injured and a dog or dogs set on it to finish it off. It was unfortunate that the keeper never managed to get the registration number of the Land Rover. Without it that particular enquiry was at an end. I found out the registration number several weeks later, but too late to gather any worthwhile evidence.

A few weeks later Jock saw another vehicle using a spotlight in the middle of the night and managed to get its registration number as it took off from him. It was a car this time and it was not registered to the present keeper of the vehicle. I made enquiries via a motor auction in the west of Scotland and managed to find out who had bought the car. This was what put me on to the Greenock and Port Glasgow gang, who had also owned the Land Rover I spoke of earlier. The new owner of the car was from Greenock and I saw from looking at his associates that he was in with a group of another four people who had dogs and were involved in poaching, amongst many other criminal activities. I circulated the number to gamekeepers in the area and asked them to look out for the vehicle.

I did not have long to wait, though it was not the Land Rover that the team were using this time, it was another car owned by the Land Rover driver's associate. The vehicle had been well off the road up a farm track when its occupants were challenged by a farmer. The men stated that they were looking for rabbits to chase with their dogs and said that they were sorry for being on his land. What they really meant was that they were sorry that they had been caught. In any event they cleared out, no doubt to continue their illegal nocturnal activities elsewhere.

Within a few weeks, when Jock was out at night patrolling the roads, he saw a suspicious car parked at the roadside. He stopped to speak to the occupants, who were four men with west of Scotland accents, accompanied by at least four lurchers. They threatened him with violence and he wisely backed off and called the police. By the time the police arrived the car was long gone. The vehicle registration number again checked out to the Greenock and Port Glasgow gang.

Shortly afterwards keepers on another estate disturbed a group of men using a spotlight from a Land Rover in the middle of the night. The Land Rover took off and disappeared out of sight in a matter of minutes. It was obviously a far more powerful Land Rover than that of the keepers, who were left well behind in the pursuit. When I got the registration number from the keepers and checked it out it was a diesel turbo Land Rover and registered in the name of one of the associates of the man who had bought the car used in one of the previous escapades. I circulated this new registration number to the keepers and to the local police officers and sat back to wait again.

Within a few weeks the Land Rover was back and the lamp was spotted by a farmer, who contacted the police. The farm where the lamp was seen operating was a good half hour from the nearest police station but luckily the officers on duty happened to be in the area. They left their car at the roadside and walked in on the lamp beam, to find a Land Rover in the middle of a field of winter cereal and three men returning to it with three lurchers and carrying spotlamps with battery packs and a dead rabbit. The men admitted they had no permission to be there so were committing an offence under the Night Poaching Act 1828. This outdated Act unfortunately does not give the police a power to arrest (though it would have if one of the three had a weapon of some sort) so they had no option but to deal with the men in the middle of the field, obtaining their details and checking them out, before charging and releasing them. This ridiculously difficult situation has now been addressed by the Wildlife and Natural

Environment (Scotland) 2011 Act, which brings poaching under the Wildlife and Countryside Act 1981, with all its associated powers of search and arrest.

It was a good capture except for the fact that the officers did not seize the spotlamps. They were of value as evidence in the case, but even more importantly they could have been forfeit by the court. I have no doubt that the men would have gone on to take hares, roe deer or both during the night but it appeared that they were caught at the start their foray. A charge with one rabbit under the Night Poaching Act was better than nothing but I doubted it would see the court.

To complete the investigation I had a post mortem examination carried out on the rabbit; this to prove that it had been taken by dogs rather than having just been picked up dead in the field. Sure enough the injuries were consistent with having been taken by a dog and this evidence would help the case.

It frustrates me that rabbits were not included as mammals for the purposes of the Protection of Wild Mammals (Scotland) Act 2002, despite my recommendation to this effect prior to the Bill being enacted. I could foresee the excuses that would be used to wriggle out of cases where hares were being coursed by dogs: 'We were just out hunting a few rabbits and the dog took off after a hare.' There are situations when it is expedient to use a dog, mostly a terrier, to catch rabbits that are bolted by ferrets, but surely a general licence issued by the Scottish Government that would cover people using dogs on rabbits *where they had permission to do so* would have closed this loophole. Had this been the case the difficult job of the police in dealing with poachers would have been made much easier.

I discussed the rabbit case with the specialist wildlife prosecutor and she dealt with it by a fiscal's fine, probably the best option in the circumstances. I was still frustrated that the men had been left with their spotlamps and battery packs.

The spotlamps and battery packs turned up again a few months later, this time with the other half of the team. Night shift police officers in the west of Perthshire were well aware of the activity and were keeping a lookout for any suspicious vehicle. They spotted a car driving along a country road at 4.00 am and thought it was worth a stop and check. There were two men in the car and two lurchers in the space behind the back seat. At four in the morning this was certainly worth further investigation. The nervous men were asked what they had been doing and admitted that they had been out chasing rabbits with their dogs. The car was searched and what looked like two dead rabbits were found on the front passenger foot well of the car. Two spotlamps and battery packs were lying on the back seat. There was no doubt in the officers' minds that this was a pair of poachers.

Driver and passenger were interviewed separately about their activities, under caution since they were suspects. They did not have a clue where they had been coursing the rabbits and had no permission to do so anywhere in the area. Their details were noted and checked out, and it became clear they were part of the Greenock and Port Glasgow gang. The officers did well making the stop check of the vehicle but, dealing with a situation that was new to them, were rather unsure of their powers. I've no doubt had it been a more respectable time I would have been contacted for advice but I really would not have relished the phone ringing in my ear at 4.00 am.

After the previous experience the first thing I asked was, 'Did you keep the spotlamps and battery pack?' If my response was, 'Oh bloody hell, not again,' you can guess the answer. I learned that once the officers took possession of the two rabbits, it turned out that – without any magic, top hats or metamorphosis – they had suddenly become a rabbit and a hare. Because one turned out to be a hare, I was hoping that this time the men could be charged under the Protection of Wild Mammals (Scotland) Act 2002 so that we had a better penalty available to the court, but it was going to be down to the interview of the two men by the officers. Unfortunately the interview was carried out before the second 'rabbit' was identified as a hare. When the officers pointed out the hare, one of the accused said, 'I thought that was a daddy rabbit.' He obviously knew damn fine what it was but he was sticking to his original, but ridiculous, story.

The problem we now had was to prove they had taken the hare *deliberately*, the offence being to *deliberately* hunt a wild mammal. There was nothing in the interviews about coursing hares or even searching for hares; all references were to rabbits, which as you well know are infuriatingly not 'mammals.' The wording for offences in the Wildlife and Countryside Act 1981, as it was amended by the Nature Conservation (Scotland) Act 2004 is to commit an offence *intentionally or recklessly*. There are not too many differences between an intentional and a deliberate act but both are much more difficult to prove than a reckless act. I had also suggested to the legislators at the time of the draft Bill that the offences under the proposed Protection of Wild Mammals (Scotland) Act should include the term *reckless*, which at that time was almost certainly going to be implemented into the Wildlife and Countryside Act. The term *reckless* was agreed for the latter Act but not for the former. I have often wished that the legal boffins who make legislation had a wee turn from time to time at trying to enforce it.

We had two options. The two men could either be charged under the Night Poaching Act 1828 or with a contravention of the Poaching Prevention Act 1862. The Night Poaching Act is, as its wording suggests, the unlawful taking of game or rabbits, or unlawful search for game during the hours of darkness. The Poaching Prevention Act allows police to charge (but still not to arrest) people that they reasonably believe to have come from land where they have been in unlawful search of game, and who are found in possession of game (including rabbits), with or without instruments for the taking of the game or rabbits. The maximum penalty that can be imposed by the court is the same in each case: Level 3 on the standard scale, which is £1000. In either case the court could also forfeit spotlamps and battery packs. . . had the bloody things been taken by the officers. In any event we decided to go for the Night Poaching Act offence.

I have lost count of the times that farmers, landowners or gamekeepers have bemoaned the fact that nothing ever happens to poachers. From their point of view it seems such a logical procedure from which to get a result. The witness sees the offence taking place and reports the matter to the police. The men have left in their car but the witnesses note the registration number. The police officers attend. The witnesses relate the events to the police and give them the registration number of the car involved. It is, to them, so straightforward that a conviction should automatically follow. Welcome to the real world!

It can never be assumed that a conviction will be obtained in *any* case. I have had many cases over the years that have slipped through my grasp because of a technicality, or more likely a slip-up in procedure. I was never the most enthusiastic at reporting road traffic offences, with drunk drivers and disqualified drivers being exceptions. I dealt with a road traffic accident on the outskirts of Perth, in the early 1970s. The driver of the car at fault was slightly injured and was requesting hospital treatment as he stated he had pains in his chest. I didn't think he needed to go to hospital but didn't argue. I had smelled alcohol from his breath and he was a bit unsteady on his feet, the latter fact *he* put down to having been involved in an accident. I suspected that he wanted to avoid being breathalysed but I was obliged to accede to his request and he was taken away in an ambulance five minutes later.

My colleague and I dealt with the accident then attended at the hospital. Since he now was a hospital patient I had to wait until he had been seen by the doctor, then ask the doctor if the driver was fit to give a sample of breath. The doctor agreed that the man was fit to supply a breath sample and in fact was being discharged. I required the driver to supply a breath sample, which he did. His breath turned the crystals in the tube red, meaning he was over the limit. The next part in the procedure was to arrest him and take him to the police station where he was required to give either a sample of blood or two urine samples. He agreed to give a sample of blood, which when tested showed that he was twice over the limit for driving.

The case seemed clear cut. He was the registered owner of the vehicle; there were several witnesses to identify him as the driver of the car; the car was being driven on a public road; he was twice over the limit to drive. An easy conviction? Not so.

In court his defence solicitor was Charlie Smith, a solicitor who was one of the regular court agents and who eventually became a sheriff. I had given my evidence-in-chief, then it was Charlie's turn to cross-examine. He asked me about the accident and of his client being taken to hospital for treatment. He conceded that I had the authority from the doctor to request a breath sample from his client, but asked why I had requested such a sample. I thought this was a strange question considering his client was found to have been twice over the limit to drive but I answered in any case. My response was that I had been of the opinion that the accused had been drinking. Charlie's response was, 'Are you sure that is the reason?' I confirmed that this was the reason, whereupon he addressed the sheriff and asked that the case be dismissed. The sheriff asked why that was, and Charlie stated, 'My client had been taken by ambulance to the hospital M'Lord. It was there, as the court has heard, that he was required by Constable Stewart to supply a specimen of breath. The Road Traffic Act allows a police constable, when he suspects a person to have been drinking, to require a breath sample *at the locus or nearby*. The reason for require-ment of a breath sample *at the hospital, which was not the locus of where he had been driving* (or in fact anywhere nearby), should have been because my client had been *involved in a road traffic accident*. I submit that Constable Stewart was not entitled to require that my client give a sample of breath at the hospital for the reason that he was suspected of having been drinking, and that the crown case should fail.' Charlie was absolutely correct and the court had no option but to return a verdict of not guilty!

Charlie made up for this when he was sheriff at the Angus town of Arbroath. I was by this time detective sergeant and giving evidence in a drugs trial where the defence solicitor was well known as a pretty unpleasant individual. I had a previous experience of this solicitor tearing paper up into small pieces, rolling them up into balls and flicking them across the court during a sheriff and jury trial in Dundee when I was giving evidence led by the fiscal. This illustrated the extremely low calibre of the man. The correct questions can be asked of the witness without the need for unpleasantness but in this court Charlie obviously had the measure of the defence. At the first sign of nastiness Charlie rounded on him and instructed him that trials would be conducted in a civilised manner in his court. He continued to scowl at the solicitor throughout my evidence, which went as smoothly as it ever had with this guy. At the end of the trial his client was found

A Lone Furrow

guilty. Sheriff Charlie Smith and I were even again.

Getting back to our night-time poachers who pretended not to be able to tell the difference between rabbits and hares, they each pleaded guilty and were dealt with by fines. One of the men was fined £150 while his nocturnal *socius criminis* was fined £125. This was a plea of guilty at the first court hearing and of course, rightly, they got discount on their penalty. What still rankled me was that their spotlamp and battery pack was not available for the court to forfeit. And it would crop up yet again.

I found an old copy of the Night Poaching Act 1828 and realised that the two were lucky to have committed the offence nowadays rather than when the legislation was first formed. The original legislation began,

> And whereas the Practice of going out by night for the
> purpose of Destroying Game has very much increased of
> late years, and has in very many instances led to the
> commission of Murder, and of other grievous offences:
> and it is expedient to make more effectual Provisions than
> now by law exist for repressing such practice.

Note that the maximum penalty nowadays is a fine not exceeding £1,000. The original legislation continued :

> Persons taking or destroying game by Night to be
> committed, for the first offence, to the common gaol or
> house of correction, for any period not exceeding three
> calendar months, there to be kept to hard labour, and at
> the expiration of such period shall find sureties by
> recognizance, or in Scotland by bond of caution, himself
> in ten pounds, and two sureties in five pounds each or one
> surety of ten pounds, for his not offending again for the
> space of one year next following; and in the case of not
> finding such sureties, shall be further imprisoned and kept
> to hard labour for the space of six calendar months, unless
> such sureties are sooner found.

On a second conviction the legislation doubled imprisonment to 6 months hard labour, with sureties doubling and the time over which the poor chap must not take the master's pheasants increased to two years, with a year's hard labour if he couldn't find the cash as surety. Hopefully most transgressors learned by the second time they were caught and had gained sufficient 'correction'. If the 'correction' had fallen on deaf ears, the legislation went on:

> and in case such person shall so offend a third time, he
> shall be guilty of a misdemeanour, and being convicted
> thereof, shall be liable, at the discretion of the court, to be
> transported beyond seas for seven years, or to be
> imprisoned and kept to hard labour in the common goal or
> house of correction for any term not exceeding two years.

In the Act there is an increased penalty available to today's court (up to a fine of £2,500) if the night-time poachers are three in number and one is armed with a weapon of some sort, held in one case to be a walking stick. In 1828 the penalty was, for this misdemeanour, at the discretion of the court, to be transported beyond seas for any term not exceeding fourteen years nor less than seven years, or to be imprisoned and kept to hard labour for any term not exceeding three years.

Funny, I always thought a misdemeanour to be a petty crime.

Chapter 3

Trapping Buzzards and Burglars

POISONED baits and their victims found on Edradynate Estate near Aberfeldy in Perthshire featured several times in *Wildlife Detective*. Since the charging of the headkeeper and his rookie apprentice in 2002 and the subsequent abandonment by the procurator fiscal of the case two years later (the trial had not started after 2 years and on the basis of human rights legislation the delay was deemed unfair to the accused) we'd had no further calls to the estate. This was not to last.

In February 2006 I received a call alerting me to suspicious activity by a man on a quad bike on the estate. Not many people on the estate have quad bikes; they are limited to a couple of farmers, and of course the head gamekeeper or his apprentice. The caller thought that either something was being buried or poisoned bait was being set out, and described the person involved as wearing a green waterproof jacket. I asked if any further investigation could be made by the caller since she was a few hundred yards from the scene and I was about 25 miles away. My instinct was that something illegal was likely to be happening and provisionally arranged for Constable Graham Jack, the on-duty Divisional wildlife crime officer, to make himself available once I had an update.

I had confirmation of my suspicions within about fifteen minutes, being told that a buzzard had been caught in a trap and that, when in due course the trap was checked by whoever had set it, the witness's belief was that the bird was likely to be killed. My informant did not elaborate on the type of trap, nor did I ask. I should have asked but somehow I assumed that the trap was a crow cage trap and that the buzzard had entered to investigate the bait set out to entice carrion-eaters to enter its one-way access. Any bird entering then had to await either its fate or its release once the trap was again checked. I made a quick call to Graham and we set off for the estate.

I phoned ahead and we were guided into the spot by the informant, who was able to see us while still remaining out of our sight. My assumption that the trap was a crow cage trap was wrong; in fact it was one I hadn't seen for years. The buzzard was caught under a net encircled by a loop of heavy wire. The net had sprung over the hapless bird when it had landed to investigate an easy meal of a dead wood pigeon. The wood pigeon was tied by wire to a metal plate, with a catch that was released when the bait was tugged by the beak of the bird as it started to feed. This then released the spring holding the loop of net, which sprung over and trapped the buzzard. The buzzard was lucky in that it had been caught in the centre of the net and had not been struck by the loop of wire, which could have killed or severely injured it. My recollection of this type of trap was when I was a boy and there was a smaller version baited with grain that could be used to catch sparrows. The principle was the same: when the sparrows picked at the grain the catch was released and in a twinkling they were enclosed by a fine net

On this occasion the buzzard was lucky on two counts. It had not been injured by the trap, and we intended to release it back into its territory and its natural way of life. Had its captor not intended to release it, removing it from the net would have been easy. It first would have been killed by being hit over the head with a stick and the limp body could then almost have been shaken out of the net.

Our situation was slightly different. The bird was determined to make life as awkward as possible for its rescuers and it gripped the net tightly with its talons. These are the dangerous parts of a large bird of prey, not its beak. I have never felt threatened by the beak of a bird of prey, yet a starling, gull or crow would give a good nip or peck with its beak if it got half a chance. A bird of prey relies on the four curved daggers on its feet and we had to ensure that we kept clear of those.

Graham lifted the bird and I took the scissors from my rucksack and started to snip at the net that was tangled round its talons and its wings. I was not in the least bothered about damaging the net as we were both sure that it had caught its last bird. I wish we could have transmitted our confidence to the buzzard as its struggles made its extrication just a bit more difficult than it should have been. In cutting the net I wanted to make sure that we did not release it with part of the almost invisible net still somehow tangled round its body but in the end, after some intricate snipping with the scissors, it was set free.

Now that the buzzard had been released and we had possession of the trap as a production, we needed to find out who had set it. I took a series of photographs of the field, the gate through which the suspect was seen entering the field after he had parked his quad bike, and photographs of the quad bike tracks in case we needed to match tyre patterns. We then carried out a scene of crime investigation of the area looking for any other evidence that might be available. A ditch partially bisected the field and on the wet earth on the sides of the ditch we found recent sole impressions. We photographed these with a signed label beside them, which also gave a scale if we were able to recover the footwear. Graham recognised the sole pattern as those of Hunter make Wellingtons, so that was a good start. On the other side of the ditch, where the witness had first seen the suspect, there was a scattering of white down feathers from a wood pigeon. It looked like the suspect had moved the trap from this point to where we had discovered it. I couldn't see an obvious reason for this unless the suspect thought that the trap might have been visible in its first position by someone at the farm at the top of the field.

So far we had the link with a quad bike, photographs of quad bike tracks, photos of sole impressions, a description of a man with a green waterproof jacket, and the recovery of the trap. If we could find the user of quad bike and the Hunter wellies we had a case, especially if the suspect had a green waterproof jacket.

From what we had, including the description of the person involved, the suspect was the gamekeeper. Graham and another officer called on him the following day. The keeper was wearing Hunter wellies and had a green waterproof jacket hanging on a peg in the house, one which I had seen him wearing several times. He also had access to a quad bike. With this evidence we would not have been unduly bothered by a denial as we could have matched the quad bike tracks and the sole impressions. It seems always to be the case that where there is the plenty evidence a suspect admits responsibility.

This was exactly the case here. The keeper admitted having set the trap but stated he was of the opinion that it was legal. When Graham passed me that information it could almost have been believable. He then told me that the keeper said he used the trap to catch crows. Again this could almost have been believable. He finally related that the keeper said he sometimes caught buzzards, which he tagged with wing tags before liberating them. Well, that was just stretching the imagination a bit too far. From the times this keeper had complained to me about the amount of 'hawks' in the countryside I did not have him placed as a buzzard's benefactor. Catching birds to tag or ring them also requires a licence, something our suspect did not have.

Graham came back to Perth and later conferred with me regarding the legal situation with the trap. It incorporated a net as part of its operation and birds may not legally be trapped by a net except under licence. In my view the trap was illegal. Graham and I re-visited the keeper and charged him with recklessly or intentionally taking a wild bird, contrary to the Wildlife and Countryside Act 1981.

The keeper's distinctive green jacket brings to mind a previous case where the identification of a suspect came from a jacket. I was on night shift and in the early hours of the morning was aware of one of my officers being sent to a housebreaking in the Letham housing scheme of Perth. An elderly woman had been in bed when she was awakened by a noise and found a man standing at the bottom of her bed. The poor woman must have been terrified and screamed, at which the man fled down the stairs and out the front door of the house. It is fairly uncommon for houses to be violated when there is an occupant inside – in fact nowadays it is comparatively rare for a house to be broken into at all. (Crime trends tend to shift to those with the least risk and the best rewards, such as frauds, thefts of unattended property and car crime).

The thief in this case had firstly rummaged through the downstairs part of the house and had crammed the pockets of his jacket with cash that he had found lying around. I can only imagine that the cash had been jingling in the pockets and making a lot of noise in the eerie quiet, so much so that as he began to go up the stairs he took his jacket off and laid it about quarter way up. Worryingly, this told me that he expected the house to have a least one occupant and this knowledge didn't unduly bother him. After his discovery, and in his panic to flee the house, he made the mistake of not collecting his jacket.

Nowadays with DNA the recovery of the culprit's jacket would be a real boon. In the mid eighties we did not have that advantage and had to work on fingerprints, sole impressions and good detective work. As it turned out, when the jacket was brought to the police station and I saw it I couldn't believe my eyes. Two weeks earlier, a man I knew well from many of his dishonest activities had been arrested for breach of the peace. I chatted to him as his details were being obtained at the charge bar and he went to great lengths to ensure that I admired his new grey suit, which he said was made to measure and not any of this common 'off the peg' stuff. I told him that his new suit was very smart, if somewhat grubby after his recent experience of lying on a damp pavement, and he went off happily to his cell.

I recognised his suit jacket right away, and thought we better visit him to tell him it was in safekeeping lest he be concerned at its loss. In best police terminology, we 'chapped him up' and, once into his house, began to question him as to the whereabouts of his new suit jacket. He took us to the bedroom and produced a grey jacket that bore a passing resemblance to his suit jacket, but it was definitely not the one he had so proudly showed me a couple of weeks earlier. I asked him to produce the suit trousers, which he did, and it was obvious then that the trousers were in no way related to the jacket. Not even second cousins. He stuck to his story for a while and said that he'd had to get the jacket dry cleaned after he had been arrested and that it had lost some of its colour. We were having none of it but it had been a gallant and entertaining try. He put his hands up at last and began to make the best of a bad job by lifting the carpet and allowing us to recover the elderly lady's money from its hiding place.

I was greatly amused when, as we arrested him for theft by housebreaking, he put on his suit trousers and the grey (almost matching) jacket to come down to the police station!

I was not so amused that our accused in the spring-over trap case had tendered a plea of not guilty. I understood from a discussion with the defence solicitor that an expert was to be called to court to testify that spring-over traps are sold on the internet and in fact are used by bird ringers to catch birds for ringing. I was not aware of any of this, though was of the view that if it were to be true, bird ringers need to be licensed to catch birds and that this is where the difference would lie. The defence suggested that I speak with this witness before the trial to see if I could be convinced that there was a valid defence. I expressed my doubt that I would be convinced but left the defence my office and mobile number for the expert to get in touch, however heard nothing further.

On the day of the trial the defence and prosecution agreed the circumstances of the bird being found in the trap and that the trap had been set by the accused. This cut the evidence that had to be led in court considerably as the fiscal now just had to lead evidence to show that the use of the trap was unlawful, while the defence would rebut this evidence and try to put the opposite position to the court. Like the trial for the shooting of the common seal (Chapter 6), the accused in this case also had a very competent defence solicitor advising a QC, who was presenting the case for the defence. Whether or not they were successful, this would be an expensive exercise.

Graham Jack gave evidence first which, between the evidence-in-chief and legal debate, took well over an hour. This took us till lunch time and, though I never saw Graham again till late afternoon, gathered that the defence still had to cross-examine his evidence. It was therefore nearly 3.00 p.m. before I got into the witness box and was led through the evidence-in-chief by the procurator fiscal.

The examination of my evidence by the defence was an extremely good-natured and civilised affair compared to many trials in which I have been involved. The QC made it clear at the outset that he was not going to challenge my experience but simply wanted to take me through my opinions of a variety of traps and nets of different types and go over the defence view of the use of a spring-over trap. Much of what he said made sense and I conceded many of the points he put forward; points made either on the basis of legality or common sense. Despite agreeing with a large proportion of the defence position I thought that would take him no closer to establishing that the use of a spring-over trap was legal. I was unable to comment on the spring-over trap being available on the internet or of it being used by bird ringers as I had simply not heard of this.

My evidence concluded just after 4.00 p.m. and the case was adjourned till a later date. The prosecution still had one witness to be heard, Dave Dick, formerly senior investigations officer with RSPB. The defence still had to produce their expert on traps and may even have had the accused give evidence.

I had several concerns about how the case was going. Normally the police are asked to take a statement from a defence witness prior to a trial going ahead. The prosecution is obliged to disclose its evidence to the defence so it seemed a reasonable balance of fairness that the prosecution should be aware of what the defence will lead as evidence. We were clear that the defence witness – a former employee of the Ministry of Agriculture Fisheries and Food (MAFF) in England and Wales – would be stating that it was perfectly legal to use this type of trap and that they were on sale on the internet. By this time I had checked and could find similar traps with a similar principle available on the web, though for catching small birds. The caveat was that the operator had to be licensed by the British Trust for Ornithology. Nevertheless I didn't know how an expert witness could possibly believe that the use of the spring-over trap in the context of this case could ever be legal.

I was aware from a much earlier conversation with an expert on birds of prey from RSPB, Brian Etheridge, that he had used a spring-over trap over a period of 45 years under licence. I discussed the possibility of calling him as a witness with the procurator fiscal. Even after 40 year's policing I had no idea if a witness for the prosecution could be called part way through the Crown case, though the answer was that he could. I passed details of the witness to the fiscal dealing with the case and left it to him to make contact. Rules in relation to evidence prohibited me making contact since I had given evidence and might have been able to influence what Brian Etheridge said in court.

With the prosecution rather in the dark at the line the defence would take, and therefore at a disadvantage, the trial resumed on 1 May. The first witness was Dave Dick. Dave's evidence was that he was familiar with spring-over traps and had only ever seen them used to catch birds of prey, never carrion crows. He was able to state that the bait, a dead wood pigeon, was significant and had a high chance of luring a bird of prey. Dave stated that he had no doubt that the use of this trap was illegal except under licence and that it would be difficult to catch a corvid in the trap as they are extremely wary, much more so than a buzzard.

Brian Etheridge gave evidence next. He was able to tell the court that when he had used this kind of trap he had caught over 100 buzzards but, significantly, never a crow. He added that a person would require training to tag and mark birds and in order to qualify for a licence to use this trap. The defence QC stated that the Crown required corroboration to show that the accused recklessly took a bird that he did not mean to, and reiterated that the Crown was not bringing a prosecution about the legality of the trap. I was not in court to hear this but when I was told I wished that we had charged the accused with using an illegal trap as well as illegally taking a wild bird. Readers may think this is elementary but there is a balance to be struck between the scattergun approach of charging a person with everything that seems remotely relevant, against homing in on charge that seems to be most appropriate to the apparently illegal act carried out by that person. The advantage in multi charges is that it can sometimes induce a bargain plea. The disadvantage is that it can completely confuse the issue in court. The procurator fiscal suggested that witnesses had given clear evidence that these traps are not used for crows but for birds of prey, and the accused had by his own admission caught buzzards on previous occasions. The accused was using a trap of dubious legality to catch crows. At a minimum this was reckless.

The sheriff commented that the legality of the trap was not the charge libelled but the way in which it was being used, and this could not be ignored. The evidence led by the Crown witnesses was that the trap was more likely to take a buzzard than a crow.

In the defence case the first witness, the ex-MAFF man, a consultant on traps and trapping, stated that he had used this type of trap exclusively for catching crows. He also accepted that the trap could catch buzzards and that if buzzards were all that was caught while using the trap to catch crows then the trap would be illegal. Continuing the defence, the next witness was a director of a shop supplying traps and other items to estates. He stated that he sells a 'flip-over corvid trap' identical to the one that had been used by the accused and that he regularly consulted with the police and the Crown Office regarding their legality.

In the summing-up, the procurator fiscal accepted, rightly, that there was a difficulty proving intentionality though there was clear evidence of recklessness, whatever the legality of the trap, stating, 'This is a trap that will catch buzzards in a way that is reckless.'

The defence questioned whether the Crown case had been proved beyond reasonable doubt, while admitting it was an unusual case. Their client had used this trap believing that it was a legal means of catching crows. In the circumstances the Crown had not proved recklessness and that the accused should be found Not Guilty.

The sheriff concluded that the accused was entitled to take crows under the terms of the Scottish Government general licence. He stated that the trap could possibly be defined as a net under Section 5(1) (b) of the Wildlife and Countryside Act 1981 but the evidence that it was more likely to catch buzzards than crows was not satisfied beyond reasonable doubt. He rightly defined *recklessness* as *somewhat above carelessness or negligence*, and found the accused Not Proven.

There is a lesson in every single case taken to court. The lesson may be to the accused, his defence, the procurator fiscal or the police officer(s) involved in the case. There are seldom two identical cases, more especially with wildlife crime cases where there is a dearth of case law as guidance. I certainly know now to give an option of charges to the court if we ever get a similar case. The difficulty with wildlife cases is that they are so few and far between that we may never get another chance of a similar case. I did in fact get another chance, though in slightly different circumstances.

Since 2002 I have organised a training day at the Scottish Police College under the Continuous Professional Development Programme on wildlife crime investigation. This takes the form of two wildlife crime 'trials', where evidence is led by police wildlife crime officers, the 'trial' is prosecuted and defended by procurators fiscal, generally those with a remit to prosecute wildlife crime, and sheriff Kevin Drummond of the Borders Courts presides over the 'trial'. We are lucky in Scotland in that there is a room at the Scottish Police College set out as a mock courtroom, exactly in the manner of a real courtroom. In 2007 I made one of the trials a resumé of the one we have just discussed. Almost.

The difference in this case was that I added in an additional charge of using a trap that was illegal, for all of the reasons already given. This, of course, was the spring-over trap. The case was prosecuted by Pamela Rhodes, procurator fiscal depute in Dumfries and a wildlife specialist prosecutor. It was defended by Vicki Bell, the then wildlife specialist procurator fiscal depute from Tayside. The evidence came out in exactly the same way as in the trial at Perth Sheriff Court, though I had done a bit more research by this time and pretty much knew what the verdicts would be.

Sheriff Kevin Drummond was very detailed in his explanations at the end of the trial. Even though there was evidence that the 'accused' had caught buzzards in a spring-over trap in the past and expected to catch them again there was no evidence that he was trying to catch them *intentionally*. Similarly, general licences issued by the Scottish Government make allowances, if traps are set by *authorised persons* to catch pest species, for them to release any non-target species. There was therefore no recklessness involved in the catching of a buzzard. The accused was therefore Not Guilty of the charge of intentionally or recklessly catching a buzzard.

Turning then to the new charge of using an illegal trap, there were three general licences issued by the Scottish Government under which an authorised person could control crows. The licences set out a variety of methods that can be employed, one including the use of a net. It is very clear under the Wildlife and Countryside Act 1981 that a net cannot be used to catch birds unless it is operated manually or is used under a licence issued by the British Trust for Ornithology *and* used by licensed bird ringers. One of the main components of the spring-over trap is of course a net. By dint of the wording in these general licences our imaginary accused was therefore not committing an offence in using a net to try to catch crows. Not guilty.

Of course someone setting a spring-over trap and killing any non-target species, such as buzzards, clearly commits an offence. I'll leave the reader to assess what the fate of the buzzard in the spring-over trap would have been had we not intervened.

After the case I wrote to the Scottish Government, and the general licences were almost immediately re-written to specifically exclude the use of a spring-over trap in the variety of methods used to control pest species. Another legal loophole had been plugged.

Chapter 4

Beavers and Wild Boar

I HAD kept a close eye on the consultation to re-introduce the once indigenous European beaver to Scotland. The beaver was hunted to extinction in Britain in the sixteenth century and suffered a similar fate elsewhere in its European range. It's yet another example of how man has interfered with and completely altered biodiversity and our natural heritage either for sport, greed or in ignorance. Proponents of European beavers claim that they are much less destructive than North American beavers and lead a different lifestyle. In Europe, in places where they remained in existence, or in the 13 countries to which they have been re-introduced, they are regarded as water engineers. They are claimed to benefit wildlife by building dams and creating wetlands and ponds that support a wide range of species. European beavers are alleged to regulate flooding and improve water quality as any silt coming down a river or stream is held behind their dam. In addition they benefit from and live happily alongside another species that is having an exceedingly hard time in Britain holding on to suitable habitat, the water vole: Ratty from *Wind in the Willows*.

Those who oppose their re-introduction say they will destroy salmon rivers, though this is countered by claims that they prefer slow-moving water rather than the much faster-flowing waters preferred by salmon. What may be a genuine complaint is that a dam may prevent salmon passing further upstream to spawn. There is also no doubt that beavers fell trees, which may be a negative factor in some cases but in other areas may be a benefit. In any event, despite a positive response for their return under controlled circumstances by Scottish Natural Heritage, the Scottish Government initially vetoed the return of the beaver to Britain, though a trial release began in Argyll in the spring of 2009. When the decision to release beavers was first knocked back, I was disappointed as I would love to have seen beavers back again in the environment they once shared with many other species before man's interference. My wish came true sooner than I expected!

In November, 2006 I had a call from the proprietor of a trout fishery near Perth. He told me that over the previous few months – in fact since the summertime – several trees had been chopped down round his loch. At the beginning he thought it was local youths running amok with an axe and replicating George Washington's demolition of the apple tree, though in this case the felled trees had mostly been willow and alder. As time went on he began to wonder if the culprit was a beaver, and consulted various internet sites to gain more knowledge of a beaver's lifestyle. By the time he phoned me he was able to say that the internet photographs of the trees felled by beavers bore a striking similarity to those felled round his loch. I was intrigued but doubtful and agreed to meet the trout fishery owner and witness the evidence first-hand.

My visit left me in no doubt that the loch had a new inhabitant: one with chisel-sharp teeth and a flat tail used to clap against the water surface as a warning signal to its relatives of danger. About ten trees had been taken down round the lochside. Most were saplings but one in particular was about twelve inches in diameter. That really surprised me and was clear vindication of the axiom *as busy as a beaver.* The fishery owner had some concerns about the presence of a beaver in his fishery, the principal one being the difficulty of getting a large tree out of the loch once it had been felled. Casting a fly near to a toppled tree and hooking a large stocked trout which would immediately make a dash into the branches was not conducive to increasing the numbers of paying anglers. He could foresee a drop in profits.

In the meantime I was snapping away with my digital camera, at the back of my mind thinking I would email the photographs to Dr Andrew Kitchener, curator of mammals and birds at the Royal Museum of Scotland in Edinburgh, for absolute confirmation of the presence of a beaver. I suppose this was a belt and braces approach as I could clearly see the teeth marks on the trunk of the trees and the pile of multi-faceted wood chips beneath, lying like a pile of giant wooden gem stones. To my knowledge there was no other mammal that had a capacity to munch with that power. Andrew confirmed that it was a beaver and just to double-check emailed my photos to a friend in Norway, who concurred. The first wild beaver in the UK in Perthshire! Interesting. Even exciting. Nevertheless someone somewhere may well have committed an offence by allowing it to escape.

At section 14, the Wildlife and Countryside Act 1981 states, if any person releases or allows to escape into the wild an animal which (a) is of a kind which is not ordinarily resident in and is not a regular visitor to Great Britain in a wild state; or (b) is a hybrid of any animal of that kind, he shall be guilty of an offence.

This seems quite straightforward, though I was amused at the *regular visitor* part. Beavers are good swimmers but I hardly imagine they have regular – or even infrequent – sojourns across the North Sea. *Regular visitors* is a term relevant to the part of the Act that relates to birds.

Within a couple of days I had a further call from the fishery owner: there were two beavers. He was in absolutely no doubt about this as both had been seen at the same time. This put a more positive slant on our investigation. It was much more likely now that if there were two beavers they had been brought to the fishery and released. For two beavers to escape – even from the same place and at the same time – and finish up at this fishery, would be unusual to say the least and anyone who believed that would be naive. If there *were* two beavers I had no doubt that someone wanted to kick-start a wild colony and also that the beavers would be male and female.

This was a difficult investigation as in reality the beavers could have originated anywhere. We did have three places in Tayside where European beavers were kept in large enclosures by private owners but asking them if they had lost any was completely different to asking someone who had two rabbits in a hutch or half a dozen budgies in an aviary if any had gone missing. Beavers are mainly nocturnal, secretive and for the most part, even when active, are underwater. Population statistics and breeding dynamics are not easily obtained.

In the meantime the fishery owner was keen to get rid of the beavers and I made contact with one of our local beaver-keepers, who volunteered to bring down a live-catch trap to assist. The trap was left open so that the beavers could enter and become familiar with it. In due course the safety catch would be taken off and the next time one of them entered the doors would drop and it would be again a captive beaver.

We almost never reached this stage. The fishery owner had begun to consider diversification into environmental interest. He had realised that the presence of beavers would not, as he had first thought, ruin his fishery, and he reckoned that their presence may provide a small additional income but more importantly could help to educate local young people about their environment, especially as the fishery already hosted an active badger sett, otters, kingfishers, herons and much more. He wondered about erecting a fence round the loch but was advised that the beavers would then be captive. If they were captive and he intended visitors to come and see them he would need to register them with Perth and Kinross Council and would require a zoo licence. Too much red tape put an end to this innovative vision.

How the fishery owner coped with the beavers was not a police matter though I allocated PC Doug Ogilvie, the divisional wildlife crime officer for that area, to monitor the situation. In addition there was some pressure from elsewhere to capture the beavers to at least determine whether they were the once-native European beaver or the more destructive North American beaver. There was also the question – especially if they were the latter species – that they may be carrying disease that could transmit to wildlife or even agricultural livestock here. They were an unknown, though hopefully benign, quantity.

I visited the fishery on several occasions hoping to catch a glimpse of the errant beaver. The elusive beastie never did appear, but the walks round the loch were well worthwhile. The highlight one morning was finding the evidence of a visit by an otter. Otter droppings, referred to as 'spraints' are black and oily. Those who have put their nose anywhere near may be surprised that the otter's toilet has a rather sweet smell. They spraint regularly in the same place, marking their territory. I had found such a place, which was on a mossy covered boulder beside a ditch running from the loch to the nearby River Earn. This must be the favoured route of otters moving between the two stretches of water, and the nitrogen in the spraint and urine had killed and discoloured what should have been bright green moss. Like foxes, the otters depend on the scent from these marking posts to advertise their presence to visitors of the same species. The signal will be loud and clear. Our sense of smell is crude, a dimension that we have either lost or never truly developed. It is our loss that we can only guess at what the otter (or the fox) might be telling its rivals, or indeed prospective suitors.

The fishery beaver was trapped soon after this. All went quiet and I suspect it had been on its own. It is much more likely that, if two were thought to have been seen, they would have been otters. In the meantime there was an issue with an escaped beaver developing elsewhere in Perthshire.

In early January, 2007 I had a telephone call from a person who was concerned about wild boar roaming over woodlands in north-east Perthshire. He had seen them on frequent occasions and even if I did not see one he could show me evidence on the ground – spoor in native tracking terms – that could confirm their presence. I suddenly remembered a conversation I had with a gamekeeper who had been driving home one dark night in this area and encountered a wild boar running across the road in front of his car. I don't often forget snippets of information I am given but this had been an exception. I had completely forgotten the wild boar story till this latest report stirred my ageing memory. 'And there are beavers on the loose as well,' my new informant assured me, 'I can show you a tree that they have been chewing at, and a dam that they've made on the burn!' The presence of beavers was almost a throw-away remark. It was something I was least expecting and one I could have well done without.

My helpful informant was willing to show me the evidence of escaped wild boar and escaped beavers but apparently had two very busy weeks ahead before he could do so. His report to me was simultaneous to a report from Scottish Natural Heritage of wild boar and beavers at the same location. This turned out to be the same incident and the same person reporting. He was not aware that the frolic in the wild which these species were enjoying could have constituted a crime and his first port of call had been SNH rather than the police. We have tried hard within Tayside Police to put the message about that wildlife crime should be reported to the police, who have the statutory enforcement role under the Wildlife and Countryside Act, but it was evident we had not yet reached everyone.

My informant met me on a date in early February and pointed me in the right direction to see evidence of the Tayside Two, boar and beaver. I saw plenty evidence of wild boar, first of all in the form of a grass field well rooted up by the snouts of the beasties in their search for bulbs, invertebrates and any other juicy morsels that lay under the healthy sward of grass. The gate of the field was open and the estate from which my informant stated the escapees had originated was just at the other side of the narrow country road.

As I was taking a few photographs I was enthralled by one of the earliest avian songsters – apart from the robin – and a real harbinger of Spring: the mistle thrush. Strangely I was not really aware of mistle thrushes until I was well into my twenties. Their song is not unlike the blackbird's but instead of a full-flowing aria like the blackbird, the mistle thrush sings in short bursts. The first time I was aware of hearing one in full voice I was walking up a steep hill with a heavy game bag full of rabbits on my back and I thought that I was wheezing. It took me a while to realise that when I stopped walking the wheezing should also have abated, and only then I knew that the sound was from a different pair of lungs. I suppose this description does a disservice to the singing ability of the mistle thrush but the bird was probably about a quarter of a mile away. When heard close up, very often on a day when it is miserable with rain and all other birds are seeking shelter, the mistle thrush must surely lighten up the day of anyone who takes the time to listen, even if they don't know the species that is giving them so much pleasure.

To digress further, we had a pair of mistle thrushes nested in the garden at home in 2005. I watched the female building a nest on the limb of an apple tree (not in a fork in the tree as text books suggest) while the male perched on top of a nearby larch tree singing for all he was worth and proclaiming his territory to birds of all other species, not just rival mistle thrushes. He showed no antagonism towards smaller birds but if he saw another member of the thrush family – a blackbird or a song thrush – or a bird he recognised as a predator such as a jackdaw, he was off his perch and viciously mobbing and scolding it, all the time making a loud *churring* call.

Eggs were laid in the nest and the female began to incubate. All seemed fine until one day I came home to find feathers scattered across the path between the lawn and one of the borders. I recognised two of the long white feathers as the outer feathers from a mistle thrush's tail and realised my bird still sitting on the nest was now a single parent. I doubted it would cope on its own and was amazed every time I passed that I could still see the tip of the bill sticking up at one side of the nest and the end of the tail at the other. I was sure when the eggs hatched that the female could not collect food for the chicks and at the same time brood them to keep them sufficiently warm.

Within a few days I could see a bit more of the bird on the nest. I realised that the eggs had hatched and that the bird had to give a bit more space to the chicks by sitting higher in the nest. I was sure that within a few days all the chicks would be dead, but this was not the case. The valiant female mistle thrush managed to rear a single chick despite all the odds being stacked against her. The chick eventually fledged and on its first day out of the nest, the most vulnerable period before it is able to fly back to the safety of a tree, I watched it hopping around on the lawn. I was devastated in the morning when I came out of the house to find the chick lying dead on the lawn. It had been caught in the night by a cat, used as a plaything until it had died, and had been discarded once it no longer provided any fun. I have never liked cats, and I dislike cat owners who put their felines out at night with the milk bottles. And this latest incident strengthened my views.

Returning again to the wild boar hunt, there was ample evidence on the estate, and also on adjoining farms, that porcine ungulates were at large. Cloven hoof (or trotter) marks, droppings, freshly rooted areas and inverted U shapes under netting fences where the netting had been pushed up to create a pig-shaped runway all bore testament to their presence. The evidence extended across the estate and there must either have been a good number at large or a single one that was one helluva busy piggy. *As busy as a piggy* is not a common simile but that brings me neatly back to beavers. I found not one but two trees that bore the same chisel-teeth marks as I had earlier found at the trout fishery just south of Perth. There was also a dam across a burn near one of the trees. A beaver had indeed been busy! Too busy!

I intended to visit the estate owner – the owner of the beavers and wild boar – and make him aware of the law regarding allowing the escape of non-native species, but another incident took place before I could arrange my visit. I was staying overnight in a hotel prior to attending the Scottish Police Wildlife Crime Conference and ordered a morning newspaper. I was amazed to see a photograph depicting a beaver and the remains of 5 apple trees in an orchard. Just the stumps remained and I could easily see the handiwork as that of a beaver. This had taken place on a farm adjoining the estate in which I had an interest. The story was then covered on the news on television and on radio. I had to get moving.

I met the estate owner by arrangement a few days later. He is a really pleasant individual and makes no secret that he would like to see beavers and other formerly native species back in the wild. On the face of it he seemed to be making a good start at ensuring this took place. Had there been evidence the releases were deliberate then the action I took would have been substantially different. I had already discussed the issue with the Scottish Government, with Scottish Natural Heritage and with the specialist wildlife procurator fiscal in Tayside. All agreed with my decision that the estate owner should be warned; advised that he had to take all steps not just to round up the escapees but to ensure there were no further escapes.

The estate owner and I made our way round the estate and he was particularly proud to show me a new grid placed on the fence line of one of the beaver enclosures where the stream runs out. He had commissioned a local firm to install this grid but it was apparent that the employees had no idea of the size of beavers, maybe thinking they were the size of bears! A triangular gap at each side would easily allow beavers to escape and neither the contractors nor the owner had noticed this. This was the first issue for immediate attention.

We parked at the top of the beaver enclosure to then walk into the pond in the middle, but were confronted by a wild boar – a very large male – behind a pile of earth. Thankfully it seemed a canny sort of beast and just stood snorting at us as if it needed to be fed. Behind it lay the gate of a deer fence which looked as if it had been lifted in the air and off it wooden hinges by the boar's strong snout. The owner told me that his wild boars had escaped during a gale on Hogmanay 2006, when a large number of trees were blown down, flattening and uprooting the security fencing. He explained that though he had managed to capture and contain the sows and their year-old litters the boar, having tasted freedom, just could not now be secured in any enclosure. It had lifted off wooden gates, metal gates, and electric fencing now held no fear for it. We put the boar in the woodland and replaced the gate but I doubted it would stay there very long.

After I left the landowner I had a quiet walk around the estate – regrettably cut short as the rain was teeming down. Even though the estate was a bit run down and I suspected might not be making much profit, the habitat was as natural as you could find anywhere. I found the largest mixed bed of snowdrops and aconites that I have seen anywhere. It was an amazing mosaic of white and yellow and completely carpeted a chunk of very open mixed birch and alder woodland; a part that the wild boar had obviously not yet found. It was a tranquil spot and I tried to visualise it with shafts of bright sunlight coming through the trees, lighting up the woodland flowers rather than the blasts of almost horizontal rain that appeared to be making them indulge in a reluctant and un-coordinated dance as the heavy raindrops bounced off their petals.

I had a further thrill on one of the estate roads when I met the wandering boar again. It was at the side of the road and saw me before I saw it. It was walking towards me at a fairly brisk pace and I was glad that I was not far from my car. I took a series of photographs as it came towards me, though until I reached my car I never allowed the distance between us to decrease. My last photograph was when it was about 10 metres away. It had stopped by that time and was eyeing me up. Had I not met the boar earlier and had some confidence that it was more likely to be inquisitive rather than threatening I might well have been pretty frightened. In any event I was not taking any chances and jumped into my car. By the time I had closed the door it was within touching distance outside the door, with its back higher than the bottom level of my open window. It must have reached that point in a flash. I wondered how I or anyone else coming face to face with this beast without the safety of a nearby car might feel. A truly wild boar may well have faded quietly away into the woodland. The trouble with semi-domestic animals is that they have little fear of humans and this can in many cases make them extremely dangerous. I fervently hoped that on my next visit the boar would be safely enclosed. I really admired its character and independence though I suspected that its determination to remain a free spirit would bring its life to a premature end.

The beaver story continued in December of 2007 with evidence of another beaver on the River Tay near to Dunkeld. A number of saplings on the riverbank had been cut down, the chisel marks of the extremely sharp teeth of the beaver being evident on the stumps. At the end of January in the following year there was yet more evidence on the banks of a small burn in Angus just on the Perthshire boundary. This was too far away for it to have been the same animal, though it may have been the one that had demolished the orchard the previous year. Evidence in the form of toppled saplings showed that the beaver was still a resident of this burn in February and efforts were put in hand to capture the animal by Edinburgh Zoo and my long-time friend Dr Gill Hartley from the Wildlife Management section of Science and Advice for Scottish Agricuture in Edinburgh. Plans were barely arranged and suitable cages sourced when a further beaver was spotted at Tentsmuir Forest, across the Firth of Tay into the neighbouring county of Fife. Since this was a coastal beauty spot regularly visited by large numbers of people the catching of this beaver took precedence.

Gill kept me up to date with progress, or in fact lack of progress in the first couple of weeks. The beaver had been visiting the trap but would not go in. It then did enter the cage but somehow had managed to get out again. Modifications were made and an infra-red camera was installed to see what was happening. The beaver was seen to be coming to the cage to feast on the apples left at the entrance but still seemed reluctant to enter. While it was making its mind up a dead beaver was found many miles away on the shoreline on the Black Isle in Easter Ross, an area policed by Northern Constabulary.

At last the Tentsmuir beaver succumbed to temptation, this time being held securely in the cage. One down but how many to go? In January 2009 the beaver on the River Tay was still leaving its trademark of gnawed saplings. In the following month a new beaver had appeared on the River Earn to the south-west of Perth. This one had been reported by the keeper, Bill McIntosh, another long-time friend, and I went with him to see the evidence for myself. There were two locations where the animal had been active. At the first, on a spit of land that would normally be covered by high water, there were a dozen or so willow saplings neatly taken down. I was impressed, but Bill told me that the next site, half a mile away as the crow flies but probably double that following the course of the river, was much more interesting. Indeed it was. I was flabbergasted at the sight of a huge beaver lodge. It was at the side of the main river and had an entrance coming directly from the river. It stood about 4 feet high, with each willow or alder branch that was part of its elaborate construction neatly chiselled at the bottom and interlinking with its neighbours. The cutting, dragging and intricate building must have taken many hours. Bill told me, 'this one's good, but there's another one over here.' We then walked across to the bank at the side of a field, crossing an area that is flooded regularly when the water rises. This second lodge may have been built for an escape during flooding; a holiday home if the main lodge nearer the river became waterlogged.

Although already a fan of beavers, I now knew that they really were incredible creatures. Their vegetarian diet means that they don't adversely affect other wildlife; in fact the wetlands they create benefit a whole range of other creatures. Despite the fact that I was involved in the investigation to establish how the beavers came to be living free, the circumstances of which were reported for consideration of a prosecution in 2011, beavers most certainly deserve a place back among the wildlife of the UK.

I took a call later in February, this time about a beaver on a small ox-bow lake just off the River Isla near Coupar Angus in Perthshire.

This was probably the one that had preferred the small burn on the Angus/Perthshire boundary the previous year since that waterway is a tributary of the Isla and about 6 miles away, not too long a swim for a beaver. I visited the site and there were freshly felled saplings, though no lodge. I passed all of the information to Gill, though we both realised that an itinerant beaver such as this would be very hard to catch.

Allow me to digress: it's New Year's day 2010 as I write this and want to capture the moment. We are still enduring 12 inches of snow that fell between Christmas and New Year and I'm barely able to type for looking out of the window. There are literally hundreds of birds in the garden, and they're costing a small fortune in a variety of bird food, which of course I don't grudge one bit. Most are greenfinches and chaffinches, with the greenfinches on the black sunflower seed feeders and the chaffinches scavenging below where I've shovelled away the snow to let them feed. They're joined by an assortment of tits: great tits, blue tits and, in the larch trees, long-tailed tits. In summer we had the highest number of coal tits I have ever seen, but for some unknown reason they don't seem to favour the garden in winter. Among the chaffinches there is a pair of bramblings, winter visitors from Scandinavia that look remarkably similar to chaffinches. Comparing the two, bramblings definitely give the appearance of a bird from cold climes. Their plumage is somehow distinctively wintry, with more speckled grey where the chaffinch is a summery orange. I make a similar visual comparison between the redwing and the song thrush; the fieldfare and the mistle thrush.

I've put some wheat on the path through the wood and this attracted a horde of wood pigeons, and some more timid, less pushy collared doves in the quieter periods. A pair of cock pheasants flew into the garden, one determinedly chasing the other, and so engrossed in their pugnacious avian conflict that they missed out on the wheat supply. Lastly, under a bower of honeysuckle that has kept the ground underneath clear of snow, I've treated some of the less gregarious birds, robins, dunnocks and wrens, to some grated cheese, mealworms and smaller seeds, with some half apples spread round in the lighter snow for blackbirds, a single mistle thrush and fieldfares. It's a veritable treat of birdlife and well worth the effort of regularly replenishing their supply of lifesaving food.

On the following morning I was at the computer again, this time treated to some different avian visitors to the snow-covered garden. In addition to the usual birds, a great spotted woodpecker appeared. He slowly made his way up some of the larch trees looking for insects, that would probably be frozen to death if they were anywhere near the surface of the bark. He then flew across to another set of feeders not 10 metres from me, where he quickly grabbed a peanut and went back to a larch tree to break it up and swallow it. He knew exactly where the peanuts were and he had obviously been a visitor well before I saw him that day. I was surprised that I'd never seen a sparrowhawk in the garden for a while, since they are quite regular visitors; after all a garden-full of birds is *their* bird table. As I was thinking about it, a buzzard flew into the garden and perched on a tree above the main feeders. Had this been a sparrowhawk the birds would have been gone in an instant and would not have returned for at least half an hour. I was surprised that they showed little regard for the buzzard, probably realising that unless they were unfit and weak, the buzzard, not nearly as agile as a sparrowhawk, would be little threat to them.

The next day I was at work, but when I came home I saw that the sparrowhawk *had* visited. A fieldfare had been the victim and the raptor must have finished up with a full belly since there was very little left. The garden visitor I felt most pity for, though, was a heron. It landed on one of the larch trees on 9 January, two weeks exactly after the main fall of snow. The countryside had changed very little during that fortnight and we still had a foot of snow. Most of the burn running through the garden was frozen over after nights of frost ranging from zero to minus 15C and I wondered what the heron had done for food. It looked a bit of a sorry sight, sitting there hunched up, looking down at the window with its yellow-ringed eye and somehow redolent of a visitor in a smart grey suit who was not part of the celebration. It certainly wasn't a guest of the party that the birds were having below; there was nothing that would have suited it. My wife and I watched it on and off for an hour, before it at last lifted its head, stretched out its massive wings and ponderously flapped off down the burn to see if there was any better hunting there. It was as remarkable in flight as it had been on the tree branch. Its long dagger bill pointing the way ahead, its snake-like neck curled into an S shape and its stilt-like legs stretched straight out behind it. There would be thousands of birds dying of starvation during this extreme cold spell. I hoped the heron wouldn't be one of them.

Coming back again to beavers, the River Earn beaver had moved on during the spring and summer, though I got a call from Bill in mid-December 2009 to say that it had returned to what seemed to be its winter abode. The efforts will begin again to try to catch it. I was interested to listen to an update by Simon King on the release of the Knapdale, Argyllshire, beavers on the Autumnwatch Update programme in late December. Simon reported that they are doing extremely well and have built a lodge, the first beaver lodge to be built in the UK for 400 years. You and I know differently!

CHAPTER 5

Education
and a Drug-Sniffing Turkey

DESPITE the level of enforcement in which Tayside Police wildlife crime officers become involved, I am convinced that education and awareness-raising must be on an almost equal footing.

It may be because of these beliefs that I was appointed Chair of the Partnership for Action against Wildlife Crime (PAW) Scotland Training and Awareness Group in early 2009. We have gradually built up a number of public events we regularly attend, the most valuable of which is possibly the Game Conservancy Scottish Fair, but has included over the years the Bowmore International Horse Trials at Blair Atholl and the Festival of the Countryside at Glamis Castle. There is great camaraderie among stall holders at these events and our stand is always well attended. As well as meeting the colourful and interesting characters who work in occupations associated with the events, who take part in pursuits that the events represent or who simply have come along for an enjoyable day out, we answer a huge range of questions about which the inquirer wouldn't necessarily telephone us or come in to a police station to ask. I think our very presence there gives encouragement to those who look to us for support.

We seldom get a visit from anyone we suspect to be sailing close to the wind crime-wise, though there was an exception to this in 2009. I was on the stand at the Game Fair at Perth on my own when a young chap in his early 20s came in and started to talk about hare coursing. He admitted that he was involved in coursing but thought that the way he carried it out – with only one dog – was perfectly fair. I recognised him immediately as one of the half dozen or so rogues from Greenock and Port Glasgow mentioned earlier who have regular nocturnal and nefarious forays to the Crieff area of Tayside. I asked where he went coursing and his reply, probably to annoy me, was, 'All over Tayside.'

When I asked where he was from he lied, 'Fife.' We discussed coursing for a few minutes until other visitors came on to the stand and he decided to go. As he went down the ramp from the events unit I said, 'See you then, John.' It took him a few more steps until he realised I had referred to him by name. When he turned round he saw me smiling at him. Bewilderment was written all over his face. He was still puzzled when I saw him turn round for a second look after another ten paces. John will re-appear in a later chapter.

These events also offer a good chance to sample some of the delightful cuisine of the countryside and a stand that sells wild boar pies and game pies does a roaring trade. The pies are about nine inches in diameter and about two inches deep. The wild boar pies in particular are scrumptious, so much so that I decided at one event we should have a bit for breakfast. There were two of us on the stand, my colleague Gordon Nicoll being another retired inspector. As a quarter of a pie is enough for one sitting, I called at the busy pie stand and asked for two quarters of wild boar pie. 'I'm sorry but we can only sell half a pie or a whole pie' was the response. I laughed and looked for some sort of reciprocal facial reaction but the vendor maintained a blank expression. *Glaikit* would be the apt Scots term.

Determined to have wild boar pie for breakfast and salivation beginning to trickle down my chin at the thought of a pie between my teeth, I tried again. 'OK could I have half a pie please?' 'Certainly sir,' the serious voice answered, as he proceeded to press a gleaming knife through the centre of a lovely meat-filled brown-crusted pie. I had a flashback to zoology lessons in school and the reproductive system of the amoeba, which multiplies by binary fission; splitting itself into two, then four then eight so that the world is suddenly filled with millions of amoebae. I had a vision of the wild boar pie, at the touch of Sheffield steel, suddenly becoming lots of mini pies, quickly multiplying so that there were plenty for everyone.

Coming back to my senses I said to Professor Glaikit as he was about to hand me half a wild boar pie, 'Would you mind cutting that in two for me please?' 'Certainly sir' he said, as the moment was lost over the top of his head.

At these events we normally have some sort of quiz for young folks, with everyone who participates leaving the stand with a wee prize of some sort. At one RSPB event a man from Fife came into the stand with three boys who would be about ten or so. When they saw the prizes they were keen to try the quiz and soon got to work on a quiz each, using their advance prize, a free Tayside Police wildlife crime pen. The first question was *Name three birds you could see in your garden*. I was looking over the shoulder of one of the boys and saw him writing *Canary*. When I gently suggested to him that might be the wrong answer and that there were no canaries in the wild in Scotland, he answered, 'Aye there are but. My neebor keeps them in a shed in his gairden an' they're aye gettin' oot'

It got worse. Another question was *Name a bird in Scotland that eats fish*. Three juvenile faces were blank and were looking for inspiration at their mentor, who I learned was not a father or uncle of any of the boys but another 'neebor'. His knowledge of wildlife appeared slim and may even have been limited to the birds and the bees. If he had been part of a team competition he would have been as good as a man short. The boys contemplated for a while then one said, 'It's an os, os, os something or other isn't it?' I whispered to him 'osprey' in encouragement and he started to write. He either wasn't a great speller or had short memory retention. He wrote *os* then started to struggle. Doctor Mensa noticed him starting to write and tried to help with the spelling. It had suddenly clicked with him and he said, 'Yer right so far, son, it's os...t...r...i c...h.' They still all went away with a prize!

As readers of *Wildlife Detective* will be aware, Tayside Police also runs a schools' wildlife crime project every year with the pupils from P5 to P7 of schools who elect to participate. This project began in 1997 with two small classes in country schools taking part, and since 2004 there has been annual involvement of somewhere between 1500 and 2000 pupils. The only downside of this increase in numbers is the time it takes me to mark their projects, especially 1500 to 2000 nature diaries meticulously kept by each enthusiastic pupil over a 5-day period. For a time I was just about visible at my desk over the pile of boxes of nature diaries stacked on the floor and somewhat resembling high-rise flats hastily built by a team of drunken builders. The upside is the clear benefit to a large number of young people in observing and appreciating their environment.

Though not at all my area of responsibility, I was often asked by the pupils about the use of horses and dogs in policing. Most were aware of the use of police horses, which have a real threatening, and consequently deterrent, effect on a hostile crowd. The use of dogs is even more widely appreciated, with a variety of breeds now being used for crowd control, tracking, detecting drugs, explosives, money and even pesticides. But we had a less well-known animal assistant. In my drug squad days we were searching a Dundee house for drugs. The suspect was a small-time street dealer and not the brightest button in the box. We were sure he would have a few ounces of cannabis for dealing in grams or other small amounts to his friends and neighbours, though never suspected him of being a dealer who could turn over much more than that.

As we started the search it was obvious that it would take some time. The house was a midden, with dirty dishes and clothing lying everywhere, and cupboards so crammed full of junk that they should have had avalanche warnings on the doors. It was the kind of house where you would wipe your feet on the way out. The bedrooms would have done justice to a tornado strike, except that an accompanying whirlwind would have removed – or at least disturbed – most of the dust and grime that coated the floor and chairs. The only item in the house that looked new and well cared for was the huge colour TV in the corner of what could loosely be described the living room. None of us were looking forward to a rummage through any of this, and there would have been plenty of volunteers to stand with the clipboard and keep the search log.

Jim Cameron, a detective constable at the time, and in more recent times a detective superintendent before he retired, was always the comedian in the team. His skills as a joker came to the fore when he earnestly said to the dim householder, 'Look Clint, (or whatever his name was; it has always amazed me the number of drug dealers I've encountered named after a butch film star or football player who would have been flavour of the month about the time of their conception or birth) I think you should just tell us where you keep your drugs. That would save us all a lot of time. If you don't, I'm going down to the van to get the drug-sniffing turkey.' Jim went into detail about the superb olfactory senses of this non-existent beast; how it was more efficient than any dog since its nose was much more finely tuned; how it never missed drugs, especially cannabis, no matter how well hidden. 'The only problem with the turkey that lets it down is the mess it makes. The bugger shits everywhere. It seems to get excited and just seems to crap all the time it's searching. We've tried not feeding it before we take it on a job but it makes no difference.'

Unbelievably this efficacious tale worked. I forget now where the dumbfounded and duped man said the drugs were hidden but he directed us to them. It may have been that he only gave up a smaller stash of an ounce and had more elsewhere, but on that day it was good enough for us. More importantly we hadn't had to reveal our secret weapon. It would keep for another day.

CHAPTER 6

The Conservation of Seals

THERE ARE certain mammals and birds, loved by some people, that are hated by others. Rabbits, foxes, buzzards, stoats, corvids, herons, weasels, bullfinches and even hen harriers are examples. They are often considered pests by different sections of society, for example farmers and rabbits; gamekeepers and foxes; fruit growers and bullfinches. The mammal discussed in this section is the seal, loved by most, but hated by many people involved in salmon fishing.

There are two kinds of seals in the United Kingdom: the Atlantic seal, often referred to as the grey seal, and the common seal, often called the harbour seal. For many years seals had a complete piece of legislation all to themselves: the Conservation of Seals Act 1970. This changed when the Marine (Scotland) Act 2010 took effect on 31 January 2011, a part of the new Act giving seals much more apt protection.

Many who favour seals more than salmon are of the view that the Conservation of Seals Act 1970 was a toothless piece of legislation. It certainly seemed to allow the general culling of seals for a considerable part of the year provided a person had a rifle suitable for the purpose and a firearm certificate conditioned by the granting chief constable to allow the shooting of seals.

There are several interesting scientific publications reporting on the interaction between seals and salmon and seals and white fish. Nevertheless the police have to enforce the law as it is (or at least as it was before 31 January 2011.) Unfortunately there were grey areas in the Conservation of Seals Act, not least the killing of seals to protect fishing nets. Very few seal-related cases have come before the court and there is an almost complete absence of case law to rely on for clarification. In one important 2009 case in Shetland the procurator fiscal shied away from the Conservation of Seals Act and used the more appropriate Wild Mammals (Protection) Act 1996 to convict a fisherman of the killing of 21 grey seal pups, a case I related in *The Thin Green Line* (Argyll Publishing 2009).

Salmon nets in tidal waters of rivers and along our coastline are now rare, many having been bought over by District Fishery Boards so that their removal would allow more salmon to reach the spawning grounds in the upper reaches of the river system, thereby improving the lucrative rod fishing. In Tayside we still have coastal nets near the mouth of the River South Esk at Montrose and there have been several instances where complaints have been made by the public of the illegal shooting of seals. To establish a crime we have to determine what species of seal was involved, that the seal had wilfully been shot (or shot at), that the shooting was illegal, and who shot it. This is difficult enough with the shooting of a bird or mammal on land where the carcass or injured animal may be easily recovered. In rivers, estuaries or at sea the evidence in the form of the dead or injured seal, in almost all cases, is impossible to recover. The body may be washed ashore a couple of days after the shooting but identifying it as the particular seal shot in the earlier incident is extremely difficult.

I should explain that under the old Act there was a closed season for killing or taking either of the species of seal. This was the period during which the species is breeding and during which time it was protected. Under the 1970 Act the closed season for the common seal was from 1 June till 31 August, and for the Atlantic seal from 1 September till 31 December. Except! This is the dreaded word which must not be overlooked in legislation, and means that if a particular act carried out is an excepted act, then the person has not committed an offence. Almost every piece of legislation has exceptions.

The exception in the 1970 Act allowed the killing of a seal during the closed season to prevent damage to fishing nets or fishing tackle provided the seal was in the vicinity of the nets or tackle. This allowed salmon netsmen to protect their nets and their catch, which does not seem too unreasonable a concession. The netsmen are trying to make a living and seals are trying to seek an easy way to catch their prey. Seals that try this easy method and visit the phocine equivalent of 'Salmon King' or 'McSalmon' risk being shot. I have no argument with this as it's what the 1970 Act set out.

You will note that there was a qualification in this exception: the seal must be *in the vicinity* of the net. 'Vicinity' was not defined in the Act, nor is there any case law or court decision that could be used to determine how close a seal must be to fishing nets to qualify as being *in the vicinity*. In the absence of any legal direction on this term, my own interpretation, from a common sense point of view, would be to report anyone for prosecution if there was evidence that a seal had been shot within 200 yards or so of the nets. A court may agree with this interpretation or may disagree completely, reducing or extending this distance, but it seemed a reasonable starting point for a prosecution until there was some legal basis from which to work.

Almost all offences relating to seals shot *in the vicinity* of a net were likely to relate to common seals. Common seals are in the middle of their breeding time when salmon netting is still in high season, so it is the common seal that would feature in any case of this nature. By the time the former closed season came round for Atlantic seals on 1 September the netting season had ended so they *should* have total protection while breeding.

In a very early morning in mid-July 2005 a seal enthusiast who is a member of the British Divers Marine Life Rescue (BDMLR), was checking on some seals at the River South Esk estuary at Montrose. She was on the private road leading to Scurdieness lighthouse, a quiet, narrow lane high above the south bank of the estuary. There were eight adult common seals hauled out on a sandbank in the estuary and the seals still had a couple of hours or so to rest before the sandbank would be covered by the incoming tide. The woman became aware of a 4WD vehicle parked further along the road, then saw the driver of the vehicle emerge with a rifle. She alternated her line of sight between the seals and the man and saw two jets of water spurt from the sea just short of the seals on the sandbank. She was convinced that the man was shooting at the seals though she did not hear any rifle shot.

The woman watched the man get in to his car and drive along the road a bit further. The seals were still on the sandbank, undisturbed and presumably unaware of bullets hitting the water just short of where they were hauled out. The vehicle stopped again and the witness watched while the man leaned his rifle over the bonnet to steady his aim. With the aid of binoculars, the woman again saw spurts of water shoot into the air just short of the seals, then saw the seals launch into the water. Seven seals made it to safety; one remained, unmoving, on the sandbank.

The man got back into his car, turned at the lighthouse, and drove back up the road. In the meantime the woman had telephoned the police to report the incident, including the registration number of the car. She had also recognised the man driving the car. Evidentially this information was extremely important, but it still did not prove that a crime had been committed. The woman was unable to say what species the seals were at that stage, which meant that the whole shooting operation may have been legal.

I was contacted by the police in Montrose shortly after this and gave advice on what was required to establish that a crime had actually taken place. I must give full credit to the police officers who attended. The two officers, the original witness and another more experienced member of the BDMLR, Elaine Roft, acted swiftly in getting out on to the sandbank. The seal was identified by Elaine as a common seal and it was secured as evidence in the case. To obtain this crucial evidence the four stalwarts already had waded knee-deep through the South Esk to reach the seal, tied a rope to it and hauled it back to the shore just ahead of the incoming tide. Had they not been able to do that we would not have been able to put a case to the procurator fiscal.

As the four were roping the seal a boat drew up alongside them. This was the brother of the person identified to the police as having shot the seal, who wanted to take the seal to dispose of the carcass. This, he stated, was their common practice after shooting a seal. Needless to say he had to leave empty-handed. This visit by the man in the boat was important to the case, especially since he allegedly stated to the police officers that it was his brother who shot the seal.

I received a further update at this stage of the investigation. I was at a meeting in Edinburgh but was happy to keep in touch by telephone. I requested that the seal be taken to the Scottish Agricultural College vet lab at Perth so that a post mortem examination could be carried out to confirm the cause of death, and to try to recover the bullet for ballistics examination. If a bullet is not too badly damaged it can be compared to another bullet test-fired through the rifle used in the crime and a comparison made. Each bullet has unique marks, called striation marks, caused by the rifling of the barrel through which it is fired. Each round fired through that rifle has exactly the same marks and in that way a bullet can be forensically linked to the rifle. This type of evidence is crucial in the use of handguns in murder cases, where the same gun can be linked to cases that took place at different times and sometimes in completely different parts of the country.

That afternoon a post mortem examination was carried out by a veterinary pathologist. There was a clear bullet entry wound on the seal's back and its injuries were consistent with it having died as a result of this bullet wound. Even better, the bullet was recovered so now there was a chance of obtaining further incriminating evidence. This was the good news, but the bad news was that at this point the prosecution case – when it came to trial – could have collapsed. Where evidence is crucial to obtaining a conviction, it must be corroborated. Though a police officer and the two BDMLR members had been present at the post mortem, had taken photographs and could speak to the recovery of the bullet, they were not vets. None were even experienced enough in the examination of injuries to have provided part corroboration of the results of the post mortem and of the cause of death of the seal. We managed, however, to rectify this at a later date. In the same vein, we still did not have corroboration of the fact that the seal was a common seal, as the vet was not sufficiently experienced in seals to provide this identification. This crucial fact we also established later.

On the day following the recovery of the seal the suspect was interviewed by the police officers dealing with the case and his rifle was seized. The rifle was a .22/250 and was fitted with a silencer, hence the reason no shots were heard being fired. The rifle and the bullet were forwarded to our ballistics department at Police Headquarters but the bullet recovered from the seal was too badly damaged for a comparison to be made.

One further factor we had to establish for the court was the location of the nearest nets to where the seals had been hauled out on the sandbank. I left this to the local officers, who knew the area far better than I did. They established that the nearest nets belonged to the suspect and were a mile away round the headland to the south of the estuary. I therefore did not think in the circumstances that the court would consider the sandbank to be *in the vicinity* of the nets, but then this had never been tested. Additionally, might the court take into account that seals resting on a sandbank were not at that time a threat to anything, and that when they left the sandbank they might indeed have swum away in the opposite direction to the salmon nets?

As in most wildlife cases, I discussed the evidence with the procurator fiscal. Most fiscals seldom deal with wildlife cases and a case under the Conservations of Seals Act 1970 was particularly uncommon. There had only been a handful through the UK courts since the legislation was framed in 1970 and as far as I am aware, only one had resulted in conviction. The fiscal asked that we obtain corroboration of the species of seal, crucial because the charge related to shooting a common seal while it was protected by the close season. She also asked for corroboration of the cause of death.

Both of these matters were in hand in any case and I had made contact with the Sea Mammal Research Unit at St Andrews to try to find an expert in seals. I did manage to find an expert, Callan Duck, and arranged for him to view the dead seal. This was in the large freezer at the Scottish Agricultural College vet lab at Perth. Though the seal took up most of the space in the freezer, we had never considered disposing of it; cases in the past have been lost when a solicitor acting for the defence has asked to see the dead animal or fish that is the subject of the charge, and it was no longer available. If the defence are denied the chance to examine the evidence on which the crown case is relying to convict their client, then that is unfair and the crown case will almost certainly be thrown out.

Callan arrived at the vet lab and I spoke with him before he viewed the seal, asking him about the different characteristics by which he could tell a common seal from an Atlantic seal. He told me that there are several methods of telling the difference between the two species but the teeth are the most failsafe method. Seals' teeth are modified for grasping prey rather than for chewing it; as a result most prey is swallowed whole. With common seals they have tricuspids on the canines, premolars and molars – in other words three points on these teeth – compared to the Atlantic seals' single cusp. As with legislation, sometimes there are exceptions: in both species sometimes there is no obvious distinction between the premolars and molars. My method of identifying a common seal is that its head has a resemblance to a spaniel's head, while an Atlantic seal's head looks like the head of a horse. This was schoolboy stuff, though Callan did agree that it was a reasonable guide in most cases for adult seals but not necessarily for young seals. Callan then looked at the mouth of the seal and gasped in amazement. He was ready to show us the distinctive teeth but every single tooth in the seal's mouth was worn down to the gum; it was impossible to use that method of identification. I asked why that could be, and was told that the most likely reason was that the seal must have enjoyed playing with stones, picking them off the bottom, dropping them, catching them again and rolling them around in its mouth. It was not an old seal and should have had a full set of teeth in reasonable condition. Despite its absence of teeth, the seal was identified as a common seal.

The next task was to corroborate the SAC vet, Colin Adams, in his determination from the post mortem examination of the seal that it had been killed by a bullet. I made a telephone call to Professor Ranald Munro and explained the position to him. He was prepared to come and see the seal, and if it was thawed out prior to his visit, he would conduct a second post mortem examination. He said, however, that this might not be necessary and he may be able to establish a cause of death from the photographs taken during the post mortem examination and the report from Colin Adams. I obtained these and posted them to him. Within a short time I had a response back from Ranald that from the evidence I had sent him he was able to concur with the conclusion of Colin Adams: that the seal had been killed by being struck by a bullet. We were now ready for trial.

The accused, during the trial, was represented by a solicitor and a very experienced Queen's Counsel. The crown was represented by a young procurator fiscal. I am convinced that this situation is neither fair on the fiscal nor fair to the public interest, which she represented, however my views on this don't count as it's a practice that is not uncommon. Neither is it the case that the defence always achieve a not guilty verdict, though the odds seem to be in their favour.

On the first day of the trial, evidence was heard from only three witnesses: the woman who witnessed the man with the rifle shooting towards the seals; Elaine from BDMLR who joined her to help recover the body of the dead seal and vet Colin Adams. Since we had run out of time the case was continued until another date two months later.

On the second day I spoke with the fiscal before the proceedings started as I had suggested I should bring the file relating to the man on trial from the Firearms Licencing Department. The entries in the file would show that he had considerable experience of shooting seals, having first been authorised to shoot them more than twenty years previously. I thought if there was an excuse offered that he had been unable to tell an Atlantic seal from a common seal then the fiscal could challenge that effectively because of his experience. I asked the fiscal if she was aware of what the QC might be relying on as a defence but she had no more knowledge of this than I.

The brother of the accused, who had turned up in the boat to retrieve the seal, was called to give evidence. I later gathered from others who were in court that unexpectedly he had led evidence that he had lobster pots in the area of the sandbank, much closer than the nets, though for whatever reason the distance they were situated from the sandbank was never brought out. No one had been aware that the accused or his brother used lobster pots, though it was known that there were some round the coast used by another fisherman. Whether they were there or not is largely irrelevant; the witness said that they had been there and no-one was in a position to challenge this.

The fishermen were entitled to use the statutory defence to shoot seals that were protected by the close season *provided that at the time the seal was in the vicinity of nets or fishing tackle.* We had focussed too much on nets since the accused was a salmon fisherman, and had not considered *fishing tackle* as we did not know that he used lobster pots. The brother apparently also gave a different version of why he had gone in the boat to collect the seal. In court he said that he had been mistaken when he said that his brother had shot it. This, he claimed, had been an assumption on his part but in fact he recollected that his brother had simply told him that there was a seal which had probably been shot lying on the sandbank.

An interesting point arose in discussions with a seal and fisheries expert since the trial. It appears that most areas on which seals haul-out are traditional and seals return to them again and again. This includes sandbanks, though by their very nature sandbanks may move about a bit in an estuary. The expert view is that if someone put lobster pots in an area near a traditional haul-out site then the operators would *not* be entitled to rely on the defence that they were protecting their tackle against seal predation. This makes absolute sense. As analogies, a farmer would not expect to have a harvest from a crop of peas sown in a hen run or would dissuade his children from keeping their pet white mice in an open run under a pair of nesting owls. In all cases disaster would not only be inevitable but would be predictable to anyone with any common sense. (It is interesting that under the Marine (Scotland) Act 2010 that now replaces the 1970 Act, it is an offence to intentionally or recklessly harass a seal at a designated haul-out site).

Getting back to the trial, the next witness was the police officer who had investigated and reported the case. She stated in evidence that what the brother of the accused had said to her was quite unequivocal: that the witness was there with his boat to collect a dead seal which his brother had shot. It was unfortunate that this corroborating evidence had not been led from the witness who watched the accused shooting at the seal. She had also heard the comment, and it was in the statement she gave to the police, but she had not been asked about it in the witness box. The police officer was also unable to say exactly where the nets were situated on the day that the seal had been shot. She had not measured the distance that day but in fact had gone three days later to measure the distance between where the seal was and where the nets were.

When this witness finished giving evidence the QC addressed the sheriff and stated that there was no case to answer. When this happens the defence has to state the reasons for this motion and the prosecution, conversely, has an opportunity to state why there *is* a case to answer. The court adjourned for a short time to let everyone gather their thoughts and the fiscal came to the witness room to see me. I was at the case in the capacity of an 'expert' witness and as such the case could be discussed with me. I learned something of what had happened in the court from the fiscal and was devastated by the new 'evidence' about the lobster pots. Surely it would have been sensible for the accused to have made mention of this at the time. Had it been the case, and had it been demonstrated to be so, he may not have been charged. I didn't believe it but could do nothing about it. I also thought that the evidence of where the nets were on the day was irrelevant as the nets are fixed nets. It would be reasonable to assume if they were in that fixed position two or three days before the shooting and still there three days after, then they would have been there on the day the seal was shot. The opportunity to give this evidence from the witness box was lost. The fact remained that the distance from the seal *on the day it was shot* to the nets had not been established in evidence, though I was still puzzled by what difference this could make.

The defence motion of no case to answer was based on two factors. Firstly the QC claimed that it had not been established that the accused shot the seal. He was only seen shooting towards the seal and no-one saw a shot strike and kill a seal. Secondly it had not been established by the prosecution that the seals on the sandbank were *not* in the vicinity of nets or fishing tackle. The fiscal argued against these points. The evidence of the shooting of the seal by the accused came from the sighting of him with his rifle and the surrounding facts and circumstances. To corroborate this we were relying on the account of the brother as to why he turned up to collect the seal. The fiscal could not disprove the allegation by the defence of lobster pots in the area and could see the case rapidly going down the tubes. I wondered also if lobster pots could really be classified as fishing tackle, since lobsters are crustaceans, not fish.

The sheriff adjourned to consider her decision, which took more than two hours. I began to realise that it was not clear cut or she could have given her decision in a matter of minutes. When she returned to the bench she admitted that the issues were complex and asked a further few questions of the QC and the procurator fiscal. As I feared, she agreed with the defence and upheld the motion of no case to answer. The accused was acquitted.

More lessons are learned from lost cases than from those that succeed. The clear issue here was that the Conservation of Seals Act 1970 no longer seemed fit for purpose. Firstly there was no power of arrest given to the police in the Act, nor were any of the offences punishable by imprisonment. This meant that any interview of a suspect by the police almost had to be conducted on the suspect's terms; he could not be arrested or detained and taken to a police station for interview.

Secondly there was no real protection for seals. They could be shot all the year round except during the breeding season, when they could still be shot in the vicinity of fishing nets of other fishing tackle. This case demonstrated how difficult that was to prove. Had the situation been that seals were protected by the law but could still be shot by a fisherman *provided he could justify the shooting in defence of his nets or fishing tackle* that would be workable. This reverses the burden of proof so that the fisherman would have had to demonstrate that nets were in the vicinity of where the seal was shot. In genuine cases that would not be difficult. From the interpretation of the outcome of this case the police had to prove first of all the species of seal shot, no easy task if it sinks to the bottom of the sea; that it was during the breeding time of the seal, and that there were no nets or other tackle – or maybe even lobster pots – in the area. Since lobster pots are under water the best person to tell the police where they are situated is the suspect, but the minute he becomes a suspect he must be cautioned that he is not obliged to say anything and that anything he says will be noted and may be used in evidence.

With the experience of the problems in this case and the unsuitability of the provisions of the Conservation of Seals Act 1970 I wrote a report for the Scottish Government outlining the issues. I repeated them during the consultation period of the Marine (Scotland)

Bill. I also learned in early 2007 that in the Firth of Tay, not too many miles down the coast from the South Esk, common seal numbers had dropped by 48% since 2002. I wonder why?

However, with every tale there is good news and bad news. I've already narrated the bad news. The good news was that the case was to be appealed by the Crown on the grounds of a wrong decision by the sheriff in response to the defence submission of No Case to Answer. Wildlife cases seem to drag on forever.

In mid April 2007 the appeal was due to be heard but was not contested by the defence. The case was remitted back to the sheriff, who was then bound to repel the 'no case to answer' submission and proceed with the trial. The trial continued on 3 August 2007. The prosecution evidence had been completed and it was now down to the defence to either concede, or argue against the Crown case. An accused person has no need to give evidence on his or her behalf: it is up to the Crown to prove the case. In this particular trial the accused had agreed to give evidence.

His evidence was initially surprising, as he did not dispute that he had shot a seal on the sand bank, his argument being that the seal was within half a mile of his salmon nets. He also produced a letter to the court that his father had received in 1971 – 36 years previously – from the then MAFF (Ministry of Agriculture Fisheries and Food, now in 2007 after several name-changes Scottish Government Rural Payment and Inspections Directorate with the unpronounceable acronym SGRPID). The MAFF letter referred to half a mile as a reasonable distance for a seal to be a potential threat to salmon nets. This was not a definition of the term 'vicinity' in relation to seals and nets, simply the view of an individual in the then MAFF. The salmon netsman further admitted that the seal, along with its companions, was basking on a sandbank when he shot it. He also agreed that the shot seal's companions probably swam off in the direction of his salmon nets rather than away from them after the shot.

Some of this was good prosecution evidence but the 1971 letter had thrown a spanner in the works. Though I wasn't in court to hear the legal arguments I'm a bit surprised that the introduction of the letter was admissible in evidence. The prosecution must disclose to the defence everything that is to be led in evidence. It seemed that this was not so with the defence. I often feel in criminal investigations and the subsequent legal proceedings that we are not playing on a level playing field; that the rights of an accused are well safeguarded but less so the rights of a victim, in this case the public interest. I may be wrong but this is certainly the way that court proceedings sometimes come across to the public – and even to seasoned crime investigators.

The accused stated in evidence that he had measured the distance between the nets and where he had shot the seal, which he averred was .32 of a mile. Though police had measured the distance at a mile this evidence had not been given in court as the officer who measured the distance was not called as a witness. The prosecution case was already closed and the version of the distance put forward by the accused could not be contested by the fiscal.

At the conclusion of the trial the sheriff found the accused not guilty. She stated that she had found him a credible witness and said that he had acted within his exemption. She went on to state that, 'the public could well be appalled at someone shooting seals apparently sunning themselves, but he's in the fishing industry.'

Since this case, common seals had temporary additional protection outside the closed season on the north and north-east coast of Scotland under the Conservation of Seals (Scotland) Order 2007, as their numbers were rapidly falling, though the 'netsmen's defence' as discussed was still applicable. The need for the Order surely begs the question of why the numbers had declined.

Returning briefly to my other fisherman, the heron up the tree in the garden, I was interrupted by Jan, my wife, to say that she had been watching the heron on and off for an hour and a half. It had been busily preening as if it maybe had a date with another heron later in the evening. I was called to see it just as it flew down from the tree to the burn. It was an immature heron that in October still seemed to have down on the top of its head. Since herons are one of the earliest nesters this couldn't be down and I wondered if it could have been the beginnings of the beautiful crest it would have as an adult. We watched it from the window for another 20 minutes. It was in the best pool in the burn for small trout and it varied its concentration on looking for fish with looking skywards for predators. I considered predators of such a big bird and wondered if the herons' habits have changed since the introduction of white-tailed eagles to the east coast, its only avian predator I could think of, or had this innate alertness never left it over the last hundred-and-a-bit years since these eagles last soared in our skies. Its patience (and ours) paid off and within half an hour it stalked and caught a small brown trout that wriggled its way down a lengthy gullet to a gruesome death in an acid bath that didn't bear thinking about.

The South Esk tale was not my first seal-related incident on the coast of Angus. The first related to the same salmon netsmen but was substantially different in the form that it took.

I was at home early one evening, probably around 2003, when I received a telephone call from Fife Coastguard. They had received a telephone or radio report, I'm not sure which, from men in a launch who were diving off the Bell Rock lighthouse. The Bell Rock lighthouse sits on top of a collection of jagged rocks, which would have been a terrifying hazard to shipping without the famous light, and is situated 12 miles out into the North Sea off Arbroath. The men had reported that there were two people on the rocks at the lighthouse who were shooting seals. They were concerned for the seals as they had photographed one swimming in the water with a head injury, probably having been grazed by a bullet. I thought their concern may have been more relevant for their own lives rather than those of the seals, as the men had been diving in the water round the lighthouse while the shooting had been taking place. The men had noted the number of the boat, which the coastguard ascertained came from an Angus coastal village.

I arranged for local police officers to watch for the boat returning to its home port and to check the occupants and their rifles. This they did and were able to verify that the rifles were owned by the two men. I followed this up the next day and verified from our Firearms

Licensing Section that the men had a condition on their certificate allowing them to shoot seals. I then asked if the men were restricted to shooting seals in any particular part or parts of the coastline but was told that they apparently had salmon nets in a number of places and the condition on their certificate allowed them to shoot anywhere round the coast. Several days later I spoke with the two men, who told me that they had shot something like 40 seals that day. In effect they had carried out a seal cull, but had done nothing that was illegal.

This may have been a conservation issue but it was not a policing issue. I am very conscious that my role is policing and that I should not stray from this field into other fields that are neither any business of the police nor in which police officers – even wildlife crime officers – usually have any form of training sufficient to voice opinions. From time to time I pass information to a conservation body if I think that the reason for, or the outcome of, some particular act may need investigation by them but it is a matter for them to decide on the most appropriate action, if indeed any action is necessary. Horses for courses.

Seal incidents formed only a very small part of my day-to-day work but there was yet another situation that I was drawn into. I'm now about to make myself popular with salmon anglers and may find myself as an effigy with seal enthusiasts, throwing darts in my direction. I intervened – mediated is maybe a better term – in a decision by our Firearms Licensing Department after the factor of an estate well upstream on the River Tay had applied for permission for seals to be shot by their gamekeepers. A handful of seals were regularly coming upstream with the tide and, in his words, were wreaking havoc with salmon in some of the pools that were popular with anglers paying a hefty price for the privilege of catching salmon. I'm not an expert in the ecology of seals but I would imagine that salmon are a lot more easily caught by seals in a pool in a river in times of low water than in an estuary or at sea. It is therefore logical that anglers would not be at all pleased that seals were at worst eating, and at best disturbing, salmon that they wanted to catch.

The estate had been told that their authority to shoot seals was likely to be refused on the grounds of public safety, hence their telephone call to me. I could appreciate the public safety concern since the estate was close to Perth and there was a path, albeit on the opposite bank from the estate, where people frequently walked. I tried to be unbiased in my opinion. I appreciated the potential danger to the public, which was the over-riding concern, but I thought that other issues had also to be considered.

The first question was: how can seals be controlled without a risk to public safety? None of those who were about to refuse permission were shooters. I had considerable experience both with a rifle and a shotgun and knew that every shot loosed off by responsible shooters did not necessarily pose a risk to human life. I wondered if there was a compromise and suggested a riverside meeting with Fiona Windmill, the head of Firearms Licensing, the estate factor, and the gamekeeper who would be carrying out any shooting. If we could agree that early morning or late evening shooting could be carried out, and that there were places on the riverside where the bank was high enough for the bullet to be directed steeply down towards the water and the shot to be safe as a consequence, then there may be some room for manoeuvre rather than just a blank refusal to grant the required condition on the certificate to allow the shooting of seals.

While the first question might easily be answered in the affirmative, as there were indeed several high banks, what about the second question: is the culling of seals in that particular area justified? The answer was that it seemed entirely reasonable. Only a small number of seals were involved, these seals may have had a 'taste' for easy pickings and as such were likely to return time and time again. Since they were unlikely to invite their relatives from the estuary, if they were dealt with the problem was resolved. The culling of this small number would be insignificant to the overall population, whether they were Atlantic seals or common seals. Lastly, their presence so far upstream had a marked negative effect on salmon angling and the local economy.

The third question was: if a seal is shot, how can it be prevented from being carried downstream by the flow of the river and ending up on the banks of the River Tay at Perth city centre? This would certainly result in a deluge of phone calls to the police and the media by concerned, but not necessarily enlightened, members of the public.

The riverside meeting took place and two sites were identified where shooting of seals could take place safely. With the keeper agreeing that he would only shoot in early morning or late evening we were nearly there, only the recovery of any seals shot had to be addressed. This necessitated a meeting with seal experts at the Sea Mammal Research Unit at St Andrews. Their advice was that if a seal is shot just before it dives and has its lungs full of air, it is likely to float. This would make for a far easier recovery of the carcass and minimise the risk of the body sinking and being washed downstream to alarm Perth citizens. The keeper was schooled by the experts in the art of recognising the stage when the seal was about to dive, which meant that, in a somewhat limited but acceptable fashion, the seals could be controlled. In addition the public would be relatively free from having to encounter, on their way to Marks and Spencer's or to their day's work at the office, a seal carcass with a bullet wound to the head.

This was put in place and in the (so far) nine years that it has operated the public has been safe from being shot and so far as we know only one seal was lost and floated down to the city centre waters where it received minimum publicity. Rather than moaning about the intransigence of the police, the anglers and the estate are now happy that they can exert some form of control over what they term rogue seals. Single issue interests or organisations can sometimes be blinkered in their views and it is important to look at the wider issues. No matter how unfortunate the situation, it is a fact that we do not live in an age where we cannot or must not interfere with nature. A balance can occasionally be struck where no-one – or no species – comes off too badly. I was pleased that I could help to bring that about.

CHAPTER 7

Operation Lepus

OPERATION Lepus is a joint initiative between Tayside Police and country-dwelling communities to target the main people involved in hare coursing. Its effects were beginning to be felt in the hare coursing community. Because of increased pressure on the criminals, reports of hare coursing became fewer in the closing couple of months of 2006 and fewer still in the first two months of 2007. Besides, we were keeping up or even improving our detection rate. One of the November 2006 incidents was interesting in that we located a man I had been looking for in relation to an earlier coursing incident in July. It involved a wee thin fellow, his diminutive size being exaggerated by the fact he was very often involved in hare coursing exploits with a large heavy-set chap with a real bull neck. I'll refer to the antihero of this tale as the 'Wee Man', which will make it easy to distinguish him later from the 'Big Man', whom he joins in yet another incident. The Wee Man was an incorrigible hare courser. He had been caught several times before, though not always convicted, since groups of people caught at the same time for any sort of crime have a habit of sharing out the sentences, taking turns to plead guilty and no doubt sharing the cost if a financial penalty is imposed by the court. I doubted that he would ever give up keeping lurchers and using them to catch hares. In a story related in *Wildlife Detective*, one of this pair had been so engrossed in filming their coursing activities that their car ran off on its own down a country road, pursued by the erstwhile cameraman now filming the car upside down from a dangling camcorder until it collided with a roadside tree. Unfortunately the film did not show the extent of the damage, though the voice on the soundtrack indicated the car owner was not best pleased.

In the July incident the Wee Man and two others had been seen releasing three lurchers into a grass field on the outskirts of Perth. A car containing the three men plus a young boy had stopped at an open gate and immediately the three dogs were out and in pursuit of a hare the men had spotted sitting contentedly in its form in the middle of the field. Hares make a shallow scrape a few inches deep in which they can sit and be partly hidden, yet retain the ability to see almost all round them. If a predator approaches they often sink down deeper into the form relying on camouflage to safeguard them, and often only run off at the last minute when they realise that their first survival strategy has failed. They sometimes use the same form for several days and the earth becomes smooth and shiny, with fine hairs embedded into the earth like lace as the hare sits and shuffles about.

At this time a public-spirited part-time gamekeeper was driving along the road and stopped to tell the men what they were doing was completely illegal. He remonstrated with them, all the while getting abuse and threats for his interference. Meanwhile he saw two of the dogs catch and kill the hare, while the third was off in pursuit of a second hare. The gamekeeper flagged down another car, with a man and woman as occupants, coming along the country road. He desperately needed corroboration of what was taking place: the offence being committed against the hares and potentially towards his own safety. The effect was instant. Now that there were three people aware of their illegal activities, the men began to shout on their dogs to come back. They were coming back right enough but all three by this time hard on the heels of hare number two, which ran through the open gate, past the mixed crowd of spectators, across the road and into a field of rape. The fate of the hare was unknown but I suspect that it would have been caught by the dogs as the height of the rape in early July would have been a hindrance to its progress, while it would have little effect on the dogs with their much longer legs.

By this time the woman in the second car had called the police and officers were en route. The dogs returned from the rape field, were bundled into the car and the gang set off, the whole episode lasting not much more than five minutes. Because of its proximity to Perth, a police officer arrived at the incident a few minutes later but even though he circulated the registration number of the gang's vehicle, it had disappeared without trace.

I learned of the incident shortly after it happened and carried out a check on the registration number of the car. It was registered to a person I knew to be a female relative of the Wee Man and this right away put us on his trail. I had suspected that it was this gang in any case because of the presence of the young boy. So far I was aware this was the only crew who regularly exposed kids from about 7 years upwards to teenagers to this cruel practice. I arranged for sets of photographs of the Wee Man and his known associates to be prepared and asked the police officer dealing with the case to show them to the gamekeeper. The Wee Man was immediately picked out as having been the driver of the vehicle, and another person was identified as being one of his cronies. Since they were travellers with a number of addresses to fit in with their itinerant lifestyle we failed to catch up with them and it appeared that they were off the hook. Or were they?

Late one Saturday evening in early November an alert farmer near Brechin in Angus saw the beam of a spotlamp playing back and forth across one of his fields. From previous experience he knew that it would be men out after hares. He contacted the estate gamekeeper and the police, then set off to see if he could find what vehicle was involved and where it had gone. The area is a web of extremely narrow country roads but by good luck the gamekeeper spotted the beam in a field half a mile further on and reported the new location to the police. Officers had been in the area in any case and quickly homed in on the vehicle.

It was the next day that I learned of this incident and of the fact that it was again the Wee Man from Aberdeen, this time accompanied by the Big Man plus a youngster. The two men were from towns over a hundred miles apart and this demonstrates the network of travellers addicted to coursing. The car involved was that of the Wee Man and the same as had been used in the Perth incident. The two men had been arrested and were to appear at Arbroath Sheriff Court on the following Tuesday. It was their misfortune that the Monday was a public holiday and that they had a long weekend ahead of them, each in a cell with no view and little by way of furnishings except for a toilet, a bunk and a couple of blankets.

Our friends' bad luck was our good luck. We now knew the address at which the Wee Man was now in residence and that he would definitely be at home for selected callers for the next 48 hours. He was visited in his Arbroath cell by police officers from Perth and interviewed about the July hare coursing incident. Rather surprisingly he admitted the whole thing! It may have been that he was just glad to have the chance to chat to someone. It was not just a chance to chat but the subject was something close to his heart: hare coursing. He was charged with a contravention of the Protection of Wild Mammals (Scotland) Act 2002 and told he would receive a summons in due course. Under this Act cases have to be with the procurator fiscal within 6 months of the incident. We were now close to 5 months and I asked that the case be reported urgently.

On the Tuesday morning I discovered that the Wee Man and the Big Man's luck had improved slightly. They did not appear in court from custody but were released before court. I made contact with the fiscal to ask if there was a problem. The fiscal said that she had been just about to telephone me to ask if I could look over the case as she wondered how we could prove it was hares and not rabbits (bloody non-mammal rabbits again) that Messrs Large and Small were after. This is always the sticking point in these cases and I undertook to re-interview the farmer and the gamekeeper to ensure that we could prove that there were no rabbits in the area.

The area where the two men had been lamping is all arable and is mostly used for growing wheat, barley and potatoes. Because of this specialisation most of the fields were bigger than average. In addition they were cultivated regularly; ideal for hares but no use for rabbits as they had long since got fed up of their burrows being ploughed up and disturbed and had moved onto woodland, rough pasture and any parts of the extremely scarce field margins that may have been suitable. I made a check of the fields in which the suspects had shown an interest and found no evidence of rabbits in any of them except a small part of the very last one the men had been seen at, where there were a few signs of rabbits emerging from woodland, though this was well away from the public road. I took a series of photographs and my statement complemented those of the farmer and the gamekeeper.

The Wee Man appeared in Perth Sheriff Court in early February for his first case. He pleaded guilty but because of his record the sheriff deferred sentence, possibly considering handing out a jail term. He advised the Wee Man that when he reappeared in court two weeks hence for sentence he should not bring his car with him but should ensure to bring his driving licence as he was going to be disqualified from driving. I was not in court but word reached me that the diminutive chap had nearly collapsed in the dock at the threat of disqualification. It was something that he had never considered in relation to hare coursing and a matter that I have absolutely no doubt has been well discussed since by many – if not all – of his lurcher-owning friends. The Wee Man most certainly didn't have a good day out at Perth!

In the event the sheriff did not disqualify him from driving, stating that 'it might be a step too far' as his lifestyle required him to have a driving licence. He was fined £150, since he claimed to be unemployed. Most interesting was the comment from his defence solicitor when he was making a plea for leniency on his client's behalf. He told the court that hare coursing was recognised as a traditional activity in the travelling community. He continued, 'These hunting skills have traditionally been passed down from father to son. It is incumbent upon my client to pass on these skills but he is aware he can't do so where very young members of the travelling community are involved.' Could this be interpreted as 'The Wee Man does not recognise Scottish Law in relation to hare coursing?' Despite what he told the court, he regularly encourages the participation of children, and hares and country dwellers can be assured that the next generation of this family of travellers will almost certainly continue as before.

While we were awaiting the trial of Messrs Large and Small for their nocturnal adventure, there was another night-time visit by our Greenock and Port Glasgow team. In mid-February the night shift officers at Auchterarder in Perthshire were called to investigate a person with a spotlight in a field about 10 miles away outside the village of Comrie. A man living on the edge of Comrie had been awakened by a beam of light criss-crossing his bedroom window and had looked out to see what was happening. He saw two men in the field with two dogs, both of which were at full speed after a hare. An hour before, the same police officers had investigated an identical report near the village of Muthill, half-way between Auchterarder and Comrie, but had found no trace of anyone. It appeared likely that the men had now moved location and luckily the officers were already half-way there when they received this second call.

The officers briefly saw the beam in the field then saw a car parked in a field gateway. The light immediately went off as the police car stopped at the parked car. Without having a spotlight themselves, it is very difficult for police officers to find anyone in the pitch black of the night and their idea at that time was to take possession of the car. It is likely that the men realised that and after half an hour or so they came out of hiding and returned with their two dogs to their car. They had a spotlight and a battery pack, which one of the men had in a rucksack on his back. It was a bit stupid to have brought the lamp out with them rather than having hidden it in the field but they had twice already had the lamp and battery pack returned to them by the police and I presume they by now considered this standard practice. This time they were wrong! I had vented my frustration about the last two spotlamp fiascos and the officers had learned by their mistake. The men were interviewed and admitted having been after rabbits rather than hares – the standard tale – but said their dogs had not caught any; that they were too slow. 'The dugs widnae chase hares anyway cos they're wee dugs and they're feart o' them. That's true. Honest sur.' What piffle!

The two were charged with an offence under the Night Poaching Act 1828. This was in the early hours of a Saturday morning and I wasn't made aware until the Monday morning. By my interpretation of the wording of the Act, a charge under the Night Poaching Act was not valid. The wording is that anyone by night time on any land or roads intersecting such land *and taking* any game or rabbits without permission commits an offence. There was no evidence that the men had *taken* any game or rabbits. The wording continues that it is also an offence by night time and without permission to be on land *for the purpose of taking game*. The men had been chasing a hare but that activity had only been seen by one person: the man from his bedroom window. There was no corroboration, either from an admission by the men or from the finding of a dead hare in the field. Further, there is no mention of rabbits in the part of the Act that relates to being on land *for the purpose* of poaching; just game, which does not include rabbits in its definition. Had I been told about the incident (as I should have been) first thing on the Sunday morning I would have spent a couple of hours looking for dead hares or rabbits in the fields to provide the much needed corroboration.

Had this taken place in daytime, the Game (Scotland) Act 1832 would have been perfect, as the men were on land in pursuit of game (whether rabbits or hares did not matter) without the landowner's permission, but this legislation is replaced by the Night Poaching Act an hour after sunset. However all was not lost. The last resort was the Poaching Prevention Act 1862, which gives power to a police officer to search any person in a street or public place if they have good cause to suspect the person has come from land where he was unlawfully in search or pursuit of game and having in his possession any game unlawfully obtained or any instruments used in the killing of game. Different Acts have different interpretations of 'game' but this time rabbits were included within the definition. I confirmed that the search of the two men and their vehicle had taken place in a public place, in other words on the road, and we were back in business.

For a charge under this Act to succeed in court, an Oath of Verity must be sworn in front of a sheriff or justice of the peace and submitted to the procurator fiscal with the police report. I am not absolutely clear of the relevance of this and can only assume that, since the Poaching Prevention Act is one of the few in which the evidence of one witness, accepted by the court as being credible, can secure a conviction, the Oath of Verity may form part-corroboration of the evidence given. It is a relic of the past and no longer included in the poaching offences now within the scope of the Wildlife and Country-side Act 1981 as amended by the Wildlife and Natural Environment (Scotland) Act 2011. Nevertheless it was an essential component of this ancient Act and took the following form, signed at the end by the sheriff or justice and the police officer:

At _____ in presence

of _____ Justice of the Peace

for _____

compeared _____

_____, Police Constable, a credible witness, who, being solemnly sworn, depones that what is contained in the foregoing Complaint is true as he shall answer to God.

_____   _____
Police Constable   Justice of the Peace

The report was submitted to the fiscal as a charge under the Poaching Prevention Act, but the fiscal decided that the Night Poaching Act was the better option, a matter that is entirely the prerogative of fiscals as the lawyers who will have to prosecute these cases in court. At the end of the day it didn't go to court and was dealt with by a fiscal's fine, an entirely satisfactory conclusion. Court time was saved and the two men received punishment that was appropriate to the relatively low level of offence that they had committed. And the spotlamp and battery pack? They got the bloody things back again!

We had a further night-time visit in roughly the same area of Perthshire two weeks later, but this time the team of four came from Fife. Gamekeepers patrol their area of responsibility in the same manner as a police officer patrols his or her beat. Like police officers, they miss very little of interest that is happening, and are always inquisitive, if not suspicious, about any parked vehicle. This time it was a van parked at the side of a country road that sounded the alarm with a beat keeper. The van looked suspiciously like a van that had made a quick getaway in the middle of a December night when a number of spotlights were seen in a field. At that time, when the spotlight operators became aware of the keepers nearby, they ran to their van and they and their dogs were in and away in a flash. In the morning the keepers found over 50 dead rabbits in piles round the fenceline of the field ready to be collected. It looked like they were back again.

The beat keeper summoned the head keeper and before long they spotted a beam of light in a field. The police were contacted and were given the location of the van. The keepers then went to the far side of where the men were working and used their own spotlight to see what was happening. The four men and three dogs bolted back towards their van to make an escape just like before. It was thwarted this time, as by now there was a police car parked beside it. Their escape was foiled but they were not yet caught.

Very few criminals are willing to give up their vehicle and before long the four plus their mutts came walking along the road to their van. 'We stopped to let the dogs out for a pee and they just took off. We had a helluva job catching them, they're such wild buggers.' More piffle! They had ditched their spotlight, though this was soon found in a ditch along the road by one of the officers. The men denied ownership of the lamp, saying it must belong to someone else. The strange thing was that the glass was still hot!

I *did* get notified of this incident. I was sound asleep but was not in the least put out, just pleased that the message was at last getting through! I said I would join the dayshift to help gather some evidence, though I would not be free until about 8.00 am as I had to do a live interview on BBC Good Morning Scotland about the batch of beavers that had descended on Perthshire. (The media were not aware of the wild boar and I had no intention of enlightening them at this point).

My advice to the officers dealing with the case was that if there was sufficient evidence the men were after hares then they should be arrested, photographed, fingerprinted, have DNA swabs taken, (all of which is standard practice with someone who has been arrested) then released on an undertaking to appear in court in a further week or so. The fact that they appear in court on an undertaking allows the procurator fiscal to request bail conditions. This procedure also has the advantages of giving both the police and the procurator fiscal some breathing space to consider the evidence in advance of the appearance in court of the men accused. Importantly I added the caveat that if it appeared to be rabbits that were the intended target then there was no power to arrest the men and that they should be charged under either the Night Poaching or the Poaching Prevention Act and we could decide in the morning which would be the better charge.

The morning – 2 March, 2007 – was one of the very few frosty mornings of that winter. By 8.00 am the sun was beaming down and it was a delight to be out. On this occasion I was satisfied as soon as I saw the terrain, that rabbits, not hares, were the target. This estate was an absolute haven for rabbits. The owners and many of their friends were enthusiastic falconers and they were happy to have a good number of bunnies about on which to test their birds of prey. The place was absolutely alive with rabbits, all reluctant to go to bed and sitting out at the burrow entrances enjoying the early morning sunshine.

Searching over the area in which the men had been seen by the keepers for evidence was really a delightful task. It was yet another situation in which I had to pinch myself to realise that I am actually lucky enough to be getting paid for this job. The staccato hammerings of woodpeckers, both green and great-spotted, reverberated through the trees like machinegun fire as they searched for insects, but equally importantly defined their territory to other woodpeckers. A single grey partridge rose at my feet, still a fairly uncommon sight nowadays, yet these birds, one of my favourites, were so plentiful when I was young. They have succumbed to the many changes in farming, practices that in some places are now being reversed to allow birds like the grey partridge, the skylark and the corn bunting a chance to gradually increase in number. Two whooper swans flew low over my head, making their lovely bugling *whoop-whoop* call, which was answered by others on the nearby loch. Within a few weeks they would be returning to Iceland and Scandinavia to breed and we would be left (apart from a very few in the most northerly part of Scotland) only with our indigenous mute swan until their return the next autumn.

Part of our search took us near to the loch, and a couple of hundred duck rose from the surface and circled round twice before landing at the far end. Most were mallard but on the fringe of the group were some teal, with their *krriks* and *quacks* much higher pitched than those of the mallard. The loch is a refuge for many geese at night but the only sign of geese that morning was one that had collided with overhead wires and had been well predated by foxes, buzzards and crows. Several buzzards flew over and there were some carrion crows and lesser black-backed gulls circling. I doubted that there would be much left of any rabbits caught by the men and dogs the night before.

As it happened we did find three freshly killed rabbits, though well predated as I expected. I took possession of them but because there was little left, doubted that they could be linked to the four men, even though I was in no doubt that their dogs had killed them. What really concerned me was that men would let lurchers run at full tilt, in the darkness, in this area which was a mass of rabbit holes where a dog could so easily break a leg. The keepers told me that the dogs the men were using absolutely stank and must have been kept in very dirty conditions. I knew the poachers and this didn't surprise me.

Since it may have been difficult to prove the dogs had killed the rabbits, we found this case was best to be reported under the Poaching Prevention Act 1862. The reporting of the case turned out simply to be a paper exercise. Due to the fact that the men had been arrested and spent several hours in police cells (unlawfully if they had wished to press the point) the fiscal considered this was punishment enough for the low level offence they had committed. She marked the case 'no proceedings', a decision with which I entirely agreed. Justice had been meted out in an unusual manner. The four men involved would be happy with the result and hopefully learned from being caught that gamekeepers and police officers will take action against poaching. Lastly, the public benefited by the whole episode taking little from the public purse.

The trial of the Wee Man and the Big Man took place at Arbroath Sheriff Court in early April 2007. Because of other court matters the trial did not start until well after 11 a.m. and I thought we might manage two witnesses – the farmer and the gamekeeper – through the court before everyone adjourned for lunch at 1.00 p.m. Not to be. By the lunch recess the procurator fiscal, Sandy Mitchell, had just finished his examination of the farmer and the defence had yet to go. Since there were two accused there were two defence solicitors. I knew the trial would not finish that day.

There was a major surprise in the afternoon: the cross examination of the farmer only took 15 minutes! I had no idea who was defending but there are only be a handful of solicitors in Scotland who have a good grasp of wildlife law and I had a suspicion that none of those were in Arbroath Sheriff Court that day. The remaining witnesses were taken in chronological order, with the gamekeeper next, then the three police officers who had been involved in the stopping of the Wee Man's car.

The farmer's evidence was that he had watched a very powerful lamp being played systematically back and forth across his fields from a vehicle, had shortly after driven down the road, at the same time phoning the gamekeeper and had followed the vehicle that had been lamping for a short time before losing it. The gamekeeper's evidence was that he had found the car just after the farmer had lost it, had followed it but had the powerful spotlamp directed at his face and had to fall back. He had contacted the police who stopped the car shortly after.

Evidence had been given by the police officers that when they stopped the car there was a powerful handlamp on the front passenger's floorwell beside the Big Man, with a cable between the door and the body of the car and attached to the car battery. There was also a hand lamp and a battery pack in the car that would be ideal if the men had to go out on foot after a hare. There was a young boy in the back seat and there were two lurchers in the boot of the car. It was a hatchback and the parcel shelf was concealing them from general view. The whole unit could aptly be described as a hare courser's rig.

For my part the trial was absolutely fascinating – if I leave aside the fact that I sat in the witness room of Arbroath Sheriff Court until 4.45 p.m. on the first day and a further half hour on the second day before I gave evidence.

Eventually I was led through the evidence in chief by the fiscal, which took about 40 minutes. I was initially asked to give an account of the ecology of the brown hare, then had to relate my search of the areas in which the lamp had been targeted, where I was able to say that apart from one very small corner where there was a wood with signs of rabbits emerging no other sign of the brown hare's smaller cousin existed. I was amused at one point when the fiscal asked me, obviously to rebut an earlier question from one of the defence agents, if the whole set-up with Little and Large could not have been to course rats and stoats. Since I couldn't be in the court until it was time for my evidence I have no idea how this originated but the very thought of going after rats and stoats with a spotlight and two large lurchers was preposterous. My response was that if anyone believed that they would be extremely naive. After I said this I hoped that the sheriff wouldn't think the comment was directed at him. I should maybe even have conceded that the two could have been after stoats as the inference from the question was that stoats were rodents, which of course they are not. Rodents, like rabbits, are not mammals for the purposes of the Act, though stoats would be.

The male solicitor appearing for the Big Man cross-examined me next. Through no fault of his own, his knowledge of wildlife was limited, which must have made his defence of this case extremely difficult. His main thrust was in relation to the breed of dogs used. I had not seen the dogs, though had been informed by the police officers that they were lurchers – greyhound-type dogs – so I could only speak in general terms. I was asked what my reaction would be if I was told that one was a chocolate labrador. The defence should never ask a question unless they know what the answer is, though I sympathised in this case, but my response was that it did not really matter as long as the second dog was a fast lurcher-type dog. One fast dog may well be sufficient. I also related another recent incident (with Double D) where a lurcher and a springer spaniel had been used in coursing. The spaniel had been very much an observer, much as a chocolate labrador would have been. 'A springer spaniel is a gundog of course,' said the defence solicitor, blissfully unaware that so is a chocolate labrador.

The lady solicitor was next and she was keen to know exactly where I had seen evidence of the rabbits, though when I told her she was unable to use it to any advantage. I explained the use of the large lamp to spot hares some distance away, and the small hand lamp and battery pack that could be used if the men had to set off on foot for a hare further up a field. She asked if there was easy access to the fields for the men and dogs, which there was through the many large gates that were open, then asked if access could be obtained other than through the gates. I explained that there was a drystone dyke on both sides of the narrow country road and that would be an obstacle that would pose little problem. That finished the questioning, but I didn't know why the questioning finished there until during a short adjournment of the court a few minutes later I heard her asking the fiscal what a drystone dyke was!

At the end of the crown case there were four submissions – two by each defence solicitor – that there was no case to answer. Very briefly they were:

1. That the court was not entitled to presume that hares were the target unless all other animals had been excluded.

2. That there was no evidence to show that the Big Man was other than an innocent observer in the car as he was not driving, and it could not be shown that it was he (rather than the small boy who had not been charged) who was operating the lamp.

3. That there was no evidence to show that the dogs had been in the car at the time the lamp was being used to sweep the fields, as the farmer and the keeper who followed the car had not had it in continuous view. The dogs may therefore have been picked up after the event.

4. There was no evidence to show that either of the accused had the experience necessary to establish that the type of terrain they were scanning with their lamp was land suitable for hares but not rabbits.

With regard to the first submission the sheriff pointedly enquired if this included such small mammals as stoats and bats. With regard to the second submission, the sheriff thought it was highly unlikely that the Big Man had found himself an unwitting onlooker in a hare coursing expedition when one of the dogs crushed in to the boot was in fact his. In submission number three the sheriff clearly wondered where in the middle of the countryside in the dead of night the Wee Man and the Big Man might have been able to pick up their own dogs. Might they have been waiting at a bus stop? In the last submission the sheriff pointed out that the type of dogs in the boot of the car were consistent with coursing hares, not for chasing rabbits, where the dogs were much more likely to have been whippets or terriers as had been given in evidence by the gamekeeper and by me.

All four submissions of *no case to answer* were repelled and the trial continued with the final submissions by the fiscal and the two defence agents. The sheriff concluded that there was an element of doubt, ever so slight, that the Big Man had not been the operator of the spotlamp and gave him the benefit of that doubt with a verdict of Not Proven. I had earlier watched the Big Man biting his nails to the quick and I'm sure he was mightily relieved. I also heard him talking politics earlier, probably for my benefit as he knew I was in earshot. He said loudly and authoritatively to the Wee Man, 'I'm going to vote Tory in the Scottish Elections as they'll bring back that you're allowed to go poaching.' I've no doubt he meant hunting with dogs rather than poaching but I rather suspect he has no chance of either.

The Wee Man had a different fate. He was found guilty and was fined £300. The spotlamps were forfeit, which would add at least another £150 to the penalty. In addition the sheriff contemplated disqualifying the Wee Man from driving for using his vehicle in the commission of a crime but a plea by his defence that this would cause a problem with his nomadic lifestyle persuaded the sheriff to relent. This was the second time within a matter of a few months that the Wee Man had been threatened with disqualification. He is building up a horrendous list of coursing convictions and must surely be jailed the next time. You would think he would learn but he was heard to say as he left the court, 'Well if that's all you get for coursing I'll be back out tomorrow.' Bravado or stupidity? I think the latter and I'm sure he'll be a customer again before too long.

This really was a landmark conviction. It was the first time in Scotland that anyone had been convicted of hunting wild mammals without either they or their dogs leaving the vehicle. The case rested on the legal definition of the term 'hunt' – *to search for or to course*. The Crown position that the sequence of events that had taken place constituted a *search* was not disputed, the defence argument being that the search had not been for hares. I found this most intriguing. I've already said that I enjoyed the trial (or at least the legal arguments at the end that I was party to). I know that the fiscal, Sandy Mitchell, enjoyed prosecuting the case and I have it on good authority that the sheriff thoroughly enjoyed it as well.

CHAPTER **8**

Getting it Wrong

NO-ONE has a monopoly on perfection. No-one can be right all of the time and this short chapter exemplifies where I, and sometimes others, fell just short of the mark. There are some, of course, who delight in ensuring that others are wrong (or at least are perceived to be wrong) and use seniority to their advantage. In 1980 when I had not long since broken through into the ranks of the CID one of my first jobs was in ensuring the safety of VIPs during the Conservative Party Conference in Perth. Many of the VIPs, including the then Prime Minister Margaret Thatcher, were staying at the prestigious Station Hotel and much of my duty was at that venue.

As the most recently-appointed detective constable I was some-times left behind at the hotel while everyone else was at the conference. The hotel was empty though I still had to maintain a presence in the foyer to ensure that no-one with any criminal intent could infiltrate the place. I stood about for a while, sometimes at the door, sometimes in the foyer, and eventually decided that I could carry out my role equally efficiently from the comfort of one of the armchairs in the foyer. As it happened I hadn't long sat down when who walked in but the detective chief superintendent. I admired his ability as a detective officer but he was renowned for his determination to be awkward. I stood up and met him half-way between the expensively comfy chair and the door and he asked what was doing. As he well knew there was bugger all doing and apart from the staff I was probably the only person in the hotel. I told him all was quiet and was surprised that he agreed. His brief meeting with his newest detective officer at an end, he was about to leave when he suddenly turned and instructed, 'Just in case anything happens you'd be better to stand at the door.'

Stand at the door I did and I watched the cars parking in the car park outside, the many passengers coming and going from Perth Rail Station and the taxis queuing up in the rank awaiting their custom. I watched a forlorn cock house sparrow picking at a crumb of bread on the pavement outside and a male pigeon puffing his chest out till he looked like a balloon; a balloon that walked round and round his female consort continually dipping his head almost to the ground, tilting his tail in the air and bubbling *rickety-coo, rickety-coo, rickety-coo* in his efforts to entice her to stand still long enough for him to mate. This was all that happened. But after all I was guarding the door; nothing else *could* happen.

I was on the same duty the following day and after the hotel disgorged its VIPs to the conference I stood at the door *in case anything happened*. I was standing at the door when the detective chief superintendent made his visit again. Like the day before he asked what was doing, which I was able to tell him in half a dozen words. This time he said, 'Well dinnae hang aboot the door. Away and get a seat somewhere!'

I had a call one day in early August 2002 from a man who had been in woodland studying birds and who told me he'd found an unusual type of trap tied to a post at the corner of a pheasant release pen. He had some difficulty in describing the trap but said that he had untied it and had handed it in at Auchterarder Police Station where I could no doubt see it for myself. I said I would have a look at it and phone him back to let him know its purpose and whether or not it was legal. In the meantime he gave me a six figure map reference, augmented by the mandatory landmark that I always request. In this case the landmark was the fencepost on the south east corner of the pheasant pen.

The following day I went to Auchterarder and had a look at the trap. It was a Fenn Mk IV trap, legal for rats, stoats, weasels, mice and grey squirrels. I had no doubt that grey squirrels were the target as the trap had been set in an open-topped box with some barley in it and according to the witness had been tied to the post about 2 metres off the ground. Despite the intended victims being grey squirrels, a pest species, the trap had been illegally set. Had it been set on the ground in a tunnel with the entrance width restricted to only allow entry to mammals the size of the target species it would have been OK. Baited with something dead it may also have been pretty effective against grey squirrels.

I drove round and parked my car about a mile or so from where the trap had been found, put my rucksack on and headed through the fields towards the location. It was a grand day and as I walked along the edge of a field several young rabbits that had been stretching out basking in the sun reluctantly sat up as I got closer and eventually scurried down into the darkness of their burrows. Nearer the wood a stoat was methodically hunting the hedge-side, disappearing from time to time down a burrow, while the occupants bolted out of another burrow. Two adults rabbits bolted simultaneously, one heading right towards me seemingly blind to my presence and almost running over my foot in its panic, while the other ran a few yards into the field and thumped a warning loudly with a hind foot. With so many young rabbits about it is unlikely the stoat would be interested in the pair of adult rabbits and sooner or later it would manage to trap a small one in a burrow and that would be its meal for the day. I have several times watched stoats go back time and time again to a burrow with very young rabbits, killing one at each visit and emerging with its head high in the air and a limp wee rabbit in its jaws and trailing between its forelegs, carrying it off in this manner to its kits hidden somewhere nearby. They must have tremendously strong neck muscles to carry such a weight and remind me of leopards carrying a wildebeest calf; the same feat on a larger scale on a different continent.

As I cut through the wood towards the pheasant pen I disturbed a roe buck, which ran off, showing its annoyance by giving vent to the dog-like barking that they make during the mating season. The *buff buff, buff buff buff* echoed through the wood and I hoped that my suspect was not in the area as he would be able to interpret warning signals as well as I could. I reflected on the stoat I saw earlier and female roe deer, realising that they have something in common that is very unusual: they both utilise the phenomenon of delayed implantation.

In both cases when the female is mated and the egg is fertilised it reaches the uterus but is not implanted in the uterine lining, therefore does not begin to develop. This allows the animals to mate when they are in the best possible condition, and have no undue strain on the body over the winter as there is still no foetus developing. The egg then implants in the uterine lining early the following year, allowing the offspring to be born at the optimum time to ensure survival.

When I reached the pheasant release pen I walked past it at a distance at which I could see the fence in case there were any more traps set, but not close enough to disturb the pheasants inside. When I came to the post at the south east corner of the pen, from which the witness told me he had taken the box with the trap, there was further evidence pointing to the person I had in mind as a suspect. The quad bike tracks of the person tending the pheasants ran past the pen no further than 5 metres from where the trap had been set on the post. It would have been impossible for him not to have seen it on his daily visits. Had it not been under his control then he would have removed it.

It annoyed me that someone had the opportunity to trap grey squirrels effectively and legally, yet had resorted to this method where red squirrels, birds and even a pine marten, were it to have been in the area, could be a victim.

I am always reluctant not to remain hands-on in an investigation but on this occasion I passed it to one of the then divisional wildlife crime officers to continue the enquiry and to interview the suspect, who was a part-time gamekeeper. Mistake! Without my knowledge the investigation had been re-delegated to two officers who had no experience of wildlife crime and who in fact had asked the suspect to come to the police station to be interviewed.

To an experienced police officer this type of arrangement has two main flaws. Firstly it gives the suspect time to think and time to make up any sort of story that can deflect suspicion away from him. A suspect is far better interviewed cold and the response he gives then is much more likely to be the truth, the part-truth or something like the truth. This advantage had been lost. Secondly, by not seeing the suspect at his home, the opportunity to see similar boxes, similar wood or even dead grey squirrels that could link him to the crime was lost. There was no use in going back with him after the interview at the police station as any incriminating evidence would have been long gone. With no lever to prompt the truth, the man denied having anything to do with the box and the trap and the matter was left pretty much at that.

I was fizzing, firstly at the matter being re-delegated by someone who had the experience to have concluded the investigation properly, and secondly that the officers who *had* attended had shown such a lack of guile and of basic interview strategy.

The first of a number incidents (unrelated to wildlife crime) where a less-than-average score for perfection was achieved goes back to my days in the drug squad as a detective sergeant. We had received information that a man in a particular house in Arbroath was dealing drugs. The information was anonymous, which meant that we always erred on the side of caution and never broke down a door but rather used guile to gain entry. On this occasion one of the group, Donald Archibald, went forward to the door while the rest of us hid round the corner. He knocked on the door, which was answered with the call from the inside without opening it, 'Who is it?' This is sometimes a good indication of a 'drug dealer in residence'. Donald said, 'It's the plumber. The woman downstairs has knocking in her water pipes and I'm checking for the source. Could I come in and turn on one of your taps please?' The door opened and Donald grabbed the occupant by an arm, an action that was shortly followed by me grabbing his other arm. The remaining two or three of our drug squad group burst into the house and began a quick check of the rooms for other occupants.

By this time Donald and I had marched the confused occupant through to the living room and had began a quick search of his pockets with our two free hands. Finding nothing of interest in the pockets, and having been quickly joined by the rest of our colleagues with negative looks on their faces, we almost collapsed with laughter when our 'captive' asked, 'What is it that's wrong with the pipes anyway?' I know little of plumbers in Arbroath but suspect that they don't normally search the pockets of their hosts when they are carrying out a repair job. Our day was made when the man asked, 'Are you not plumbers?' His naivety confirmed that he was not a drug dealer and after a short chat and a laugh over the whole episode we parted on the best of terms.

On another occasion, two traffic officers dealt with a deer poaching case. A roe deer had been shot from the roadside and the traffic officers happened along just as the deer was being loaded into the back of the poachers' vehicle. The men were arrested and brought to the police station, where I was asked for some advice on charges. I gave the advice and I later had a look at the report that the officers had prepared for the procurator fiscal. These officers were much more familiar dealing with traffic offences and the officer who had written the report was a specialist in dealing with lorries that were carrying in excess of their permitted weight of cargo. He was perfectly familiar with the weights of vehicles without their load and of the weight *in cumulo*, in other words the lorry plus the contents. I was amused to read that the two men who took the deer were found in possession of a dead roe deer and an *unladen* shotgun.

Continuing on the theme of firearms, when I was an authorised firearms officer (AFO) I was called out one summer evening to a report of two men that were allegedly encamped on a hillside near Comrie in Perthshire, being on the run from an armed incident in England. Several of us, as AFO's, met at Comrie Police Station, a very small station in a very small village with one resident police officer. Plans were going well until meddling senior police officers arrived. Being summer, with daylight at 4.00 a.m., we had decided to sit tight and monitor the tent from a distance, then mount a quiet assault on the tent just after 4.00 a.m. We reckoned that the occupants would be sound asleep, and we would have the advantage of seeing what we were doing without hindrance of half-light or risk of exposure by torches being accidentally illuminated.

This plan changed when the then deputy chief constable arrived and wanted us to carry out the arrest of the men right away. The deputy chief constable had never been an authorised firearms officer. This was plain when he suggested that we collapse the tent on top of the two men. The plan got worse when he put an unarmed superintendent in charge of the operation. You've guessed. He was not – and never had been – an authorised firearms officer either.

We found ourselves stalking up the hill, in the darkness, with guns and torches, albeit the torches unlit. We had almost reached the tent, with the superintendent bringing up the rear, when he bellowed into a megaphone, 'You are armed and we are surrounded.' That was it! We disregarded rank, carried out the work we were trained to do as AFOs and quickly arrested the two men. As it turned out they had nothing more dangerous in the tent than crossbows but we didn't know that at the time. They were collected by police officers from the English force who had wanted them arrested but we had many a laugh about the farcical supervision of the operation. The situation is completely different now with the advent of tactical firearms advisers.

I often got photographs of suspected crime scenes emailed to me. The photographers were usually hill-walkers and their participation in the detection of wildlife crime is invaluable. On this occasion I received a series of three photographs. Two were close-up photographs of a dead pine marten in a trap, while the third was a panoramic view of the area in which the trap had been set. As I have explained traps set in tunnels are legal provided access is restricted, so far as is possible, to the species permitted to be caught in the trap under the Spring Traps Approval (Scotland) Order 1996. I have already listed the mammals that may be caught in a Mark IV Fenn trap. A slightly larger trap, a Mark VI Fenn trap, permits rabbits and mink to be caught in addition to those already listed. None allow the catching of a pine marten, though a Mark VI set legally for mink may well allow access to a pine marten, a mammal of roughly the same size. I struggled with the photographs to discern whether this was a Mark IV or a Mark VI trap. The panoramic photo did not help as all I could see apart from hills and drystane dykes was a single larch tree. This needed a visit to establish whether or not the trap had been set legally.

A 'visit' in this part of Highland Perthshire is not a ten minute stroll through a field. Graham Jack, one of the Divisional wildlife crime officers, and I took a 4WD vehicle as far as we could. This was a half hour drive from Perth, a further 45 minutes drive along hill tracks, over hills and through burns till we could go no further, then about an hour's walk through lovely but tiring mountainous terrain to reach the scene. We reached the march dyke between two estates and could see the larch tree on our right hand side. We followed the dyke down till we came to. . . a burn. If only this had been in the photograph. The trap had been set in a pile of stones at the side of the burn and because of this juxtaposition had obviously been set for mink coming up the burn. If only the photographer had shown the burn in the photograph. Through no fault of his he had got it wrong. But we had enjoyed our walk. Until the mobile phone rang.

The report on the phone was that two men, believed egg collectors, were on their way up to a golden eagle nest in Glen Lyon. Glen Lyon, so far as the county of Perthshire is concerned, could hardly have been further away from where we were. We almost ran back to the vehicle. Once we were mobile we took a lot less care traversing the bogs and burns than we did on the outward journey. Once on to public roads we did not break the speed limit, only because neither the vehicle nor the narrow winding roads were up to it. An hour-and-a-half later we met the shepherd who had witnessed the men passing his house. He showed us the car, which displayed a road tax issued in an English town of interest to us for egg thieves. This in fact was what had initially made the shepherd suspicious. He had been instrumental in the catching of two egg thieves who had taken golden eagle eggs from this site in the past and if he was suspicious of the two men he had seen on this occasion then so were we. Graham and I gave him our mobile telephone numbers and asked him to return to his house so that he could give us advance warning of the men returning to their car.

An hour or so later a call from the shepherd indicated that the two men would be back at their car in a further twenty minutes. I was in a position where I could see the men approaching their car. Graham was waiting with the police car well off the road so that when I signalled him we could join up and meet the two men just at the point they were opening their car door. I saw the two of them coming round the corner but I was just a wee bit concerned: one of them was wearing a bright orange jacket. I know that egg collectors don't always have the best of outdoor gear but usually they don't go about the countryside in garish colours that can be seen for miles, and drawing attention as much as would a blue flashing light on their head. A seed of doubt was sown.

The ambush went to plan and our arrival in an unmarked police 4WD coincided with one of the men putting the key in the lock of their car. I had even more doubts now as the men were well into their seventies. We have few egg thieves of that age and most are not up to the long walk plus a climb or abseil associated with taking golden eagle eggs. We announced who we were, as did they, and we realised that we had been on the second wild goose chase of the day. I made the most of a bad job and told the men that we'd had a hell of a job keeping up with them as they'd tramped round the hills. They replied in amazement that they had never seen us the whole day and that we'd made a very good job of our surveillance, especially in getting back over the top of the mountain rather than through the pass to get back to the car at the same time as they had. I let this story run for a short time then told them the truth. We all had a good laugh and they explained that they were very interested in wildlife and thought that we were doing a great job in trying to track down criminals. I take my hat of to the two of them. That was a bloody hard day's walking that they'd had and I just hope that I am up to it if I ever reach their age.

In my last tale I'm really not sure who had got it wrong. I came home from work on Monday 26 February 2007 to find a mallard duck and 6 ducklings in amongst my 20 domestic khaki Campbell ducks. Finding wild ducks amongst my domestic ducks is commonplace as I had set a clutch of mallard eggs under a domestic duck in the mid 1990s and have had semi-wild mallards nesting in the garden and wood ever since. It was the date that was very unusual. Normally mallards are not even laying until late February yet here was one with ducklings. The ducklings had obviously been in the garden before by the way they were running in and out of the shed to feed on spillage from the basin of layers' meal for my own ducks. The forecast was for snow and I doubted that the poor wee things would be there the next day.

The burn coming through the garden was already high and many early ducklings in past years have been swept away like bobbing corks to their doom with nothing I or their mother could do about it.

Next morning my wife and I awakened to about 3 inches of snow, with the snowflakes still tumbling from the sky. The mallard and the ducklings were still there but the wee ones had been reduced to four. There was no trace of any dead ducklings and I suspected the two missing ones had been swept away. I was thinking about them while I was at work. It snowed all day then rained hard all afternoon. I didn't expect to see them when I came home but they were still there, huddled under their mother among the snow. There were patches bare of snow under bushes and trees and I couldn't understand why she didn't take them there where it would be slightly safer and certainly less cold. I kept an eye on them but I am always reluctant to interfere with nature.

At dusk when I went to shut my ducks in the shed the ducklings were huddled together barely moving. They had been abandoned by their mother and left to freeze. I suspect that the mallard duck had realised that she had no hope of bringing up the brood successfully and had left them. There is no point in being anthropomorphic about animals as they don't have the same senses and responsibilities as humans. She must have had an innate pragmatism that she could have another brood later in the year and could still do her bit to keep the overall mallard numbers in good shape.

Strangely I have seen this type of reaction before when we had our first mallard duck, one that was weak and had landed near our previous house. We brought it home and packed the food into it, for which it rewarded us with many happy years as a companion in the garden, especially when I was digging and worms were coming to the surface, or on hot summer days when we had a glass of coffee, tea, wine or beer at our feet that she saw as a welcome receptacle in which to clean her beak. Her name was Jemima and she was joined a couple of years later by Donald, which meant fertile eggs and in turn ducklings. One duckling was a weakling and Jemima did everything possible when the family's backs were turned to drown this poor wee soul. My daughters rescued it several times and pumped its lungs clear of water but Jemima's determination paid off and the duckling was eventually drowned.

Coming back to the four ducklings about to succumb to hypothermia I caught them easily due to their torpor and brought them in to the kitchen, where I put them under a heat lamp. Within an hour they had come alive again, had jumped out of the box and were running around the kitchen floor. I scooped them up, this time into a bigger plastic box, which was to be their home for the next week or so, placed next to the kitchen radiator for maximum heat. They grew fat on baby chick crumbs and had their own paddling pool, the contents of which they splashed all over the radiator and the wall. At the end of the first week and despite being cleaned out at least once a day, the kitchen had a very obvious duck odour when I came down in the morning, so they were transferred to the conservatory. Within a few days they went outside into a run during the day and came in at night, their nocturnal home in time being transferred to the shed.

In the meantime their mother returned to the garden with her boyfriend and began looking around for a suitable place to lay a second clutch, one much more likely to hatch in weather conditions suitable for the ducklings' survival.

At a month old the ducklings began to lose some of their resemblance to giant bumble bees as they replaced down with feathers, and once they were fully fledged I introduced them to my Khaki Campbells. If anything the Khaki Campbells were more afraid of them than the reverse situation so I was happy to put them in at night along with the domestic flock.

By mid April the wee ducks were standing on tiptoe flapping their stubby wings to build up their muscles and looking very like brown penguins. By early May they were taking their first short flights. The first flights were only over the fence from the wood where the domestic ducks are housed to the lawn, where they did a great job of removing the moss that had accumulated over the winter. Their landings were extremely bumpy, always finishing with their well-filled crop hitting the ground and their tail in the air. This would improve with practice, though I see adult mallard still having an occasional bad landing. Within a week they were circling the house, which is always the most vulnerable time, as in the excitement and enthusiasm of early flight some in the past have hit a telephone wire. Invariably this results in a broken wing and is the end of the road for the apprentice flier. Three have met with this fate so far including one that I was particularly keen to see into adulthood as it was pure white.

On 4 May the mother appeared back in the garden with a brood of 10 ducklings. She was now bringing up 10 and I had brought up 4. The duck had certainly got it wrong with the timing of her first brood. I had interfered with nature but hopefully I can be excused.

I have to finish this chapter with an apology. In *Wildlife Detective* I devoted a chapter – entitled The Myth of the Big Cat – to my extreme doubt that there are leopards, pumas or lynx wandering the Tayside hills and glens. I have been sceptical of alleged sightings, and while I believe that the reports are genuine, I think they are mistaken. Until now!

The factor of a Perthshire estate emailed me in mid-February 2010 to say that there was a big cat on a particular estate, though he did not want this publicised. Included in his email were three photographs. The first was a paw mark in a light fall of fresh snow, with a ruler beside it showing that it measured about 4 inches in diameter. There will be some dogs that could leave a paw mark that size but this was definitely a cat's mark; I was 100% happy about that. There were no claw marks, (cats, with the exception of the cheetah, retract their claws when they don't need them; dogs can't do that) and the mark was round like a cat's: in fact it was a giant cat. It was also a giant cat that had been running. It was so big that in the second photograph the gamekeeper who found the marks had walked alongside them and it took three of his paces, about 12 feet, to cover the area from where the first of the cat's paws hit the ground to where that paw hit the ground next.

I spoke to an expert in Scottish wildcats, Keith Ringland, who had seen and photographed the paw marks. He was even more convinced than I was that it was a big cat. When I asked him what kind it could be he said a leopard (the famous black panther, which is in fact a melanistic leopard), a puma or a lynx. I immediately thought back to a talk I gave in 2009. There was an audience of just over 100 and at the end, at time for questions, a lady asked me my view on big cats. I told her what my thoughts were and as I was doing so I could see that she was a believer. She was not at all pleased with my answer and shunned me during the tea and biscuits afterwards. If I knew who she was I'd be phoning her up now.

Even though the owner of the huge paw marks in the snow was never found, I should have hedged my bets and entitled my earlier chapter The Myth of the Big Cat? A question mark can make a huge difference and makes a U-turn easier!

CHAPTER 9

Salmon Poaching

THE WAY that police respond to salmon poaching has seen considerable change over the years. In Scotland there has been no shift of responsibility to another agency to deal with salmon poachers; the situation as I write in 2010 is exactly the same as it was when I dealt with my first of literally hundreds of salmon poaching cases from 1966 till about 1980. Roughly equal power is given to the police and to water bailiffs to deal with issues they encounter. This was the case under the Salmon and Freshwater Fisheries (Protection) (Scotland) Act 1951 and is little different under the more recent Salmon and Freshwater Fisheries (Consolidation) (Scotland) Act 2003. In the 1960s and 1970s in particular police and water bailiffs took proactive measure to deal with salmon poachers, often joining forces for some of the bigger jobs or when dealing with poachers who were more likely to be violent (though to be honest violence among salmon poachers in Perthshire was rare). Nowadays water bailiffs deal with many more salmon poaching cases than do police officers.

I carried out many operations where only police officers took part. In most of these just two of us were involved, as the more officers there are the more noise is made and the chance of ambush reduced. Nearly all of these took place at night, since the poachers' view was that they were safer under cover of darkness. They may also have thought that police officers were much more likely to be patrolling the streets or sitting in warm police cars. This was true of many but there were a good number of us, in the 1960s in particular, who had been brought up in the country or had formerly worked on the land and just loved to get out into the county in connection with policing. Daylight or dark made no difference.

Having stated that most poaching was a nocturnal activity, there were always one or two stupid enough to risk daytime salmon poaching. I had a very good informant who I was sure was buying many of the fish from the poachers. For this reason let's call him The Fishmonger. His van was always parked near where the poachers were active and several times I had detected a smell of fish inside. I'd challenged him about this but his reply was always that he had run one of the poachers home with some salmon. He was lying but I couldn't prove it.

Unlike my other informants in the salmon poaching world I found The Fishmonger a sleazy fellow and to be honest I didn't have much time for him. Despite that he came up with some pretty reasonable information from time to time but I had to watch him as I caught him one time trying to use me for his own ends. He had set up a person that he didn't like by selling him a salmon with very obvious marks of treble hooks on its flank then immediately phoned me to tell me in which house to find the fish. I visited the new owner of the poached salmon – without a warrant – and convinced him that if he let me in to the house and that was the only fish he had he would be warned rather than charged. It had been cut up, placed in poly bags and was the most recent inhabitant of the freezer but the hook mark was still visible on one of the pieces when I decanted them on to the draining board.

Though the man had committed an offence by being in possession of the salmon he heard no more about it and I passed the sections of salmon on to the Tay District Salmon Fisheries Board. This took place in the month of November and I'm sure the salmon would have come from the River Almond, which often has a late run of fish. Had I charged the man, the charge would have been under an old Act, the Salmon Fisheries (Scotland) Act 1868 and the relevant section states that during the period of the year when *all* the salmon rivers in Scotland are closed for fishing (November through to 15 January) a person in possession of a salmon or sea trout has to show that it had been taken legally. He would have had difficulty with the large gash in its side.

In the mid-seventies the Fishmonger gave me another piece of information about salmon in a house. He came in to the police station very early one May morning and asked for me. I had not long arrived at work for a 6 a.m. start though I was not surprised at The Fishmonger being up and about at that time as he never seemed to sleep. His information was that there was a bath full of salmon in a house in Newhouse Road in Perth but that they would be away by 9 a.m. I asked how they had been taken and the reply was, 'By a net. That will be in the hallway cupboard. The fish are pretty fresh-run and they'll be worth a bob or two.' I asked, 'How do you know all this?' His response, 'I just heard it on the grapevine.' This was nonsense and I am sure he had provided the transport to get the fish to the address as I knew the occupant – not from meeting him at cheese and wine parties but as a regular salmon poacher – and he had no 'wheels'. I had often wondered how he got his fish from the river to the place of sale but now I had the answer. I had also no doubt that The Fishmonger was due to go back about 9 a.m. to take the fish on the next stage of their journey.

Had this taken place in 2011 I may have struggled to obtain a search warrant within a couple of hours. The on-call procurator fiscal would need an early-morning phone call and would need to decide first of all if the information justified a search warrant, (probably not in this case) and if it did was it so urgent that it would need to be granted by a justice of the peace rather than a sheriff. Since there is no pro-forma search warrant to enter a house to search for salmon I suspect the fiscal would need to be visited in any case so that he or she could write out a search warrant in longhand, which could then be presented to a sheriff or a JP, whichever was the fiscal's choice. In the 1970s (or thereabouts) there were no such safeguards to human rights. I knocked up the nearest JP, he signed a stolen property warrant, the wording of which I had adapted to read 'salmon or sea trout' instead of 'stolen property' and I was on my way to Newhouse Road.

I had adapted a stolen property warrant three or four times but none of the cases ever came to trial, the accused pleading guilty at an early stage. During a trial I don't really know how this might have been viewed by a sheriff. And now, it's something I'll never know.

The Newhouse Road occupant who answered our knock at the

door had obviously been sleeping with his clothes on. He opened the door with his eyes half shut and I am sure took a few seconds to recognise us as police officers despite the uniforms. I could see salmon scales on his jeans so I knew our information had been accurate. I showed him the warrant and he took us in to the living room, probably the last room I had any interest in. He said he had just come in from a party but couldn't quite understand why I asked him if it had been in a temperance hotel. He made the expected denials about having been salmon poaching but soon realised that he was wasting his time and said, 'I suppose the first room you'll want to search is the bathroom.' I was sure that finding salmon in a bathroom wasn't going to entail much of a search.

Eighteen salmon lay in the bath covered by a couple of wet towels. As The Fishmonger had said they were in good condition and there was no doubt they would have commanded a fair price at the back door of a hotel. The marks behind the fishes' gills made by the net were evident in all of the fish and I pointed these out to our unwilling host. He peered closely at the fish as if he had never seen net marks before and as a last ditch attempt to lessen his culpability said, 'I bought them from a guy. I thought I could make a couple of quid on them.'

My response, 'We're going to search the rest of the house to see if you have a net. Do you have a net?'

'No. Well yes, there's one in the hall cupboard. I just keep it for a guy.'

'Is this the same guy that you bought the fish from?'

'Yeh'

'You're not a good liar, are you?'

'No. You obviously know the whole story. I've had better days.'

'Where did you get the salmon?'

'On the Tay at Kinfauns.'

I had previously caught poachers at this location and the gill net in the cupboard tended to back up his claim. This part of the River Tay, only a few miles downstream from the city of Perth, would be an ideal spot for a net to hang, invisible in the water, and catch fresh-run salmon on their way up from the sea. I wondered about The

Fishmonger. Was he involved, or did he just provide the transport. Why did he turn him in? He wouldn't be ferrying the salmon free of charge and he most likely now had burned his boats, so to speak. Unanswered questions, but the 18 salmon and the man who was not having a good day shared space in the back of the police van en route to the police station.

The Fishmonger again made contact later in the year. He had phoned the police station early one afternoon and asked that a message be passed to me to meet him at what he knew would be a quiet location. This time he told me that two youths were on the River Almond, a tributary of the Tay and were 'sniggering'. This is local terminology for foul hooking salmon with a large treble hook and a lump of lead dragged through the water with a violent jerking action so that the hook sinks into any fish it makes contact with. It is a method commonly used by salmon poachers, often with very profitable results. The part of the river at which the youths were working was given. It was beside a track that ran alongside the south bank of the river and approaching them shouldn't be too difficult. The track was well used by walkers so I imagined they would be down right at the side of the river and hidden by the bank from the walkers.

I made contact with another officer, Alan Joyce, and we walked quietly up the river bank. We had taken off our tunics and thrown on anoraks, which we zipped up to hide the white shirts. We looked like police officers from a mile off but with the short notice there was little else we could do. We were 40 or 50 metres from the location given by The Fishmonger when I saw a head peeking round a tree at the top of the river bank. We had obviously been spotted and I'd have been surprised if we hadn't been recognised as police officers, but there was nothing we could do except carry on.

We quickened our pace and when we reached the spot where the face had earlier appeared two young lads of about 19 were sitting on the bank gazing out at the river. No fishing rods were to be seen, but what I did see was that the colour had drained from the faces of the youths, having recognised us not just as two police officers but two officers to whom they could put names. And reputations! Since by the way they were sitting they reminded me of a double image of

Humpty Dumpty on a wall they can for the time being be Humpty and Dumpty. The two came from the nearby village of Almondbank and were regularly involved in salmon poaching.

I addressed the one I knew best, 'What are you on today then Humpty?'

'Nothin, Mr Stewart, jist having a look at the water.'

'You both look the picture of innocence, but I don't think that's the case somehow.'

Dumpty said, 'We're jist seein' if there's anythin' jumping in this pool here,' pointing out to the river.

I followed his gaze out to the river as he spoke and saw an almost invisible line cutting through the water heading upstream. The line travelled upstream for a bit then headed downstream again. Looking further out there was the hint of a swirl in the water. Though I had difficulty seeing the fishing line I could see its action in the water and managed to trace it back to the stout branch of a tree just at water level on the bank. They had been hand-lining, in other words using their treble hook and lead but without a fishing rod, and had a salmon on that was doing its best to dislodge the hook by racing up and down the pool. They must have caught it just before they saw us and when Dumpty warned of our approach Humpty had wound the line round the branch, hoping that we would pass by.

I unwound the line and slowly played the fish in to the bank. It was a salmon of about 8 lbs, a hen fish and beginning to turn slightly red due to being in fresh water for some time. I removed the two points of the hook embedded near the pectoral fins as gently as I could, making less of a mess of the fish than I thought I might, and returned the fish to the water. I left Humpty and Dumpty with Alan Joyce and I had a search round the area for other fish that they might have taken. There was little cover at that particular part of the river and after about ten minutes I found three salmon hidden under one of the few bushes nearby. The fish were fresh and had been there less than an hour. I went back and collected Dumpty, the weaker spirited of the two, and walked him over to the fish.

'They're yours aren't they?' I said.

'It was Humpty that caught them. I'm not fishing,' he replied.

'What are you doing then,' I asked, knowing damn fine what his part was.

'I'm just the lookout,' he pleaded.

Having established the truth from Dumpty, Humpty had little option but to cave in pretty quickly. I charged the two with taking four salmon without written permission and by means other than rod and line, two of them acting together to commit these offences, and with the unlawful possession of the fish and the handline. There was little point in taking them back to the police station as that would just create unnecessary paperwork and I told them they would get a summons in due course.

Some people, when they are caught committing crime, learn their lesson and give up. This was the first time that these two had been caught and I never saw them near the river again. I just wished instead of being Humpty it had been his older brother. He was one of the most regular and one of the most successful salmon poachers. Of my list of salmon poachers it was only he and one other that I never managed to catch.

I was reminded of a poacher I caught one night on the River Tay at Moncrieffe Island, a part of the Tay famed for poaching activity. He only had two salmon and was a poacher completely unknown to me. He would be aware of that and tried give me a false name. When I asked for his name he replied, 'James Almond.' How original is that! He featured quite frequently from then on, though I never needed to ask for his name again and simply wrote it in my notebook.

I've mentioned some changes in fish poaching over the years. The fact that salmon stocks fell away in the last decade of the twentieth century meant that there was very little poaching at all, as there were just not enough salmon to make it worthwhile. As we came into the twenty-first century many of the excellent re-stocking measures were paying off and the salmon fishing industry began a slow recovery, though I'm not sure that the recovery was so strong in rivers in the north-west of Scotland, as there were issues concerned with salmon farming, the associated pollution under the cages, escaped farm salmon and of course the dreaded sea-lice. In the south-west and on the east coast rivers there seemed to be a steady increase in wild salmon, and with this increase salmon poachers re-emerged.

During times of low salmon numbers and relatively little poaching, water bailiffs were pretty much left to deal with what poaching there was and most of the time police only paid lip-service to the enforcement of the fish poaching legislation, becoming involved only when they, metaphorically speaking, fell over a poaching case. One issue that did emerge and very much involved the police working in partnership with the bailiffs was clamping down on the use of illegal gill netting for salmon in estuaries. These estuarine nets were catching dolphins as well as salmon, and the problem was particularly serious in the Moray Firth, so much so that my colleague in Northern Constabulary at the time, Inspector John Grierson, launched *Operation Fishnet* to raise awareness.

As is the way with many of these wildlife operations, the launch was well publicised through the media and the problem was lessened. It was not eliminated and gill nets are still being recovered, but the situation showed improvement. The Moray Firth dolphins, the most northerly pod of bottle nosed dolphins in the world, now have slightly less to fear from nets but there remains some disturbance from shipping.

The next issue with salmon emerged in the Firth of Clyde. This problem was again with nets, and Strathclyde Police, again with the assistance from water bailiffs, addressed this problem by the launch of *Operation Salmo*. This operation, named after the Latin name for salmon, *Salmo salar*, made full use of Strathclyde Police's Marine Unit, and their motor launch was utilised in arresting a gang of salmon netters. The launch and the capture, with the associated publicity, reduced the problem so the operation was hailed a success.

Towards the end of 2006, when reports of salmon poaching had increased sufficiently to be noticeable it was decided by the then chief constable of Lothian and Borders Police, Paddy Tomkins, who held the ACPOS (Association of Chief Police Officers in Scotland) portfolio for environmental and wildlife crime that *Operation Salmo* should be rolled out across Scotland. We were in an age when criminals travelled across force boundaries much more than they used to, and, like farmers and many other aspects of industry, they diversified. They poached salmon when the season was right and when there were few salmon running the rivers they became housebreakers, drug dealers, bogus workmen or fraudsters; after all they had to supplement their unemployment benefit somehow!

We held the first launch of the Scotland-wide *Operation Salmo* in Tayside on 1 February 2007, the opening day of the salmon fishing season on the River Earn in Perthshire. I had emailed a draft press release to our media office a few days before and had intimated that we would be pleased to provide a photo opportunity for the media at our venue at Kinkell Bridge on the River Earn. I was astounded at the response. We had BBC and STV television crews, BBC Radio Scotland, Radio Tay, Wave FM (a Dundee-based radio station), and a host of newspaper reporters. It was crime. It was wildlife. It was just a wee bit different. The media interest – and obviously that of the public – in this combination never fails to amaze me. Lothian and Borders had a launch on the Tweed the following day with similar media interest. Grampian Police had a launch a few days later on the Spey, still with plenty media attention, then we had a launch for the county of Angus in Tayside on the River South Esk with more than enough press coverage to keep us happy.

Our priority is to work closely with the water bailiffs on the various rivers in Scotland, sharing intelligence, and mounting joint operations where necessary. This is exactly as we do in Operation Easter, the extremely successful national operation to deal with bird egg thieves. It is the pooling of expertise and the sharing of intelligence that is the key to dealing with criminality. There is absolutely no reason to think that *Operation Salmo* will be any less successful in reducing the problem of salmon poaching than *Operation Easter* has been in reducing the problem with wild bird egg thieves.

CHAPTER 10

The Importance
of Being Observant

GOOD POLICING is very much about using your eyes and your ears. It's about knowing what car is regularly parked at a specific location, or ought not to be on the go in the middle of the night; who is about at certain times and at certain locations; the opening and closing times of premises; known or suspected criminals and their usual associates and much more besides. Once the police officer is aware of what is *normal*, anything out of place or different is of interest. The investigating of wildlife crime can benefit from using the same principles but in a very different context. A very practical example in the late 1970s was the catching of a man intent in removing as many fat brown trout from a Perthshire stank (a loch or pond which has been stocked with trout and from which there is no entry to other fish or exit for those stocked) as he possibly could using a bubble float and worm.

I had a call from the landowner, who had seen the man making towards the loch carrying a fishing rod. The elderly landowner had encountered this poacher on a number of occasions and described him as 'a very nasty piece of work'. I knew the poacher well and was of the view that the description of him given by the gentlemanly farmer had erred very much on the side of caution. I attended with a very young colleague, 'brand new out of the box' sometimes being the term used to describe such a rookie officer. We parked the police van a good distance from the loch so that the sound of the engine would not alert the poacher and walked quietly up through a gully towards the south shore of the loch. The loch was about 300 yards wide and just a bit under a quarter of a mile long but we had no idea where Mr Nasty had decided to fish. About 100 metres short of the loch I signalled my young colleague to stop and indicated that I was going to creep along on my belly to the lochside to see what was what. The young officer was as yet untested in stalking and I wanted to ensure that I could see without being seen.

We were in the first week of May and I had some difficulty concentrating on our poacher because of the sounds of the wildlife in the woodland. The staccato hammering of the great-spotted woodpecker was the most noticeable. As this mechanical drumming reverberated through the wood like gunfire I couldn't help wondering how it managed to batter on the trunk of a tree without finishing up with an incredible headache. I could hear a blackbird, the repetitive lilt of the song thrush, a robin, the soft cooing of a woodpigeon (that often sounds as if it has been interrupted before it finishes, like a poem with part of the last line missing), the impressively loud crescendo of a tiny wren, and at the side of the loch, the lovely, melodious sedge warbler.

The sound of a cuckoo, possibly just landed after its long migration from North Africa, drifted across the loch. I have read *At the Water's Edge* by Sir John Lister-Kaye, a man with knowledge of wildlife second to none, and a parallel command of the English language. His eloquent description of the cuckoo in his book surpasses anything I could hope to write:

> In the distance throat-pouting cuckoos would float pairs of
> muted minims into the air like audible smoke rings, notes
> that seem to hang there, directionless and slightly sinister as
> if, along with the hawks, cuckoos have been forbidden to sing.

Regaining concentration, when I peeked through the reeds at the side of the loch I could see twenty of thirty mallard and probably about the same amount of tufted duck swimming happily at the east end. That was where Mr Nasty *wasn't* fishing. Invariably these waterfowl are at the west end, which is a much more sheltered and quiet end, and I suspected they had been flushed to the less popular end by Mr Nasty. I looked towards the west end of the loch and could see three or four coots swimming about on the north shore. They are more tolerant of humans and in most cases will quite happily carry on their business a couple of hundred metres from a fisher. My guess was that Mr Nasty was on the south shore somewhere near the west end of the loch. At the west end there is woodland right down to the shore for the last 150 metres of the loch. Between where I was and the start of the woodland a field came almost to the loch side and there was little if any cover. I watched a woodpigeon flying directly up the middle of the loch making for the west end. As it came towards the wood it turned slightly left as if intending to land in the trees but shortly after its gradual left hand turn it suddenly veered off to the right and began to gain height. It had obviously spotted Mr Nasty in the trees; had he been in the field there would have been a reaction much earlier from the pigeon.

Now that I had located Mr Nasty – though had yet to see him – we needed to catch him. This entailed back-tracking, walking along the bottom of the field that ran up to the loch, entering the wood and walking slowly and quietly up to where the birds – or indeed lack of birds – had indicated the poacher was located. I told my apprentice that as we neared our goal he must be extremely quiet and not be standing on any branches that would alert Mr Nasty to our surprise visit. He did very well and, just less than an hour later, we were about 20 metres behind Mr Nasty, who was watching his bubble float bobbing on the surface of the loch waiting for it to be pulled partially under the water if a trout had a nibble at the wriggling worm on the hook somewhere near the bottom. We closed in further but when he was almost within our grasp he turned round and saw us. Quick as a flash he took a cigarette lighter from his pocket and a flame flicked from it briefly as he melted the line, casting the bubble float and skewered worms adrift.

He needn't have bothered as even without the bubble float and the hook we had enough evidence to charge him with attempted theft of trout, these being the property of the person who had stocked the loch, the elderly farmer. I could see no fish hidden round about him but again the absence of fish was not important. I don't believe for a minute he had caught none but I wasn't bothered.

We had caught *him*; that was what mattered. I arrested him and had to suffer the usual tirade of abuse that went with being anywhere near, far less arresting, this man. He really was an extremely nasty piece of work.

Birds and mammals can be great indicators of what is happening in a place. One day I was working in my garden, which is on the outskirts of a Perthshire village, when I noticed that my ducks all had their heads tilted to the side with one eye looking skywards. I had seen them do this often when a buzzard is flying high overhead. The buzzard would be no threat to them yet they maintain a watch on it so that they will not be taken by surprise. I knew they were looking at a bird of prey but I was thrilled when I looked up and saw a red kite gliding over. I have never seen a red kite from the garden before and would never have been aware of its presence had I not read the ducks' signals.

On another occasion when I was detective sergeant I was with a colleague, detective constable Willie Gibson. A man involved in a robbery had driven off in a car pursued by another two detective officers, but had abandoned the car at the edge of a large wood. Knowing the area well I decided that we would park up in sight of the far side of the wood and just sit quietly and watch. We had been sitting in the car for half an hour or so on this spring afternoon and, as well as keeping a lookout for our robber, I was enjoying the wildlife all around me.

At one point I said to Willie, 'There's a cat about Willie.' 'How do you know that?' was his response. 'I can hear the birds,' I answered. He probably though I had gone off my head but there was a chaffinch sounding a steady *pink, pink, pink* call which is always worth investigating. There was also a blackbird alarming with a regular *tak, tak, tak* call, a clear indicator of a predator on the ground (its loud and piercing chatter, a completely different alarm call, is reserved for an avian predator). I continued, 'The cat's just over there where that hedge meets that shed.' 'Can you see it?' queried Willie. 'No,' I said, 'but that's where the birds are telling me it is.' Willie was anything but convinced and said, 'Well if there's a cat appears over there I'll eat my hat.' At that a white cat appeared from the end of the shed. Unfortunately Willie didn't have his hat with him!

And the robber? He was capable of terrorising helpless elderly shopkeepers but he was out of his league in a dark wood on his own. He only ventured into the wood a short distance and was caught within an hour.

In another incident a car stolen in Dundee was stopped by police officers on the west side of Perth in the very early hours of a summer morning. One of the culprits was caught but the other ran off through the fields. I was involved in uniformed duties at that time and a colleague and I in a police van drove into the centre of a large sporting estate, parked the van in a dark corner of a wood (since it was white and might as well have had its blue flashing light illuminated), then sat quietly some distance from the van, waiting and listening. It was not long before the woodland animals let us know what was happening. A roe buck trotted out of the woods, always the first mammal to clear out when there is trouble. Shortly after the disturbed roebuck a much more wary fox came trotting out from the same direction, its departure from the wood concomitant to a number of woodpigeons that came clattering out. Our target was getting closer.

Next out of the wood was a cock pheasant, not flying up in alarm but running. On a shooting estate pheasants are accustomed to humans and seem to know when they are protected by law from being shot, becoming noticeably bolder even a week after the shooting season ends on 2 February. The chances were that our man was not too far away. Indeed that was the case and he came out of the wood at a steady trot within a few minutes. We took off – on foot – in pursuit and chased him only a short distance before he gave up and stood and waited on us catching up. He was in surroundings with which he was not familiar, tired from the mile and a half he had already covered, while we were fresh and reasonably fit (this being when I was in my thirties).

There were another couple of instances when normally urban-based criminals were well out of their depth in the countryside. The first related to yet another stolen car. This time the car had been stolen from Aberdeen and a colleague of mine, Jim MacDonald, stopped it for a routine check. Jim had a great nose for a criminal and at 4.00 a.m. this car and its occupants just didn't look right. It was not a local car and it appeared to him that the occupants were unsure of their route. When he stopped the car the occupants tried to convince him that they had rightful ownership of the vehicle but their story didn't ring true. When they saw the game was up they took off on foot, but Jim was a fit chap who did a lot of swimming and caught one within a hundred metres. The second disappeared into railway property and had made good his escape before Jim could summon assistance.

I joined the search but by 6.00 a.m. there was no trace of the second man and I returned to the police station. My own sergeant had gone home and the day shift sergeant was Jock Thomson, a first class-officer who shortly after left the police, obtained a law degree and within a short time was an eminent QC. Jock said that he was surprised that I was abandoning the search and jokingly commented that I had no interest in the job. My reason for wanting to knock off on time was that I was carrying out a bit of rabbit trapping and I had several hundred snares to check before too many crows and other diurnal predators that would share my spoils were up and about, a mere detail that I omitted to tell Jock.

I went home, changed into old clothes and traditional green wellies, and set off to check my rabbit snares. I was driving on the A9, westwards, about 3 miles from Perth when I encountered a man thumbing a lift at the roadside. As I slowed down I could see that he was wet up to the knees and had either been through dew-laden growing crops or a burn. He certainly didn't get as wet as that on the trimmed roadside verges. This was very obviously our missing car thief.

I stopped alongside him and as he jumped in to the passenger seat he said, 'Thanks pal, could you drap me anywhaur in Glesca.' When he shut the door I turned the car about on the road and replied, 'It's not your day. I'm one of the cops who's just been looking for you in Perth after you cleared out from the car you nicked in Aberdeen. You're arrested for stealing it.' His reply? 'For fuck sake. Just my luck to thumb a lift from a cop.' I drove pretty smartly back to the police station for two reasons. First was I was still needing to get to my snares. Second, I didn't want him trying to jump out of my car and escaping for a second time.

I rang the bell at the back door of the police station, a signal that it had to be opened to allow a prisoner to be brought in. Jock Thomson came and opened the door. My comment to him? 'Who has no interest in the job now then?'

The second incident occurred a few years later and would be around 1981 as I was in my early days in the CID. On a night shift there was only one detective officer on duty and whoever was on duty teamed up with a uniformed officer. We had been in Blackford in Perthshire and were suspicious of a Ford Transit van that was parked with three men in the front. We drew in behind it to go to speak to them but neither our unmarked car nor the fact that we were in casual clothing fooled the van's occupants; they knew we were cops! They took off in their van heading towards Perth and we radioed ahead for some assistance to stop the van, then checked the vehicle registration number on the Police National Computer. The van had been stolen in Glasgow so we now had a reason for its occupants not being keen on exchanging pleasantries with other night-time travellers.

Before any assistance reached us the van turned left off the A9 up a very steep, narrow and winding country road. We relayed this information to any unit coming to help and kept on the tail of the van. It suddenly stopped in the middle of the road and the three men jumped out and ran off into a wood. Luckily they set the handbrake before jumping out, as an unanchored van, a steep hill and a very narrow road was a bad combination that could have caused us real problems. We abandoned our car and took off into the wood after them. It was pitch dark and in our haste we had not grabbed our torches off the back seat of the car. Bob White, my colleague was in the wood somewhere on my right so I headed further left. It was pitch dark but I felt I had two advantages. Firstly I had been in this wood several times in daylight as I used to help the gamekeeper in this area – Gask Estate – years before, so I knew the layout. Secondly I was convinced that I would fare better here than would people from the city. I decided to stop and listen, which would give me a further advantage. I could hear Bob in the distance still on my right but suddenly I heard a person coming crashing through the trees much nearer. One of the men must have heard Bob and had doubled back towards me. I stood listening behind a tree as the crashing got closer. Seconds later I was aware of a figure passing the left hand side of the tree I was standing behind. Instinctively I reached out with my left hand, grabbed him by the jacket, birled him quickly round and hit him as hard as I could on the jaw with my right hand. Police officers are only allowed to strike people in self defence. I had no idea whether this chap was a big lad, of violent disposition or whatever. I was taking no chances and was prepared to argue my corner later if need be. In the meantime I had knocked the chap out and he was lying on the ground. I heard further crashing and shouted loudly, 'Bob?' 'Yeh, where are you?' was the reply. 'Over here,' I answered. Bob joined me seconds later. Our prisoner was still on the ground apparently out for the count, so we took an arm each and dragged him out to the road, by which time he had started to come round. It reminded me of dragging a stag off the hill after shooting it!

Our assistance had arrived in the form of two other police vehicles. One took the man-with-the-sore-jaw back to Perth and we continued the search for his colleagues, this time with torches. We caught a second man shortly after, though he was keen to give himself up and was probably glad to get out of the wood. They admitted having stolen the car and the man-with-the-sore-jaw told us that they were en route to Aberdeen where they had a housebreaking planned. Tools in the back of the van confirmed their story, though as recipients of 3 months in jail their housebreaking project had to wait till another day. The third man had either made good his escape. . . or is still in the wood yet.

On occasions, the inanimate environment can also aid a police investigation. I was night shift detective constable when I was informed that there had been an armed robbery with a sawn-off shotgun at a lovely loch-side house at Foss near Pitlochry in Perthshire. As I was on my own I contacted the detective officer who had not long since finished duty, Roy Sommerville. We made our way to the scene and en route made a note of all the vehicles that passed us on the road south as we headed north up the A9. (At midnight in Perthshire the roads are not exactly alive with cars.) Roy read and noted the first part of the registration and I read the second to make sure that we got the complete number of each vehicle. One vehicle that we had seen coming out of a quiet side road was of particular interest and we asked officers further south to stop and check it out. This turned out to have been two of the people involved and they were arrested.

We continued to the house, where we found that the two men resident in the house had been tied up. They had a huge mutt of a dog, a great Dane, that was still soundly sleeping on top of its own bed, oblivious to the commotion. It could have eaten the three robbers for breakfast yet slept through the whole incident.

There was a sole impression visible on the polished surface of the library of the house which I was unable to photograph as it could only be seen by looking along the floor, but disappeared when I went over it with a camera. As I had no oblique lighting to photograph it, I drew the sole pattern in my notebook, little knowing that it would eventually become crucial evidence. Other evidence was a broken tail light where someone had reversed a vehicle into a wall. We took possession of the broken glass and as it turned out the vehicle driven by the two men had a broken tail light that provided a physical fit for the glass we had recovered.

Only two of the men had been arrested in the vehicle but the third was arrested in the morning, waiting at a phone box for his girlfriend coming to collect him. He had no shoes, but these were found in the wood behind him. The sole impressions matched the sole impression I had drawn in my notebook.

Coming back to the environmental – or, to be specific, geological – clue, the men had driven to a rural quarry after the robbery, where they had hidden for an hour or so before making their getaway back to Fife. Unluckily for them they had decided to hide at what is a barytes mine, the only one in Scotland and with a unique dust that had coated the wheel arch of their car as they drove through. There was no other place within hundreds of miles that they could have collected this dust on their car. This evidence also put them right at the locus and was not far from where they had jettisoned their shotgun into roadside bushes.

Despite this overwhelming evidence the three pleaded not guilty and, as witnesses, a number of untrue allegations were put to Roy and I by the defence QC, Donald Findlay. He alleged we had driven the men's car back up to the locus and crashed it deliberately into the wall. He said it was impossible to note car registration numbers on the other side of a dual carriageway. Lastly he claimed that I had drawn the sketch of the sole impression in my notebook *after* the recovery of the shoes in the wood. We were vindicated when the weakest of the trio changed his plea to guilty half-way through the trial, which forced the hand of his now ex-friends and resulted in them also changing their plea. The two main players received 10 years each in jail (they had not long since been released from an earlier 10 year sentence for an armed bank robbery) while the weak link in their group received 3 years. Unique rock dust had been part of their downfall.

This last incident entails a slightly different type of observation. I had received word from an informant that a number of ornaments had been stolen and were to be found hidden at a particular house. We had no record of a large-scale theft of ornaments but decided to pay the householder – a man known to us for his dishonest enterprises – a visit without a search warrant and try our luck at getting access to the house.

The man allowed us into the house but denied that he had been involved in any thieving. He seemed confident and consented to a search. Looking for a few hundred ornaments is nowhere near as intensive as a search for drugs or for documents that might be required to prove a crime. Ornaments need space so the search was not going to take long. At the time of this search I was very much involved in the control of rabbits in my spare time and my activities were often the subject of jokes by my colleagues. The search took us eventually to a bedroom where I looked under a double bed. I couldn't believe my eyes as I peered into the dusty gloom. Literally hundreds of wee rabbits in the form of colourful Pendelfin figurines were peering out at me from under the bed. I was in absolute stitches, as was my colleague when I showed him. My rabbiting skills had come to the fore and we had discovered a cache of ornamental rabbits worth many hundreds of pounds.

The suspect admitted that he had been a regular visitor to the warehouse of a well known High Street store, which remarkably he had always found to be unlocked. At each of his many visits he had taken a few dozen ornaments and had built up his own private collection under his bed. None of these had been missed by the rightful owners. The man had unfortunately not kept his collection private enough and one of his friends had shopped him. I often wondered if I had been singled out to be given the information because of my interest in real rabbits

Chapter 11

Things are not always as they seem

THE POISONING of our wildlife is a scourge that is regrettably still with us. As I write this in December 2009 we have just had the fourteenth confirmed bird of prey poisoning of that year, 2008 saw the recovery of over 30 poisoned baits and in 2007 there were five red kites confirmed as having been poisoned. When I re-read the text in early 2011, I can add that there were a further seven victims of poisoning in Tayside in 2010 – three red kites and four buzzards.

Red kites are birds that are no threat to game management, farming, poultry-keeping or pigeon racing. Apart from a few pairs that remained in Wales, these exquisitely elegant birds had already been exterminated in the rest of the UK by poisoning, trapping and shooting, and had to be re-introduced to give them – and us – a second chance.

This type of crime distresses the public, who wonder why on earth someone would want to kill such beautiful birds, especially with the terrible death that poisoning inflicts on creatures. It also infuriates modern-thinking gamekeepers who, whether or not their profession is responsible, are blamed in any case. The publicity generated by the poisoning of re-introduced birds such as red kites and white-tailed eagles is well noted by the public, who increasingly make contact with the police to report any dead bird of prey they encounter on their travels. I would reckon that Tayside Police must now receive nearly fifty calls a year about birds of prey that are suspected by the finder to have been poisoned or shot. If I or one of the divisional wildlife crime officers were to attend every such report the wildlife crime carbon footprint would be huge, and the financial cost to the public would increase substantially. On the positive side I would have to walk many more miles and would have a much-needed chance to burn off calories.

But we have to use some discretion and there are several germane factors to consider before rushing out the door. My first question to the caller relates to where the bird has been found. Invariably I'm aware if this might be an area in which we have had poisoning or other related issues, in which case we most certainly go out to investigate and pick up the bird. I am always conscious that some birds die of starvation, especially from late autumn through to early spring, and if the caller can give some evidence of this, such as a razor-sharp breastbone, we might agree this as a natural death, with no need to collect the bird. If the bird is a sparrowhawk and found anywhere near a window, especially a conservatory, then this is again one that would be left, as its death is most likely to have been accidental.

Lastly, I have now seen so many birds electrocuted on electricity poles with transformers, or with power leading off to a nearby house, that this is another case where we would take no action. The most recent examples of this, in the spring of 2009 and 2010, were two ospreys killed on a pole conducting electricity beside a fish farm in west Perthshire. The birds had landed on the pole – no doubt to survey the ponds beneath for trout – and had been electrocuted either as they landed or had taken off. In each case the death had been reported by the fish farm owner. While the deaths were indeed tragic, one of the ospreys is now displayed in Perth museum; the other in the National Museum of Scotland in Edinburgh. I had left to RSPB the reporting to the electricity company of the dangerous pole and, since no birds were electrocuted in 2011, I trust the situation has been resolved.

In another incident in early August 2007, there was a report of a dead buzzard under such a pole near Kinross. The bird was picked up and put in the bin by the lady who found it. The following day she found another buzzard lying in the field under the pole and unable to fly. Both were reported as suspected of having been poisoned but I am satisfied that they were victims of electrocution. Strangely in most of these cases two buzzards are involved, though whether this is a pair of adults or an adult and a semi-dependent offspring I have no idea. My previous experience indicated that no crime had been committed and the matter was passed to the SSPCA to rescue the stunned buzzard.

I am not professing that my telephone diagnosis is correct on every occasion but I suspect I will have missed very few victims of crime and generally err on the safe side. Here is a further selection of false alarms.

Thankfully barn owls are becoming a more familiar sight again in Tayside and I encounter many more now than at any other time in my life. I know that the increase in the part of Perthshire where I live is partly due to a release scheme under licence by a gamekeeper. The owls were extremely successful and have spread widely. One wintertime call and one early spring call were to the Amulree area of Perthshire, which because of the height above sea level, might be at the extreme edge of the barn owls' range. In each case a pair of barn owls was found dead in old buildings and the finder immediately suspected poisoning as the reason for their demise. The birds had been dead for some time and there was little left of them.

At the first pair I gathered what I could of the desiccated bodies and first x-rayed them, courtesy of Dundee Airport. There was no chance of leaving maggots behind on the conveyor belt leading to the scanner as the squirming scavengers of rotting flesh would have either succumbed to the winter frosts or pupated and turned into blowflies. The x-rays were clear: I didn't really expect to see either shotgun pellets or air rifle slugs but this was all part of a thorough examination to establish a possible cause of death. Next stop was Science and Advice for Scottish Agriculture for testing for pesticides, but again they were clear; not even a trace of a residual build-up of rat poison, which is sometimes the case with birds of prey that pick up dead or dying rats and mice round farm steadings where rodenticides have been in legal use.

I was left with starvation as the most likely cause of death, and this was exactly the same with the second pair. Barn owl numbers, in common with one or two other birds of prey, burgeon during a year when voles proliferate. A pair can sometimes rear as many as 7 chicks in these fruitful conditions, but the opposite is the case when voles are scarce. In winter conditions that have long periods of very wet weather or deep snow the owls have difficulty hunting and unfortunately there can be many casualties. Despite being long dead, the plumage of these barn owls was still pristine and exquisite. Though I could accept that their deaths were natural, I was extremely sorry that the winter had taken its toll on a species trying hard to survive right on the edge.

On an unrelated investigation I visited this same area in what I hoped would be the final stages of the long, hard winter of 2009/10. Even in March there was a metre of snow at either side of the country road. I could tell where there were rabbit warrens on the steep sides of some of the hitherto grassy knolls in the fields. In a blanket of white, the dirt-stained tracks the starving rabbits had made between the burrows were etched as if someone had drawn on the snow with a pencil. The marks showed that they had travelled no distance at all from their burrows and I was sure they would be just skin and bone. I suspected that all the barn owls must have perished, but was assured by the gamekeeper, who keeps a close eye on them in the glen, that he had seen them in recent days, and that they had been hunting a lot during daylight. This was good news.

Though poisoned baits are generally dead birds, rabbits or hares, other bait might be more likely to be successful depending on the target. If mink were the target, then I would imagine that fish could be used as bait. There is no doubt that a dead fish lures a mink into a trap so there is no reason to believe that it would be less successful if laced with a pesticide. (Readers should not be concerned that I am giving those who are involved in the abuse of pesticides new ideas; they are at least as knowledgeable as I am in the preferred diet of what they may consider as pest species.) I was therefore not too surprised when a man telephoned me one November morning to say that he had been out walking on an estate and he had found three trout set out as if they were poisoned baits. The fish had been laid out at the edge of a burn running from a large pond in the middle of the estate, and were at intervals of about 100 metres. When he named the estate I was doubtful about poisoning as I knew the keeper as trustworthy, but the man was quite concerned that these fish were baits. I would normally never ask anyone to collect and deliver to me what might be poisoned bait because of the severe risk of the person becoming affected with the pesticide, but the man was several steps ahead of me. He was so worried there was something illegal going on he had collected the fish, put them in a carrier bag and had taken them home. Since he gone to these lengths I said I would call to see them. 'No need,' was the reply, 'I'm coming into Perth anyway. I'll bring them in to you.'

The man with the carrier bag duly arrived and I couped out the contents onto the drive at the side of the police station. There were three lovely brown trout, all probably about the 3lbs mark and fish that I would love to have had on the end of a fishing line, then sizzling in a hot frying pan. Each was missing its head and each was full of ripe eggs, some of which were spilling out on to the tarmac. They had been fish that had come up the burn from the small lochan to spawn, and were probably in the process of doing do when they had been captured by an otter. The trout had been so plentiful and so easily caught in the confines of the narrow burn that the otter had contented itself with eating what to it is the best part, the head. My concerned finder of fish was satisfied at the explanation and apologetic for putting me to so much trouble. I was not of the mind that I had been troubled and was pleased to have found an answer to the puzzle that had not involved a crime. What I was less pleased about was that I had stupidly handled the trout without gloves and could not get rid of the smell from my hands for the rest of the day, despite repeated washing in soap and hot water!

One animal that would most definitely be tempted by a piece of fish, or in fact any other edible morsel it happened upon, is the fox. Foxes have been frequent victims of baits over the years and I once, during a January morning out in the countryside, found two – a dog and vixen – lying a few yards apart. They had been victims of bait laced with the pesticide chloralose that they had clearly shared. Though solitary animals much of the rest of the year, the months of December and January is the time when foxes pair up for breeding, hence the reason there were two. The cold temperature of a January night would make the pesticide chloralose super-efficient in its illicit purpose, as it works by quickly lowering the body temperature and the victim dies of hypothermia.

In another incident a fox had been seen staggering about on the edge of woodland near Aberfeldy in Perthshire. The distraught animal had allowed the human observer within a few metres, then simply curled up and went to sleep. The man who had witnessed this went back to the area an hour or so later and the fox was still asleep, so it was at this point that he called me. He narrated the tale and stated he had seen foxes in the past that had been poisoned and was of the view this was what had made the fox so lethargic and unaware of the proximity of its most feared enemy, man. I didn't disagree. The symptoms sounded exactly like a fox so cold that it was oblivious to any danger and just wanted to curl up and go to sleep.

I headed for Aberfeldy and met the concerned witness, who took me to the fox. It was still curled up sleeping, but it was a sleep now from which it would never awaken: the fox was dead. I made an examination of the fox and saw first of all that it was a vixen, a female. I was surprised that it was extremely thin, in fact just skin and bone. It had an injury just behind the left shoulder, which had healed and looked like it had at one time been hit by a rifle bullet, possibly of too low a calibre to have killed it. This may have accounted for its emaciated condition.

I now had a dead fox that could have died of an old injury, or may very well have been poisoned. An injured fox continues to eat and since it would be less efficient at catching larger prey like rabbits, is more likely to rely on invertebrates and on scavenging, making it even more susceptible to being poisoned by a bait laced with pesticide.

Since foxes are considered a pest species and an offence would not have been committed by someone trying to shoot one, my intention was to explore the poisoning aspect only. Staff at SASA do not like whole bodies of larger animals, such as foxes, dogs and cats, being delivered to them and much prefer to deal with samples taken from relevant areas of the victims body, such as the gullet, stomach and liver. To obtain these samples I called in at the Scottish Agricultural College vet lab in Perth and asked if the vets there would be kind enough to take these samples for me.

Once the vets saw that they were dealing with a fox that was virtually just skin and bone and weighing only 3.5 kilos – about the weight of an adult brown hare – they were keen to find out a cause of death for their own interest, and carried out a full post-mortem examination. The teeth were examined first. Their condition and length showed that the fox was not a young fox, but neither was it particularly old. Next it was cut open and the insides examined. The poor wee vixen was suffering from acute constipation, with the large intestine being completely blocked. There was not a trace of food either in the gullet or the stomach of the animal, which immediately ruled out poisoning. The vets' view was that it was the extremely emaciated condition of the animal that had induced the constipation, though there was no apparent reason for it being thin. I pointed out the shoulder injury to the vets but when this was examined it was found to be superficial and would have had little or no effect on the animal's health.

As I watched the post mortem examination and saw the state of the gut of the vixen I was not surprised that it had been oblivious to the human presence. Its mysterious medical problem must have been developing for some time and the manner of its death must have been pretty awful.

In March, 2010, I took another two foxes for the SAC vets to examine. Poisoning had again been suspected by the finder, as he was the only person who shot on the land concerned, and there was no apparent injury to either fox. I went to collect them and found one to be a young vixen, the other an adult dog fox. The dog fox had been dead for a few weeks, though the cub from the previous year was newly dead. I photographed them and turned them over. As the finder had told me, they were in good condition, but there was one small clue as to how the dog fox had died. Though I could see no injury there was a small tuft of fur hanging from the left flank. This indicated to me that it could have received some sort of blow, and the fact that it was lying about 100 metres from a narrow country road made it possible that it had been struck by a car. The wee vixen was about 300 metres from the same road and may have suffered the same fate.

This was confirmed when David Gibson, the vet, carried out the post mortem examination. The vixen had a bruise on its shoulder consistent with having been struck by a vehicle, and the dog fox had a substantial amount of bruising over its back near the tail end. It had severe internal haemorrhaging and its lungs were almost white. Neither had been killed instantly but would have died of hypothermia in the extreme cold of the preceding weeks. I was interested to see the stomach content of the vixen. It had the lesser injury and may have lain injured for some days. The stomach was empty apart from a tablespoonful or so of black liquid and several dozen parasitic worms. Thankfully my background has made me immune to these sights!

Foxes, like rabbits, are regularly controlled by snaring. I have several times seen a fox that has managed to break a snare and escape, though I once shot a rabbit that, had it been a cat, was running very short of its nine lives. This rabbit had recovered from myxomatosis and had one eye that was now permanently partially closed due to the disease, so that it only had a small peep hole on the one side through which to see. Myxomatosis, or myxy as it is usually termed, is now only fatal to a small proportion of rabbits compared to the 99% rate of fatalities when it was first released onto the unsuspecting coney population in 1954. It is a vile disease that causes a slow death to rabbits, infecting their eyes, so that they close and fill with white pus, and the base of their ears and their genitals, which swell and become encrusted. The rabbits drop rapidly in condition and of course, with being blind, fall victim readily to predators. Those that survive usually have some tell-tale scarring, especially to the eyes or to the base of the ears.

In any case myxy had only been one problem for this rabbit. It had also been caught in a snare, which had broken and part of which was still round its neck, in places eating into the flesh though not enough to cause it serious harm. When I skinned the rabbit at home I saw that it had an earlier encounter with a firearm before my .22 bullet found its mark: it had been shot at with a shotgun, probably at long range, and was carrying two shotgun pellets just under its skin. I suppose its luck couldn't last for ever.

Snaring is an emotive subject and I get lots of calls from people who are under the impression that it is illegal. Many are concerned about their cats being caught in snares, though I am aware that a good number of rabbit trappers and gamekeepers notify cat owners when they are snaring near to their homes. Normally rabbit snares are only set for two or three days at a time and if the cat owner is asked to keep it indoors over this period they usually comply and are glad to have been forewarned. Those using snares on their own ground are not obliged to notify neighbours with cats but it is sensible and profess- ional to do so.

One of my recent calls was from a rural cat owner who had no idea that anyone was snaring nearby and was distressed to find that her cat had not only been caught in a snare but told me that the monster who had caught it had strung it up on a fence near her house. Invariably the operators of snares want to get on with their job of reducing the rabbit population quietly and without drawing attention to themselves, so I was surprised that anyone would be as stupid and unfeeling as advertise what they were doing. This seemed reminiscent of the days of gamekeepers' gibbets, when they hung all the 'vermin' that they had caught on a fence so that their employer could see how busy they had been and how efficient their shooting, trapping and poisoning skills were. I have seen many of these gibbets in my youth, and they included stoats, weasels, rats, foxes, crows, moles, jays, magpies – and of course cats and birds of prey – but these are a relic of the past. Was a new trend emerging? I set off to see.

From my telephone conversation I had a picture in my mind of a dead cat, still in a snare, having been tied to the top wire of a fence. The reality was slightly different. What had happened was that the woman's cat had been caught in a rabbit snare but had managed to pull the wooden peg out of the ground. It had headed for home with the peg from the snare rattling and bouncing around somewhere close to its tail. It had then jumped a drystane dyke against which, on the far side, was a single stand of barbed wire strung between fence posts to keep cattle from damaging the wall. Unfortunately for the cat the wooden peg of the snare had clattered against the dyke, becoming jammed between two of the coping stones. The cat had gone sailing over the strand of barbed wire but of course didn't quite reach the ground because of still being attached by the snare to the jammed peg. It was suspended, inches off the ground, and no doubt was very quickly strangled. What was reported as an act of extreme malice, when looked at more closely was an unfortunate accident. The person who set the snares was never traced but this situation was something that could possibly have been avoided by dialogue with the residents of the very few properties in the vicinity.

The next incident was in an urban situation, which often means youths with airguns. This is what was suspected when three domestic ducks on a pond within an Arbroath college were found dead and bleeding. The college tutors were rightly furious when they found their ducks and related a number of different problems recently with youths coming into the grounds. As an owner of nearly a couple of dozen khaki Campbell ducks I had considerable sympathy with the duck owners; I would be on the warpath if someone harmed them.

The ducks were brought to me at Perth and since it was during the period in 2005 just after a swan had been confirmed with avian influenza, I took the ducks to the Scottish Agricultural College in Perth as a precaution, rather than having them x-rayed at Dundee Airport or Perth Prison. That way, since the SAC veterinary laboratories across Scotland were responsible for surveillance of the avian 'flu virus in any case, and since waterfowl were most at risk, they could carry out the relevant tests and give me a cause of death at the same time.

Digressing for a moment, around the same time I had a call from the caretaker of a Perth medical centre. The conversation went like this.

'Good morning. Alan Stewart here.'

'Yes good morning. I'm Joe Bloggs, the caretaker from the Neverwell Medical Centre. I've just found three dead blackbirds outside the Centre. What should I do with them?' I knew very well what he should do but I must have been in a mischievous mood.

'Keep them till you get another 21, then bake them in a pie.' I replied.

The line went quiet for a minute and the caretaker must have thought he was dealing with some sort of lunatic, or wondered if he really had got through to the police station. Before he became too confused – or annoyed – I told him I was just joking and that he should notify the Defra helpline, giving him the telephone number, and they would decide the best action, though I told him that the birds may well have flown into the glass doors of the centre. I also told him that the guidelines advised to be more suspicious of dead waterfowl, or of 12 or more dead birds over a small area, rather than just three. We had a chat about avian influenza and wildlife crime which hopefully convinced him that I wasn't mad after all. When our conversation ended I couldn't help wondering if he was trying to remember the rest of the nursery rhyme, because I certainly couldn't.

Returning to the three ducks suspected of being shot, they were not, thankfully, carrying any strain of avian influenza, neither had they been shot. There were small puncture wounds on the bodies and neck of all three consistent with having been killed by a fox. Sometimes the fox is a victim; this time it was a successful predator. Probably a well fed predator as it did not carry any away for its supper.

If black-throated divers are victims of crime it is usually because their eggs are taken by egg thieves. It would be unusual for one to be shot mistakenly for any of the duck species as their flight is completely different to that of ducks. I was therefore not too concerned about a crime having been committed when I had a call from RSPB on a morning in late spring stating that there was a dead black-throated diver lying at the edge of Loch Rannoch in Perthshire; even when I was told that the bird had what appeared to be an injury that was similar to a bullet wound. This was another of these judgement calls when I have to decide if the circumstances merit either my attendance or that of one of the divisional wildlife crime officers. It has to be borne in mind that if a crime is suspected the police should attend to collect and label the victim, to photograph the scene or to carry out a scene of crime examination. If the wrong decision is made then valuable evidence or corroboration of important elements of a case may be lost.

I had not a clue how a black-throated diver would receive such an injury though I considered two possibilities; firstly that it had flown in to something sharp, and secondly that it could have been shot by a .22 rifle or air rifle. I thought the chances of this latter option were extremely remote. This in fact was one of my easier decisions and I left RSPB to pick up the bird and have it examined for a cause of death.

On this occasion RSPB took the black-throated diver to one of the foremost avian pathologists in Scotland at the Lasswade veterinary laboratory, Alisdair Wood. The bird was found to be a male and the result was something that no-one was expecting. Black-throated divers have extremely long dagger shaped beaks, as do their relatives the red-throated diver and the great northern diver. On this occasion it is likely that two males had designs on the same female and began to fight; a fight that ended in one being fatally stabbed by its rival. Detective work to establish the cause of death in wildlife as well as in human cases can have some surprising and unusual outcomes.

I am always pleased when a photograph can be emailed to me to give a far clearer idea of what we might be dealing with. This would have been handy when a dead buzzard was reported in 2007 lying next to a dead rabbit on the outskirts of Brechin in Angus. The month – February – conformed to the likely time for the deliberate poisoning of wildlife, but what threw me a wee bit was that these carcasses were close to a track used regularly by dog walkers and only a few hundred metres from the edge of the town. It was an unlikely place for a poisoned bait to have been set but nevertheless it required immediate attention because of the potential risk to humans and dogs as well as wildlife. I asked PC Blair Wilkie to go there as soon as she could, and received a call from her an hour or so later. The dead rabbit was indeed a rabbit, but not a poisoned bait. The dead 'buzzard' was a cormorant! In a simultaneous enquiry at the other end of Tayside, an 'eagle' tethered to a balcony of a block of flats in the town of Crieff in Perthshire turned out not to be an eagle at all but a Harris hawk.

In June of 2008 I *did* get an emailed photograph sent to me, but instead of being much help it caused me considerable distress. A hillwalker had come across an injured immature peregrine while he was walking on Invermark Estate at the head of Glenesk in Angus.

The feathers at the end of one of its wings were badly smashed up and there was no way that it would be able to fly. If it couldn't fly it couldn't eat and was destined to die of starvation. He assumed that the bird had been shot. He photographed it . . . and walked on! I could hardly believe that anyone could do this. At the very least he could have killed it rather than leave it to starve. It was two days later that I received the photograph and the rough location. I emailed the photo to a friend of mine, Alastair Lawrie, a well respected vet who specialises in dealing with injured and unwell birds, especially birds of prey and parrots. Alastair put my mind at rest in that he said that having been shot with a shotgun could almost be discounted, while having been shot with a rifle was possible but would have killed the bird or given it serious internal injuries. His conclusion was that it had suffered unknown trauma which caused it to severely self-mutilate the injured wing.

I was pleased, since we have had no reports of illegal activity on Invermark and in fact it is a well-respected estate. I passed on the information about the bird to Fred Taylor, the head keeper, who said he would get one of his underkeepers to have a look in the area. It was a bit like looking for a needle in a haystack. There was no sign of the bird and I hoped that a fox had got it so that its end was quick.

On a completely different type of call, PC Harvey Birse, another of the divisional wildlife crime officers, responded to a report of someone trying to break into a house in Forfar. It was 4.00 am and the occupants were listening to the thief trying to break through the high wooden gate at the bottom of the garden. Harvey sped there in his traffic patrol car. . . and chased away the errant badger that thought there was something much more interesting on the other side of the gate and was determined to find out just what it was. The badger lumbered away into the darkness, and the occupants fell about laughing at the false alarm.

May 2009 was a special month for unusual calls. I had a call early one morning from a man that said he had found a trap set for birds of prey. Three dead rabbits had been set out on a floating platform and were covered by a loose net set a few feet above them. His interpretation was that buzzards would fly down to get the rabbits and become entangled in the net. I was doubtful. I couldn't envisage what he was describing, plus the 'trap' was in an area of almost continual activity, being in an industrial site at the edge of a village near Perth. Anyway I said I'd meet him and he could show me where this trap was.

I met the man, who I immediately though was a rather strange character. He was keen to accompany me rather than just point me in the right direction. I compromised and dropped him off just before the location, which was a very large round tank sunk in to the ground, and which was a reservoir for a water supply to the nearby buildings in case of fire. Before I left my passenger I asked him to describe the trap again. He did so but said that he had wrecked it when he found it, as he was so angry. I thought Mr Angry even more strange now.

I went to the reservoir but there was really little to see. The reservoir was surrounded by a chain-link fence. There was a gate, though that was padlocked. A floating wooden platform with a wire netting centre, on which there were three freshly-killed adult rabbits, was at the side of the reservoir. A net had been pulled through the chain link fence and torn to bits. I could see that the platform had initially been tied in the middle of the reservoir, but the rope that had secured it to the far side had been cut and was floating on the water. I couldn't work it out, but couldn't see it as a trap for birds. I looked back towards where I had left Mr Angry. He remained there, watching.

I next went to the nearest occupied building and asked about the reservoir, to be told it was owned by the folks from the building next door. When I went there one of the occupants told me that he had just stocked it with trout. To increase their food supply he had made a platform with wood and wire mesh, shot three rabbits, and put them on the wire mesh so that in time bluebottles would lay eggs and the maggots would fall through the netting for the fish. He had covered the rabbits with netting to keep crows off, and tied the structure so that it floated in the centre of the reservoir. It had been ingenious and labour intensive. Until it had been spotted by Mr Angry.

I left the disconsolate inventor and went back to pick up Mr Angry, still waiting and watching from the same spot. I'm sure he was keen to see an arrest being made, or for police cars with blue flashing lights to attend as back-up. I was not surprised to see that he was very obviously disappointed that the law had not been broken and that he didn't get a deputy sheriff's badge to wear with pride on his jacket.

Because things sometimes turn out otherwise than what they seem initially I try to be careful not to jump in too quickly. This paid dividends in early December 2009 when I received a report of a Fenn trap that had possibly been set on top of a post. The caller said that the Fenn trap was not set when he saw it but was hanging down from the top of the post. It seemed a shiny new trap and was only a short distance from a pheasant release pen. These traps – or their earlier versions, pole traps – used to be regularly set on top of posts to catch birds of prey. Many were set near to pheasant release pens to protect the pheasant poults against birds that might be looking for an easy meal: a buzzard, sparrowhawk, goshawk or tawny owl. Though there has been an odd trap found in these completely illegal circumstances in other parts of Scotland in recent times (the last being in 2009 in the Northern Constabulary area) I have never encountered nor even heard of one being used in Tayside since I became wildlife crime officer in 1993. With this report there was a possibility that the trap had been used earlier in the year but I would be very surprised if anyone indulging in this very obvious criminality had not taken the trap away when it was not in use. Back to my old favourites: photographs.

The caller had photographed the trap but for technical reasons to do with his computer could not email it to me for a couple of days. When I eventually got the photos all became clear. The post was the straining post for a gate. From tracks through the gate it was quite well used. Not the place to put an illegal trap. The photos also showed that a well-used track ran past the gate; again not the place to carry out an act that you would not want anyone to witness. Also, the straining post was juxtaposed to a drystane dyke, an ideal place for a tunnel trap, in other words the same Fenn trap used legally in a tunnel to catch mammalian pest species. Lastly I could see that the trap was not nailed or stapled to the post; simply hung there on the hinge.

Now that I had much more information, if only from the detail of three photos, my assessment changed from the initial suspicion to the true appreciation of the situation: for some unknown reason the trap had been taken out of the tunnel trap and then – maybe by the same person, maybe not – hung on the post so that its operator could find it. The case was solved from my desk. It was, in police speak, a false alarm with good intent.

Chapter 12

Fishy Stories

FOREIGN visitors to Britain who are involved in shooting and fishing are welcomed as they make a very valuable contribution to the economy. Two Swiss visitors that I remember from some years back were much less welcome as they and a fishing ghillie from the River Tay formed a particularly unprincipled triumvirate.

The River Tay is one of the top salmon rivers in Scotland, with fishing beats between Perth and Dunkeld probably being the most productive. The river is wide and deep and much of the fishing, to get to the best parts of the pools, is done by boat. There are many ghillies (sometimes called boatmen) on a range of fishing beats on this part of the Tay. All of them have been fishing the river for many years and know every place that a salmon is likely to be lying, the optimum height of the river for catching fish, and the best lure for the particular conditions. The paying clients rely on the ghillies to provide the best possible chance of catching a salmon, and in addition to that, many regale their customers with stories of past catches and adventures on the river, some of these becoming more dramatic as more malt whisky is imbibed.

It came as a bit of a surprise one day when a couple of ghillies complained about one of their fellow boatmen. Fishing was quite good on the river at this time but while most boats were managing to land 3 or 4 fish a day, one particular boat was reported to be landing a catch more akin to a trawler. Along with the then superintendent of the Tay District Salmon Fisheries Board, Garry Gibb, I made some enquiries into the background of the skipper of the trawler and we decided to investigate further.

I was still a serving police officer at this time and had power of search and arrest if required, so Garry and I made for the river bank on this particular beat and lay down concealed with a set of binoculars each. We had a good view of the ghillie and his two guests out on the river. It was a good fishing day, with not too much wind and very little sunshine so catches could be quite good under normal circumstances. We had barely been there two minutes when we saw that circumstances were not normal: the scene was reminiscent of poachers I had dealt with further downstream on the Tay at the Lower Harbour, when they were raking the fish with treble hooks and lumps of lead on the end of their line to make the line sink. These fishermen were exactly the same, jerking the line viciously through the water in an attempt to foul hook salmon. At least the salmon poachers I had dealt with in the past had the decency to wait until it was dark; these guys were blatantly trying to foul hook fish in daylight. Each time they cast with their rods we could see that they had genuine lures – large spoons with treble hooks – on the end of their lines. The difference between genuine anglers and these guys was that they were in no way trying to convince a salmon that the lure was an appetising morsel they should try to swallow; they wanted to rake the needle-sharp points of the treble hooks into the sides of the fish and get it on board the boat as quickly as possible. Not in the least sporting, in fact out and out poaching of the worst kind, since they were outwardly respectable salmon anglers. And the ghillie was even worse, facilitating the whole episode and no doubt in for a hefty tip from the visitors after three days fishing.

Years later I compared the action we were taking with the action that would be carried out by police officers in Malta. In 2003 I spent a week helping to train police officers in Malta in wildlife crime investigation. I very soon learned that they had plenty of wildlife crime to deal with as a high proportion of the Maltese population seemed to be involved either in shooting protected birds (in addition to those that they could legally shoot) or trapping finches and other small birds (both legally and illegally) for the wild bird trade. As the police knew many of the criminals involved, I suggested that they conceal themselves at a vantage point – and there were plenty of those on the surrounding cliffs and other high ground – and watch what was happening through binoculars. They could note who was shooting which protected bird then call on them the following day and charge them. I was astounded when they told me that their law did not allow them to permit an offence to continue. Once they saw an offence being committed they had to move in and deal with the offender.

This, to me, meant that they could only deal with one offence per day. When they saw the offence happening they could run or creep down the hill and arrest the person involved, while everyone else cleared out and got off Scot-free. Relating the Maltese dictum to my present situation I saw three men in a boat committing offences but if I did anything to try to stop them committing these offences, like showing myself and shouting to them to come ashore, all the evidence would be jettisoned overboard. I therefore did nothing of the sort. And continued watching.

The illegal fishing continued for an hour or more and we saw three salmon getting hauled into the boat. Compared to a salmon legally caught by the mouth by the normal fishing method, the time taken to play and land these fish was minimal: five minutes rather than 15 or even 45 minutes. The hooks obviously had a good hold in the side of the salmon and, using strong line, a fish can be landed in no time at all with little chance of it escaping. The skipper was ready with the gaff and another salmon was added to the clandestine tally in the bottom of the boat.

In due course the boat began to head for our bank of the river and I thought it must be time for the crew's lunch. Within a few minutes they had beached the boat just downstream from our vantage point and began to unload the fish from the boat and carry them to the fishing hut. When they were all inside the hut gloating over their fish it was time for Garry and I to move in, which we did. The three men got the surprise of their lives when we entered the fishing hut and identified ourselves. There were a total of 10 salmon in the hut, not a bad haul for a morning on the Tay when other boats would be lucky to have a couple of fish. The telltale marks on the sides of the fish where they had been ripped by the hooks were obvious and any attempt they made at trying to talk themselves out of trouble was wasted. They realised this when I told them we had been watching them for well over an hour and that they were all under arrest for salmon poaching.

Most poachers, especially nowadays, would be released from custody either to receive a summons in due course or on an undertaking to attend court at an arranged date within the next week or two. This was not the case here. The Swiss visitors were due to fly home in a couple of days, and the ghillie's offence was deemed so serious that all three were kept for court the following day. Charges were: (1) fishing by means other than rod and line, which meant that even though they physically had a rod and line in their hand in the case of the two Swiss visitors, and a gaff in the case of the ghillie, they were not using them in the legitimate manner; (2) two or more persons acting together to commit this offence, which was quite straightforward and is in fact 'gang poaching'; and (3) unlawful possession of the fishing tackle in their possession and 10 salmon with marks consistent with being foul-hooked.

In the morning, at Perth Sheriff Court, all pled guilty and received substantial fines and the confiscation of their fishing tackle. The ghillie, being employed by an estate, was sacked for bringing the name of the estate and the fishing beat into disrepute. This meant he lost his tied house, a lovely cottage within the grounds of the estate. He moved out a few days later, and that night the house was burned to the ground. Police enquiries were made but the officers involved in the investigation never managed to gain sufficient evidence to bring anyone to court.

While foul hooking salmon is effective, there is no poaching method so effective as the use of Cymag. Cymag is a white powder which gives off a poisonous gas when exposed to moisture and was formerly used in the control of rats and rabbits. The use or even the possession of Cymag has been banned since 2005 though I've no doubt there will be stockpiles hidden somewhere by determined salmon poachers waiting on a good run of salmon.

Cymag was used regularly by poachers, especially in the River Ericht at Blairgowrie and the River South Esk near Brechin. Many thousands of salmon have been killed in these rivers by unscrupulous poachers. Though the Cymag doesn't gas the fish, its effect prevents red blood corpuscles absorbing oxygen and effectively suffocates them, causing them to thrash about on the surface of the river in an attempt to get their live-saving oxygen. Only a few fish would ever have been gathered up to line the pockets of the poachers, while the rest drifted downstream, dead fish that minutes before had almost completed their journey from the seas off Greenland to the place in their native river where they themselves hatched, with the single purpose of spawning and ensuring the survival of the species.

My last experience of the use of Cymag in Tayside was in the River Ericht in July 2003. Heavy rain had brought a very good run of fish up the River Tay and those that themselves had been hatched as fry in the River Ericht had returned to this tributary of the Tay in good numbers. This was perfect for poachers, who heaved half a tin of Cymag into a turbulent part of the river, causing several hundred fish to be killed. It was not known how many they took for themselves, or even who had been involved, but the devastation was obvious at daybreak for many miles downstream.

Salmon returning from the sea to spawn have other dangers besides poachers. On most days during the open fishing season on any good salmon river there will be dozens, if not hundreds, of fishers testing their skill at tempting a fish that in fact doesn't eat in fresh water to have a bite at the lure. In addition seals and dolphins love salmon, and to a lesser extent, otters will take the smaller grilse. Then there are nets. Most river netting stations have been bought out now to allow more fish upstream to satisfy the lucrative salmon and sea trout angling industry. Some coastal nets have also been bought out but those that remain must take a significant proportion of the migrating salmon as they hug the coastline seeking the smell of their natal river. It was in one of these coastal netting businesses using bag nets that we had an unusual case in 2003.

A bag net is positioned out from the shore and though visible at low tide, is submerged at high tide. Another net, called a leader, runs at right angles from the bag net towards the coast and this is used to guide fish swimming along the coast out into the bag, where their entry into the bag is quite straightforward as they are committed to following the direction of this net termed the leader. The leader will usually have weights at the bottom and floats at the top so that it can rise and fall with the tide. Once in the bag net, exit for the fish is almost impossible.

Under fishing legislation no netting is allowed between 6.00 p.m. on a Friday and 6.00 a.m. on a Monday. This gives some salmon a chance to make it safely into the rivers, where there is a further respite from danger: rod fishing is banned during the whole of Sunday, from midnight to midnight. The netting industry is obliged to comply with the legislation, and must lift the leaders by 6.00 p.m. on a Friday, not resetting them until at least 6.00 a.m on a Monday. With the leaders lifted, salmon can continue to swim parallel with the coast rather than be diverted out seawards into the captivity of the bag net.

Responsibility for enforcing fishing legislation is shared between water bailiffs and police. During one of their patrols in July 2003 a water bailiff noticed that the leaders of one of the bag nets in his area had not been lifted over the weekend. He made contact with the police, and Constable Doug Ogilvie, one of the divisional wildlife crime officers, met the bailiff to discuss the offence. In case this was a one-off offence it was decided that the nets would be checked again the following Friday. On this occasion, at 6.00 p.m., several nets still had leaders in place. Instead of improving, the situation had worsened. There was no valid reason for this as the weather was fine and the sea calm.

The person responsible for the nets was traced and charged, but claimed that inclement weather had made it impossible for him to lift the leaders. This claim was certainly at odds with the fine weather that Doug Ogilvie and the water bailiffs had experienced shortly before. It is always good to have an independent view and Doug made contact with the coastguard, who provided a copy of the local weather forecast for the relevant day and offered the view that in his opinion a professional salmon fisher would have no problem going about his normal business with such a forecast.

At 5.00 a.m. the following day the leaders were still in place and three hours later, bailiffs and police watched the salmon fishermen in a boat removing some of the leaders, but leaving one in place. This leader was left in place in fact over the next 4 weekends. As a result the fisherman, who said he was *solely responsible for the bag nets* – a term I will come back to shortly – was charged with a total of 6 charges under the Salmon Fisheries (Scotland) Act, 1868, Section 24 and Schedule D, which dealt with close times for netting at that time, though these offences would now be under the more recent Salmon and Freshwater Fisheries (Consolidation) (Scotland) Act 2003.

A date was set for trial but two issues arose just before this. Firstly the complaint (summons) from the procurator fiscal's office served on the fisherman gave the year of the legislation contravened as 1968 rather than 1868, though I doubt that this problem would have been insurmountable. Secondly the procurator fiscal had decided that evidence would be required to establish that the fisherman who had been charged was the owner or a director in the company.

This issue had probably arisen from the wording of the charge, which included 'being the *proprietor* of a salmon fishery at which bag nets were used'. I'm puzzled yet as to why this would be necessary as he had admitted being *solely responsible for the bag nets*. I don't doubt that some document proving ownership or directorship would have been beneficial to the case but since this had been missed by the police it's the type of essential element of evidence the fiscal would normally pick up on and instruct an investigating officer to obtain, or establish more fully. In any event it was not possible to remedy this the day before the trial and the case was abandoned, to the frustration of all the players involved – except the fisherman!

It is so easy to miss one essential piece of evidence in more unusual cases that it is always worthwhile for the investigating officer to look at each part of a charge to ensure that each element of the charge can be proved. Most police officers and fiscals have a heavy workload and work to deadlines, so it's regrettable, but understandable, when there is a slip up.

It is not all bad news for salmon. In an attempt to conserve salmon stocks many rivers now operate a catch and release system, where all adult female salmon caught, and a high proportion of the remainder, are returned to the water. This is especially important with large hen

Dog and hare's paw prints at full speed – Chapter 1

One of the poisoned buzzards found on
Edradynate Estate – Chapter 3

Buzzard in spring-over trap – Chapter 3

A beaver's determined attempt to fell a large tree – Chapter 4

Beaver lodge on River Earn – Chapter 4

The recovery of a bullet from a shot seal – Chapter 6

Pine marten in a tunnel trap – Chapter 8

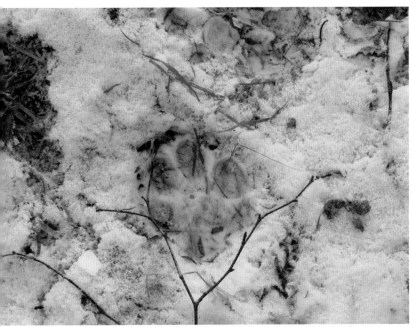

Huge paw prints suspiciously feline-looking (photo – Keith Ringland)
– Chapter 8

The length of the stride of the big cat? (photo Keith Ringland)

Two buzzards reported as poisoned, but had been electrocuted – Chapter 11

Trap hanging on gate initially though to be a pole trap – Chapter 11

Coastal salmon net near Montrose – Chapter 12

Golden eagle in back garden – Chapter 13

The 'rabbity' landscape of Glen Lethnot – Chapter 14

The hedgehog before post-mortem examination – Chapter 15

The young oyster catcher that was thrown off the roof – Chapter 16

Some of the dead rooks – Chapter 16

One of the swallow's nests inside the building – Chapter 16

The snared badger – Chapter 17

The white fallow buck shot on Atholl Estate – Chapter 19
(photo – Malcolm Whyte)

The Tamaskan shot while worrying cattle – Chapter 19

Road sign used as target practice – Chapter 19

The poisoned bait in the pheasant pen – Chapter 20

Author with the poisoned golden eagle 'Alma' –
Chapter 20

The poisoned venison cubes on top of the deer fence on Glenogil Estate –
Chapter 20

One of the 5 poisoned red kites
recovered in Perthshire in 2007
– Chapter 20

The poisoned white-tailed eagle 'White G'
– Chapter 20

Hare coursers about to slip their dogs
– see Chapters 1, 7 and 14 for discussion of hare coursing

Hare taken by dogs awaiting post mortem examination

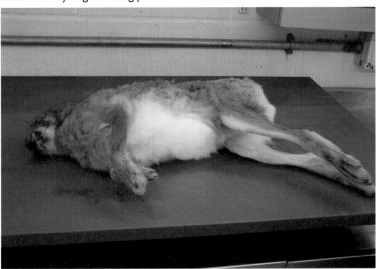

The new Tayside Police events vehicle with the author and Gordon Nicoll –
Chapter 5

Bertha Loch looking west – Chapter 10

fish that can produce copious amounts of spawn with the consequent potential of regenerating the river's stock for future years. (The benefits of this policy are beginning to show, with many Scottish rivers having record numbers of salmon during the 2010 fishing season).

A further measure to conserve salmon stocks are the provisions of the Salmon (Prohibition of Sale) (Scotland) Regulations 2002, legislation that bans the sale in Scotland of rod-caught salmon. This is to prevent less scrupulous salmon anglers taking more fish than they can eat themselves and making their fishing a commercial enterprise. Public knowledge of this ban led to a phone call to me on 7 October 2005 when a concerned person walking past a fish shop in an Angus town saw salmon cutlets displayed in the window. A flag-shaped sign proudly stuck into them declared them as *Fresh Rod-Caught Salmon.*

There were two options. Indeed they could have been salmon caught by rod and line, in which case an offence was being committed in offering them for sale. Alternatively they could have been netted salmon, but the netting season finished at the end of August. If they were netted fish they would either have been taken by poachers . . . or they had been frozen and thawed, in which case they would not be fresh.

Since I was an hour and a half away I asked two local police officers to make a check of the shop window, but by the time they were clear of their previous job and got to the shop, demand must have been such that the salmon was sold out and the sign removed. A joint visit later between police and an officer from Trading Standards, with whom I had discussed the complaint, ensured that whatever the offence had been it would not recur.

August 2005 and 2006 saw a good run of salmon in the River Tay but low water during these good summers meant that salmon that needed to make their way up the second tributary from the estuary, the River Almond, had to wait just downstream of the Almond at a part of the Tay known locally as the Woody Hole. This is a deep, fast-running pool close to the bank just prior to where the salmon would make a left turn into the Almond. It was a pool where in 1968 I had recruited one of my best informants in the salmon poaching business, Mr X, and the place where I had many successful captures of salmon poachers, who had been using darkness as their cover and big treble hooks and lead weights as their tackle.

Times had changed slightly and now the poachers had a bit more guile. There were some rainbow trout in the River Almond and the Tay, escapees from a fish farm further up the River Almond. The Tay at the Woody Hole is tidal and the poachers had worked out that it is not an offence to fish in tidal waters for rainbow trout. Not only had one or two worked this out but they had told their friends and relatives, and August 2005 saw upwards of 20 people at a time fishing this small stretch of river. Complaints from genuine anglers flowed to the local papers but by this time the long dry spell of weather was coming to an end. Before measures could be taken to counter the poaching activity rain had filled the rivers again and the salmon were on the way upstream.

The following year, we were ready for the poachers and in August, when there was again a build-up of salmon because of low water, the bailiffs and I devised a strategy. It was clear from the previous year that 'Rainbow Fishers' were using lures with large treble hooks. These may catch a rainbow trout but they were also very likely to catch a salmon. Since the Rainbow Fishers were fishing without a permit to take salmon they were obliged to return any that they caught to the river. That would be right! It was also clear from what genuine anglers had been telling us that, when they thought no-one was watching, they had been ripping the lines through the water in an attempt to foul hook one of the many salmon in the pool. If they had used this method in 2005, we assumed it be the norm again in 2006.

We agreed that I would use my unmarked car and watch for the Rainbow Fishers arriving. They parked at the edge of a housing scheme and had a walk from there of about 200 metres to the riverbank. I would note and check out the registration number of the car. At the same time I would give the water bailiffs, who were in a concealed position with a good view of the Woody Hole and any illicit activity, the warning that the Rainbow Fishers were arriving. I also passed on their description so that they would recognise the ones I had seen when they arrived at the water-side.

The bailiffs watched the fishing methods, which were exactly as anticipated. If they saw one of the Rainbow Fishers attempting to foul-hook fish they would give me his description (or his name as some were well known to all of us). Similarly if one caught and landed a salmon, by fair means or foul, and failed to return it, again the name or description would be given to me. When anyone who had committed an offence left the riverbank, returned to his car and drove off, I followed in my own car, at the same time directing in the nearest marked police vehicle to stop and deal with the offender.

This worked a treat, though one Rainbow Fisher who caught a salmon ran downstream with it then cut across into the housing scheme a good distance from where I was parked. I drove down and checked the various streets, hoping to see him heading into a particular house with his booty but he managed to vanish without trace. However by the time we had caught and charged half a dozen Rainbow Fishers their numbers dwindled and normality returned to the Woody Hole.

CHAPTER 13

Falconry and the Law

THERE ARE many people who keep and fly birds of prey. It is a sport with a long history but, personally, I much prefer to see birds of prey in the wild. Having said that, bird of prey demonstrations at country shows can be enthralling and, for people who have little chance of seeing these beautiful, graceful and efficient birds of prey in the wild, they demonstrate the skills they need on a daily basis for survival.

Likewise, one day in Angus, I was fascinated to watch a real-life flying demonstration with two unlikely participants. Golden eagles and white-tailed sea eagles are equated with formidable power; peregrines have super speed in their stoops on to pigeons or ducks; it cannot be denied that hen harriers and red kites are graceful yet efficient in flight, yet the bird I watched was a common buzzard. Buzzards are normally thought of as lazy birds, content to sit on a pole or fence post until an unwary mouse or unsuspecting vole offers a chance of an easy meal, to soar in the sky like a vulture looking for carrion, or to waddle about a field on a wet day looking for worms. The buzzard I watched was putting sterling effort and endurance into getting its meal.

I had been on an enquiry and was driving along a very quiet country road near Brechin. I was approaching a wood on my right when I saw a buzzard chasing a wood pigeon up the side of the wood at right angles towards the road. The wood pigeon cut the corner through the wood and came out on to the road in front of me, still with the buzzard on its tail. It continued along the road for several hundred yards, then cut back into the wood again, the buzzard neither gaining nor losing ground. The trees in the wood were mature conifers that had been thinned so I still had a good view. I stopped but lost sight of the chase, though I saw the pigeon veer to its left at this point and I was hopeful it would come back into view. I drove slowly, watching into the wood all the time, and was grateful that there were no other vehicles about. The pigeon re-appeared flying towards me and came out over the road. I again had a grandstand seat in my car as I followed the chase. It followed the line of the road though just off to my nearside so that for a while I was driving parallel to and no more than ten metres from the buzzard. The two then cut left and headed away from the road over grass fields. I stopped and grabbed my binoculars and saw the culmination of the chase half way down the second field, about a quarter of a mile away, when the buzzard had at last caught up with the wood pigeon and they both crashed to the ground in a flurry of white feathers. The distance involved in this chase must have been around two miles. I suspect that the buzzard would have been pretty sure of the outcome and I wondered if it was a young or a sick pigeon it was chasing. Whatever, I hope it enjoyed its meal as it was well deserved.

Buzzards are often mistaken for golden eagles and I've frequently overheard people talking about seeing an eagle sitting on a telegraph pole at the roadside. There is a high probability that this would be a buzzard, but if it excites visitors to the countryside to think they have seen a golden eagle then I wouldn't want to spoil their day. I had the same suspicions with the next report of a golden eagle.

In the summer of 2006 two Dundee-based police officers had an enquiry in a Perthshire village. They had been asking directions to the house they were looking for, and these directions were given by one of the locals, who finished his description by adding, 'It's the house with the eagle in the garden.' The officers found the house via the directions, and were able to confirm it was the correct house since there was a large cage with a wire netting top and front in the back garden, though out of sight of the road. On a block in the centre of the cage sat a large brown bird, easily identified by the officers as ... a large brown bird. They dealt with their enquiry and later mentioned the presence of this bird to Sgt Andy Carroll, the divisional wildlife crime officer covering Dundee. Andy contacted me about the bird, and told me it had been referred to by a local villager as an eagle.

This 'eagle' could have been one of several species but was narrowed down to a 'large brown bird'. A common buzzard is also a large brown bird, the difference being that a golden eagle is a 'larger brown bird'. There are not many golden eagles kept as falconers' birds, possibly because of a combination of scarcity and cost, but a good starting point for the enquiry would be Defra. Golden eagles are birds that are on Schedule 4 of the Wildlife and Countryside Act 1981 and as such anyone keeping them must register them with Animal Health, Defra, and have the birds ringed or marked in some way to confirm them as the bird to which the registration refers. I had the address at which the eagle was kept and it was no great difficulty to obtain details of the people resident at that address.

But my check with Defra drew a blank. One person at that address had in the past registered a peregrine but there was no information with Defra to suggest he currently had any other Schedule 4 birds. The address now needed a visit. For visits where evidence is required to submit a case to the procurator fiscal, search warrants are often obtained. There was no need in this case since the bird was in a cage visible to anyone going to the house door for a legitimate purpose. In good policing if an investigation can be carried out low key and without fuss then that is the route that is taken.

Along with Constable Jim Pentley, a divisional wildlife crime officer, and Stephen McGee from BBC Scotland who at the time was filming wildlife crime investigations in different Scottish police forces for a BBC 2 series *Wildlife Detectives*, I called at the address. We walked round to the back of the house and I must say that I was still expecting to see a non-Schedule 4 bird of prey. To my astonishment a huge brown bird sat on a block in the cage, exactly as the Dundee police officers had described, a beautiful adult golden eagle. I could hardly believe that ten paces off the street, with absolutely minimum security, there was a bird that was worth several thousand pounds. The large cage in which the bird was housed was clean and the bird seemed well tended. It was alert and clearly used to human observers, as it made no effort to extend the distance between us as I photographed it from about a metre away. It may seem cruel to keep any bird in a cage, though this was a cage in which the bird could fly to a perch from its block had it so wanted. As I said earlier I much prefer to see birds flying wild but I appreciate the right of falconers to keep birds of prey that are reared in captivity. Many – and none more than the golden eagle – are pretty lazy birds in any case and even in the wild, if they are well fed, are content to sit on a perch or rock for hours at a time. It was time to 'chap the door' to see what the owner had to say about an unregistered golden eagle.

The owner had a lot to say. And it was all by way of apology. He admitted that the eagle was his but that he had been under a lot of pressure with work and family commitments and had simply not got round to registering the golden eagle. He told us that he had previously had a peregrine, which had been registered, and that he knew fine that the golden eagle should likewise be registered. His profuse apology even included raising both hands in the air as if we had just pointed a gun at him, and continuing his explanation while in that pose! In the end he had to be charged with keeping a Schedule 4 bird which he had failed to register. The penalty for this offence could be up to £5000 and/or 6 months imprisonment. We told him it would make good sense to register the eagle before the police case was submitted to the procurator fiscal, a request with which he complied. It pays to be honest when you are a suspect being interviewed by police. In this case we recommended to the fiscal that the case be dealt with by means of a warning, a disposal with which she agreed.

Remaining on the theme of falconers' birds, there was an unusual situation one day in north Perthshire when a gamekeeper saw a peregrine sitting on a grassy mound amongst the heather on the hill. He wondered why it didn't fly off and as he approached he saw that it had jesses attached to its legs. Realising it was a falconer's bird that had failed to return to its handler he crept quietly closer and managed to catch it. He then put it in a run, which earlier in the season had been used to house partridges and had been left on the hill. His next move was to phone me to report that he had the bird in case its owner contacted the police.

There had been no report of a missing peregrine but in any case I let Constable Graham Jack, as the divisional wildlife crime officer for the area, know about the bird and he set off to collect it to take it to a local falconer to be looked after until it could be re-united with its owner.

I'd love to have seen the next stage of this moorland drama. Graham met the gamekeeper and the two set off to the run that was a temporary home to the bird. But the run was empty. They checked round the run in case there had been a hole through which the bird had escaped but the run was intact. No escape route and not a trace of the peregrine that he had put there not an hour before. It was a complete mystery and had the two scratching their heads in disbelief. It was not until later that all was revealed.

The peregrine had a radio transmitter fitted on its tail that had gone unnoticed by the keeper. The falconer, unaware of what was happening a few miles away over the hill, was tracking his peregrine: tracking which ultimately led to the partridge run and the recovery of the bird. Initially the falconer was as puzzled at his peregrine being inside a partridge run as the keeper and Graham were at its failure to be there. He soon realised that his bird had been caught and rescued and in due course made contact with the police. It was a comedy with a happy ending.

Later the same year a wild peregrine was not so lucky on another Perthshire estate. It was found on the ground by a walker, who quickly realised, since the bird was flapping along the ground to get away from him, that it was unable to fly. It's amazing how many kind souls there are who would never leave an injured bird or animal, and take the trouble to catch it and bring it either to the police or an animal rescue organisation. In this case the walker was aware of a man who kept birds of prey and took it to him to see if the bird could be saved.

Since peregrines must be registered if kept in captivity, the falconer let me know that he had it, reporting it as an injured wild bird that he would take to a vet with a view to eventually rehabilitating it to the wild, and which he would also register with Animal Health at Defra. The falconer explained that it was an immature bird, an easy identification since adults are predominantly blue and immature birds are predominantly brown. One wing was damaged at the tip.

The peregrine was examined by Alistair Lawrie, the specialist bird of prey vet at Falkirk. Alistair x-rayed the bird and was able to say that it had been shot. Its wing was injured in two places, at the elbow and at the wrist, and at both places traces of lead were evident in the x-ray. The prognosis for the bird was poor. Though it would have no problem in surviving, it would never be able to fly again. A peregrine is master of the air and probably our fastest bird, being able to reach speeds well in excess of 100 miles an hour in a stoop from high above a prey species such as a pigeon or grouse. This predator at the top of a food chain had caught its last wood pigeon and was now destined to a life in an aviary.

The vet's opinion was that when shot, this injury would make the bird lose height quite quickly so it was likely that it had been shot not too far from where it had been picked up. It was in good condition so had not been shot too long before it was found, otherwise through lack of food it would have deteriorated in condition rapidly. It could walk, but is unlikely to have walked very far as it was in woodland. Even in the open, birds of prey, unlike game birds, are not inclined to walk since they rely on flight. A river bounded one part of the woodland, which would restrict it even further.

An investigation was carried out by Graham Jack and several people interviewed. Its proximity to the river, the boundary between two different estates, complicated the issue as it could possibly have been shot on one side and landed on the other. There had been some visiting goose shooters on one side of the river, and there were gamekeepers on the estates on each side. There was no evidence to point to one person more than another (there may even have been others we could have been considering but were unaware of) and the case was never solved.

It was revealing that one of the keepers when interviewed told Graham that he couldn't stand birds of prey that were scavengers. 'But peregrines, they kill in the air. I would never shoot *them*.' Could this be interpreted that he would shoot buzzards? And would he have considered as a scavenger the one I saw chasing the woodpigeon for two miles before catching it?

A difficult case unfolded in mid-February 2009 when a well-known falconer called in to see me at Perth Police Station. He had been flying his peregrine x saker hybrid with some guests on land that he leases for that purpose from Braco Castle Estate. The bird flew over the top of Braco Castle and went in to a stoop, so he knew that it was homing in on a bird, but it disappeared from sight. The falconer had heard some shots earlier and was aware that someone was shooting on the estate, but thought nothing of it as it was a common occurrence. He heard two shots just after the bird had disappeared, but thought these no more than a coincidence.

The falconer went off to find his bird, using the telemetry system to guide him. He was aware from the signal from the bird that it was in a wood beyond the castle and as he got closer to the wood the signal changed, indicating the bird was within 50 metres. The signal then began to move towards the right hand side of the wood, where he then saw three people with shotguns moving from the wood and heading across the field towards a 4x4 vehicle. The signal followed the men, who were 50 or 60 yards ahead of the falconer. One of those, who we'll call Mr Lucky, got into the vehicle, and the other two made back for the wood. Mr Lucky drove in the direction of the falconer, though on the track at the other side of the fence. As he passed, the falconer told me that the signal got much stronger, then got weaker as Mr Lucky drove further away, and was eventually lost.

An hour or so later the falconer saw the vehicle being driven on the estate, but there was now no signal coming from it. He managed to get Mr Lucky to stop and told him of his suspicions – that he had made off with the falcon – but Mr Lucky would have none of it.

In the late afternoon the falconer and a friend made a search of the wood where the shooting had been taking place. They found the spot easily enough because of the amount of white feathers on the ground (down feathers from wood pigeons are shed very easily, much more than those of the feral pigeons that inhabit towns and farm buildings. The comparison is similar to hares and rabbits, with hare fur coming out in tufts even when the 'mad March hares' box in springtime. Rabbits seem to have a far better grip of their fur coat).

This was an important search for the falconer, as he and his colleague found a feather – an under wing covert – that could be shown as having come from the falconer's bird. Significantly the feather had a shattered shaft, with about half an inch of the lower part missing. It was consistent with having been damaged by a shotgun pellet passing through it.

The loss of the falcon was not the end of the falconer's troubles. Some three days later his wife said that she had been approached by Mr Lucky, who allegedly handed over to her an envelope with £200 by way of a goodwill gesture, that being estimated as the value of the radio tag on the missing bird. On the following day Mr Lucky returned to the falconer's house and was alleged to have told the falconer and his wife that the shooting tenant would make their lives very difficult if he saw a police car on the estate.

Constable Colin Proudfoot, one of the divisional wildlife crime officers, took up the investigation and eventually managed to track Mr Lucky down. He admitted being one of the people who had been shooting, but had remarkably back luck: he shot at a pigeon that was flying past and two birds fell to the ground, one a pigeon and the other the falconer's bird. He agreed that he drove off with the bird, and that when some distance from the estate he took off the radio system from the bird and flung that and the bird into a burn.

A 'Not Guilty' plea was entered by Mr Lucky in relation to charges of theft, attempt to pervert the course of justice and shooting the falcon. A date was set for trial, which I was looking forward to for professional reasons. The falcon, being a hybrid and also being a falconer's bird, did not fit the legislative definition – as I saw it – of being a wild bird. I doubted that we could prove a charge under the Wildlife and Countryside Act 1981 of killing a wild bird if the bird could not be shown to be a wild bird. An alternative charge may have been available under the Animal Health and Welfare (Scotland) Act 2006: the offence of causing unnecessary suffering to a protected animal, though there were lots of complications that a good lawyer could exploit.

In any event the trial was adjourned. And adjourned and further adjourned. A date of 2 November 2010, more than 20 months after the incident taking place, was set for trial, but yet again, five days before the date, the witnesses received notification that the trial was not going ahead. This time the reason was not a delay but the desertion of the case by the Crown. Knowing the evidence, I had anticipated this.

Under the Criminal Justice (Scotland) Act 1980, then more recently under the Criminal Procedure (Scotland) Act 1995 police officers in Scotland could detain a suspect and bring him or her to a police station for interview for up to a period of six hours. During that period of detention the suspect was not entitled to have the services of a solicitor. This position had been criticised by some solicitors and was challenged more vociferously after a landmark case in 2008, when the European Court of Human Rights ruled Turkey had infringed the rights of an 18-year-old called Yusuf Salduz, who was denied access to a lawyer when he was detained. Poland, Russia, Ukraine and Cyprus have all since lost similar challenges, and France, Belgium and the Netherlands quickly altered their legislation to let solicitors see their clients in custody.

In Scotland, in an appeal by a man Duncan Mclean, convicted of stealing a car and wilful fireraising, a bench of seven of Scotland's most senior judges ruled that Scots law was compliant with Human Rights legislation and that McLean had no rights to a solicitor until the point when he had been charged. Solicitors on behalf of a 20 year old, Peter Caddell, made the same appeal to the UK Supreme Court, a civil court that does not normally meddle in Scottish criminal affairs. In this case it did meddle and ruled against the seven Scottish High Court judges.

Despite annoyance and frustration from many quarters, new legislation in Scotland was rushed through and from Friday 29 October 2010, cases still to come to court – or those under appeal – *that depended on admissions made by a suspect while detained, and where that suspect had not had the services of a solicitor,* had to be abandoned by the Crown.

Crown Office anticipated the change, and since the early summer of 2010 had instructed police to ensure that a solicitor had been offered to detainees, thus minimising cases that might have to be abandoned. There is no doubt that defence solicitors were equally aware, and in the peregrine x saker case this may well have been the reason for delaying the onset of the trial by repeated adjournments. In any event the reader will be in no doubt now why I named the suspect Mr Lucky.

CHAPTER 14

The Three Musketeers
go Hare Coursing

GROWING UP with dubious parental supervision and guidance in the last decade of twentieth century Tayside, young d'Artagnan dreams of becoming a hare courser. With hopes for excitement and adventure in his heart, he sets out to join the elite company of Tayside's untrustworthy hare coursing fanatics. A misadventure brings him to a meeting with three of his heroes – the untrustworthy hare coursers Porthos, Athos, and Aramis. Impressed by the young man's naivety and with not a moment to lose in their determination to kill a hare, the three men enlist d'Artagnan to join them. What follows this fateful encounter brings d'Artagnan all of the danger, intrigue, and risk that any hare courser could ever hope for: a night in the cells, a criminal record, possible imprisonment. The fact that there are no beautiful and deadly women, priceless treasures or scandalous secrets all combines for a riveting tale of adventure and challenge that will put d'Artagnan to the test. Will he succeed in helping the untrustworthy hare coursers escape and earn his place among their ranks?

Maybe not quite an Alexandre Dumas tale but it gives me names for our players in this drama of the open fields.

As some readers will be aware, there are a number of men across the UK who are incorrigible in relation to their illegal pastime of hare coursing. We have several of these in my home area of Tayside whose names keep coming to the fore. They are out coursing regularly, and though they're not always caught I am pretty certain when it is this gang that has been involved. One episode that turned nasty

involved the three that I'll give the names of the Three Musketeers;
Porthos, a man in his 40s who gives his occupation as a part-time car
dealer; Athos, a slim, fair-haired man coming close to 40 who seems
pretty much to be unemployed; lastly Aramis, a smally chubby man
in his 40s who professes to be a gardener. Some might link the name
Aramis with aftershave. The Aramis in this story had a very close
shave.

During an April evening in 2007 the three, along with an impressionable 16 year-old who might loosely fit the bill of d'Artagnan, were
seen coursing in a field near Kirriemuir in the county of Angus. A
woman, passing in a car, saw them in the middle of a field with two
rangy lurcher dogs, one brown, one white, which she saw were zigging
and zagging across the field in pursuit of a hare. She made contact
with the farmer, who, along with his three sons, made to intercept the
men. When the posse arrived the hare coursers were still in action
coursing but quickly returned to and jumped into their car, an old
Skoda. Once aboard they drove off for a short distance but must have
realised that something was missing: their dogs. They stopped and
tried to encourage their dogs to come to the car so that they could
make their escape, but the dogs were not playing the game. Farmer &
Co parked in front of the Skoda and managed to get hold of the two
panting lurchers, both of which seemed exhausted by their earlier
exertions.

Taking hold of the dogs was like a red rag to a bull and the Three
Musketeers, plus apprentice d'Artagnan, jumped out of the Skoda and
demanded their dogs back. Meantime one of the sons was photograph-
ing the musketeers with his mobile phone. Coursers are a particularly
nasty lot and began to make threats, as frequently happens when they
are confronted, that they would be back to burn the farm down. Athos
picked up a large stone and threatened to brain the photographer,
obviously realising that valuable evidence was being captured but
apparently oblivious to the fact that he was making the case against
himself worse.

He then tried to hit the farmer with the stone, only being
prevented by one of the sons grabbing his hand. Meanwhile the valiant
d'Artagnan retreated to the car and bravely shouted through the open

window at Farmer and Co, loudly branding them as 'sheep shaggers.'

Unfortunately, despite the advice given to farmers and gamekeepers who encounter hare coursers to phone the police right away, no contact was made to the police till the following day. Porthos was arrested shortly after the call, but the remaining brace of musketeers and d'Artagnan had gone to ground. Athos and Aramis came to the fore again five days later when they were again identified as being involved in a hare coursing incident near the village of Eassie, again in Angus. They were not traced by the police at the time but warrants had been granted by the court for their arrest. They were arrested a few days later in the Lothian and Borders Police area, having been investigated by officers there for . . . hare coursing.

Within a few weeks the Three Musketeers and d'Artagnan appeared at Forfar Sheriff Court. Athos pleaded guilty to hare coursing and a breach of the peace and was fined £200. His plea of not guilty to the later hare coursing incident was accepted. Porthos pleaded guilty to hare coursing and was also fined £200. Aramis pleaded not guilty to all charges and that was accepted by the Crown. A close shave indeed. And d'Artagnan? He pleaded not guilty, which was accepted by the Crown. He skipped off from the court into the sunset, never to have been seen (so far) hare coursing again.

Porthos was involved in another similar incident in February 2009. After a report of hare coursing was made by a witness he was traced by police officers in a field with three lurchers. There were several inches of snow on the ground and Porthos was trying to hide beside a wire fence. This is difficult enough in snow, but with three dogs standing wagging their tails it was impossible. He may as well have waved a flag above his head. The police officers saw him easily and he and his dogs were taken away.

A short time later, during a search by other officers of the fields in the vicinity of where Porthos was found, they recovered two dead hares, still warm. It seemed to be a reasonably clear cut case, especially when I later had a post mortem examination carried out on the two hares and they were found to have injuries entirely consistent with having been killed by a dog.

At his trial Porthos gave evidence in his defence, during which he admitted being in the field without the permission of the landowner but for the purpose of coursing rabbits, not hares. Rabbits, as we all know, are not mammals for the purposes of the legislation under which he was charged. He knew well enough that he wouldn't get rabbits in the fields, especially with snow on the ground. His evidence was that he was making for the woods to course rabbits there, but hadn't quite reached the woods before being caught by the police.

Evidence had already been led by the veterinary pathologist and me regarding the post mortem examination. Porthos had three lurchers but apparently had no leads for them. Nor did he have transport. His account to the investigating officers was that he had been dropped off by some friends who were going to Aberdeen. It was probably more than coincidence that a 4WD vehicle was seen to speed away just as the police came on the scene. They concluded that this was a friend – or friends – of Porthos abandoning him to his fate.

Porthos gave evidence in court that the rabbits he intended to catch in the woodland were to feed his three dogs. He seemed to have overlooked the fact that hares are twice the size and he'd only need to catch half as many to make a good supper for his canine trio. Of course his dogs might have been extraordinarily fussy mutts and may have had a predilection for the slightly less gamey meat of boiled bunny. By this point, even if the sheriff was not aware of how difficult it would be for lurchers to catch rabbits in woodland with plenty of cover and boltholes into which the fleeing rabbits could disappear, I'm sure he was not conned by the rabbiting story. However a sheriff can only rely on evidence that comes before the court on which to base a judgement.

It got worse. Porthos claimed that once he and hounds had caught sufficient rabbits he intended to telephone his partner, 20 miles away in Dundee, to pick him up. Lastly, he carefully explained to the court that although his dogs were quite biddable there was no way that he could hold two of them without leads or some other form of restraint while the third chased a rabbit or hare. The two dead hares being found near where he was hiding was an unfortunate coincidence and they must have been caught by someone else; perhaps the mystery occupants of the 4WD vehicle the police saw driving away as they arrived. This was all important evidence for him, knowing what the defence witness would say.

The defence witness was a gamekeeper, which I found really strange considering many of the complaints about hare coursing are made by gamekeepers. This man apparently had kept lurchers for many years and had used them against hares prior to the change in the law in 2002 which banned the hunting of wild mammals with dogs. His evidence was that the hares couldn't possibly have been killed by the dogs that the accused had with him. His logic was that Porthos had no means of holding back two dogs, and if three dogs had been after and had caught a hare they would have torn it to bits.

At the end of the trial, and before the sheriff retired for a short time to consider a verdict, he asked the procurator fiscal that if he returned a not guilty verdict on Porthos for hare coursing, was there any other related legislation that she wished him to consider. I was sitting with the fiscal and advised her to ask the sheriff to consider the Game (Scotland) Act 1832 – trespassing on land in daytime without leave of the proprietor of the land in unlawful search or pursuit of game or rabbits. I learned later that this can be done provided the circumstances on which the conviction would be based were the same. The sheriff had clearly been listening intently and in fact carried out a fair bit of questioning of witnesses to clear up any queries that he had.

When he returned to the bench, the sheriff found Porthos not guilty of coursing hares under the Protection of Wild Mammals (Scotland) Act 2002, but guilty of the Game (Scotland) Act 1832 offence. It is at this stage that the sheriff is made aware of any previous convictions that an accused person has. In this case eight analogous convictions were admitted and Porthos was fined £300.

I was frustrated that Porthos had managed to avoid conviction on the more serious charge and I reviewed many of my earlier photos of hares killed by a dog or dogs. In the case of at least four of the hares photographed at the post-mortem stage I knew two dogs were involved in the chase. No injuries whatsoever were visible externally and the hares were most certainly in one piece. When I looked at photos of the carcasses after they had been skinned, in two cases there were significantly more injuries than in the recent case with Porthos, but the bodies were still intact. Still not satisfied, I discussed the debate with two eminent veterinary pathologists who had carried out numerous post-mortem examinations of hares over the years, and also with many other wildlife crime officers who had dealt with similar hare coursing cases. Their experience was no different to mine. Though I was not in a position to refute the defence evidence that day since I had given my evidence before this unusual story emerged, I look forward to a re-match with the defence expert. His evidence that day, that I found extremely doubtful, may well have saved Porthos a jail sentence.

In an earlier hare coursing escapade, and with another participant I'll call Mr Snowman, adverse weather conditions were no deterrent. On 4 January in 2008, after a heavy snowfall, a man local to the area was driving slowly and carefully along a narrow country road. He looked over the fence into a roadside field and saw a man walking a greyhound-type dog through the field. Just at this time three hares rose from the snow and ran off across the field. Mr Snowman now released his dog, which duly took off in pursuit of one of them. The dog chased the hare across the field and the hare gained some ground by being able to get through the fence at the top of the field much more quickly than Mr Snowman's dog.

The witness continued along the road but as he rounded a bend the road was blocked by Mr Snowman's 4WD car. He got out and shouted to Mr Snowman, who politely enquired, 'What the fuck do you want?' before returning to his car. By this time the witness was using his mobile phone to contact the police, and received a tirade of curses from Mr Snowman. Snowman moved his car, all the while anxiously looking up the field to see what had happened to his dog. The witness passed Mr Snowman's car and continued on his way, but at that point, unusually for such a quiet single track road, a man came walking down the road. This witness saw Mr Snowman in the field and heard him shouting, at first thinking he was calling to him but then realising when he saw the greyhound that he was calling on the dog. He also saw the farmer approaching through the fields on his tractor and realised then that Mr Snowman had been coursing hares.

As this witness approached Mr Snowman's car, it coincided with the return of Snowman and dog. Mr Snowman vainly tried to cover the rear number plate of the car with snow, all the time calling to his dog to get into the car. Snowman either didn't seem capable of counting beyond one, or didn't realise his car had number plates front and back. As the witness passed the car, he noted the number from the front number plate and saw the farmer arrive in his tractor.

The farmer told Mr Snowman he had no business chasing hares, and was subjected to a variety of threats for his trouble. As I said earlier this is just about standard with hare coursers, with the threats usually about returning and burning down a barn or opening gates to let stock on to the road. Occasionally blows are struck, with the hare courser not often coming off best. In this case it didn't come to that and Mr Snowman made his departure pretty quickly, knowing that the first witness had phoned the police.

Police officers attended and could read in the snow what had taken place. To a degree this corroborated what the first witness in the car saw. The second witness, on foot, could add other pieces to the jigsaw but did not see coursing taking place. The farmer did not want involved and refused to give a statement to the officers. Identification came from the first man, who was able to pick out Mr Snowman from a set of twelve photographs. Because the farmer had refused to speak up, the case was short of the level of evidence to convict if Mr Snowman denied being involved, which was more than likely.

Mr Snowman was a career criminal and I was determined that he wouldn't get away with this, so called on the farmer the next day. I could quite see why he didn't want involved. Apart from any threats made, the farmer was a busy man and didn't want to spend time hanging about a court. I explained that the others, who were virtual bystanders, had spoken up, and that it seemed only reasonable that the person on whose land this had taken place should stand up and be counted. I managed to convince the farmer that if he gave a statement to me of what he saw, then the case would be really solid and it was much more likely that a guilty plea would be entered. He took a wee bit of persuading but in the end I left with a statement completely backing up that of the witness in the car.

Mr Snowman was charged with hare coursing and, as I suspected he would, pleaded guilty. His record determined that a jail sentence would be appropriate, though that was replaced with the alternative option to a court: that of a community service order. Mr Snowman was sentenced to carry out 80 hours of community service. He'd missed an opportunity to work as Santa Claus but I'm sure there would still have been some snow to be cleared off pavements.

There seems to be a strong link between men from Tayside who course hares, and their counterparts in Aberdeen. The Aberdonians make frequent forays to north Angus in particular, and coursing incidents there are often attributable to these men from the North-East. Some farms are regularly targeted, and one of those featured in a case that was reported in early March 2009. The farmer had seen two men in one of his fields, probably picked because it is 120 acres and conducive to a chase by its vastness. The field was next to the farmhouse, and the farmer watched the two men walking through the oil seed rape crop and two of their three dogs out chasing a hare. He telephoned his farm worker to come out to observe (and importantly, corroborate) the coursing and his wife then telephoned the police. The men and dogs disappeared down the field and the farmer was unable to say whether or not the dogs caught the hare they were after.

The farm worker watched the men coursing from a vantage point and was able to say that they had stopped for about 10 or 15 minutes, and at this time all three of their dogs were still running loose in the field. By this time the first police car had arrived and the officer and the farmer drove round the roads to try to cut off the escape of the men in the field. The farmer was aware that in the past the coursers had gone out a gate at the top of the field and their cohort, acting as driver and lookout, drove to the other side of the farm to await their arrival.

The first officer saw the three dogs chasing a hare, which they also failed to catch, but soon after this the men spotted the police car. One man, the smaller of the two, managed to get hold of two of the dogs and put them on leads. He was beckoned by the police officer to come up to the road, and rather surprisingly, complied. His taller friend, in the assumption that he was invisible, slunk into a deep ditch and tried to hide. A white lurcher, hardly invisible either, went into the ditch beside him, but almost immediately put up two roe deer and left the cover of the ditch, instinctively determined to chase and catch one. Meantime the Invisible Man was creeping along the bottom of the ditch in the direction of the next two police officers to arrive on the scene. By the time he was caught he covered from head to toe in mud, and had clambered through brambles, resulting in his face and hands being torn and bleeding. He was not having a pleasant day out in the countryside

When the case came to trial in Arbroath Sheriff Court in February 2010 I was cited as an 'expert' witness, and sat through the first day of the trial listening to the evidence of the farmer, his worker and the police officers. In the dock the invisible man kept up his aura of invisibleness, being dressed in a ghostly white shell suit top and with a shiny shaven skull. His shorter pal, quite content to be noticed, was dressed all in black, though had a shiny hairless bonce like his juxtaposed mate. Peering out of the dock they seemed a black and white optical reproduction of two boiled eggs in egg cups on a breakfast plate. Each was represented by a solicitor, with one of those, Tom Cruickshank, being an extremely experienced and well-respected defence agent who specialises in cases that have a relevance to wildlife or firearms. The procurator fiscal depute, Arlene Shaw, was not one of the specialist wildlife prosecutors, but was enthusiastically, and very competently, cutting her teeth on her first hare coursing trial. The sheriff, an advocate depute, was on her first visit to Arbroath Sheriff Court and I rather suspect also having her first experience of hare coursing.

By the time I was due to give evidence it was half past three and it was not worth starting with a new witness. The trial was therefore continued for another 5 weeks. I met the two boiled eggs, now out of their dock eggcups, outside the court and they asked me how I thought the trial was going. As it happened I had not been impressed by the evidence and there were many lessons to be learned for the reporting of future cases. Truthfully, I told them I thought the verdict could go either way, which seemed to please them more than it did me. We would all have to wait till the next court diet.

Though in these cases we had managed to trace the people involved, there are many cases where we don't. Mainly this is because hare coursers seldom have a car that is registered in their own name. Very often it is a car that has just been bought and will be re-sold within days, with use for just a wee bit of coursing in between. Occasionally the person registers the car under a false name and address. One of these smart-alecs annoyed me for the best part of a year. He kept registering his cars under the name 'Shaggie McPhee,' with a variety of addresses in Dundee. By doing regular checks of the history of the car both before and after the incident we managed to track him down, though it took the best part of a year and the coursing incidents in which he had probably been involved were time barred. The next time there is a car registered under Shaggie's nom-de-plume involved in a coursing incident we might just be waiting for him to arrive home!

In another incident where a man and a dog had been seen coursing, the car involved was stopped a few miles from the scene by Constable Harvey Birse, one of the divisional wildlife crime officers who is a traffic patrol officer. Two of the men were local but two were from Liverpool. Unfortunately there was no evidence of identification of who had been doing what. Their luck, however, was short-lived. The Liverpudlian driver of the car was arrested for driving under the influence of drink, while disqualified from driving and having no insurance. The Liverpudlian owner of the van was charged with causing or permitting these offences. In addition to this, Harvey seized their car since it couldn't be driven on a road without insurance. I never did find out what happened to the men in court but I'm sure the penalty would have been substantially more than they would have got for hare coursing.

In due course the trial of the Invisible Man and friend continued. I gave evidence first, and explained how coursing takes place. I also told the court that I had dealt with perhaps 20 hare coursing cases (under older legislation) in the 1960s and 1970s. I had also followed the course of another 200 or so investigations in the previous five years, usually speaking with the witnesses and sometimes helping the investigating officers to obtain evidence on the ground. I was asked about the ages of the three dogs that had been with the men. Two were white lurcher-type dogs, with one clearly being older than the other, though it's difficult to put an age on a dog from a coloured photo. I later heard when the two men gave evidence that they said the young dog was four months. A four months-old dog is really a puppy, and to me this dog was a bit more than a pup. Nevertheless it was probably under a year old and I would have conceded, had I been asked, that it was too young to use against hares. In summary, I said that what had taken place in the field the previous March was entirely consistent with hare coursing.

The Invisible Man and his pal, Shorty, gave evidence. I was surprised at this, but when I heard what their evidence was I could see why they had to do so. In some cases defence solicitors are reluctant for their client to give evidence in case they say something better left unsaid, and allow the fiscal an opening. The defence was, so far as I was concerned, an unrecorded story from Grimm's Fairy Tales. . .

The older of the white dogs didn't belong to the Invisible Man or to Shorty; it belonged to a man named Georgie. Georgie came from Aberdeen but didn't seem to have a surname. Georgie's dog had been cooped up in a kennel for months since Georgie, according to Shorty's evidence, was 'crippled with knackered legs'. Feeling sorry for the dog, Georgie was going to sell it, and arranged to be picked up by the Invisible Man to take it to a potential buyer. The Invisible Man thought the buyer might also buy *his* dog, a brown lurcher, so he took it along as well. He had asked Shorty if he wanted to come for the run, and Shorty agreed. He took his dog as well in case it 'tore up the house' while left alone. So that was how there came to be three men and three dogs in the car.

Half way to the address (a caravan, probably not there now) of the mystery buyer of cast-off canines, the men stopped at a roadside café for a coffee. They were there an hour before they set off again. They hadn't gone too far when the older white dog appeared to need the toilet and allegedly began to dribble in the back of the car. The men stopped and Shorty got out to take the dog for a pee. As he opened the tailgate of the hatchback the dog shot past him, ran along the road and disappeared through the hedge into a field. When Shorty looked into the field the dog was 'miles away down the field, running about as if it was mad'. Shorty and the Invisible Man thought the best way to get the dog back was to take the other two dogs into the field. The runaway might be attracted by them and return. That was how two men with three lurchers came to be in the field. They were in the process of trying to coax the runaway back – not hare coursing – when the police came along.

Shorty said that his dog was off the lead, but it was well-behaved and never left his side. The Invisible Man said that his dog was never off the lead, which was contrary to what the police and one of the witnesses from the farm said in court. When asked why he had tried to hide in the ditch, the Invisible Man said that he had been released from prison on a tag, worn round his ankle, and just panicked when he saw the police. By the state he was in – by his own admission covered in mud from head to toe and face bleeding from bramble scratches – it must have been some panic! There was one highlight as he was giving evidence, the 'quote of the day' as I called it. The farmer and I had given evidence that the field the men and dogs were in was huge, over 100 acres. At one point the Invisible Man was asked where he was in the field when he first saw the police. His answer? 'Well, Mr Stewart said the field was over 100 acres, so I would be about 60 acres from the top'.

'Georgie' must have panicked as well, and took off in the Invisible Man's car. He, along with the transport for all three, apparently skedaddled back to Aberdeen. It can only be assumed that dog sales for the rest of the day were suspended. Neither did Georgie appear in court as a witness to help the Invisible Man and his short sidekick out of their pickle. Had he done so the fiscal would have been entitled in advance of the trial to have the police note a statement from him. The 'reason' for the two men and three dogs being in the field would have been known in advance. Not a good defence tactic.

The fiscal finished the Crown case by asking the Invisible Man if he had ever been involved in coursing. 'No,' he answered stone faced. I only wished I had been looking at him straight on. The fiscal then asked if he has seen coursing taking place. 'Only on a DVD,' he responded. Any previous convictions a person has can only be revealed to the sheriff after a person is found guilty.

The defence expert was the same gamekeeper that was called in the earlier case against Porthos. He had to leave the court while I gave evidence and I had to leave while he was in the witness box. I therefore don't know the full extent of his evidence, though I rather suspect that part of his evidence would be to back up the claim that the younger white lurcher was too young to course hares, and that a good idea to recover a runaway dog is to take other dogs into its view.

In the summing up, the defence solicitors made two valid points. They were first of all very critical that the police never interviewed their clients about why they were there (which I also found extremely disappointing). This, one solicitor said, could have given them the chance to learn about Georgie and the 'real' reason the men were in the field. The defence also adversely commented on the evidence that the farmer gave; that it was much more extensive and detailed than that given in his statement. I didn't disbelieve the farmer, but I can't understand why these extra (and important) details were not noted when he was interviewed. This and the lack of interview of the suspects were the two main flaws in the case, and the sheriff returned a verdict of not guilty, telling the Invisible Man and pal they were free to leave the dock. As they did so each reached over and shook the hand of the gamekeeper . . .

In mid-November 2009, as I was having breakfast, I noticed that my mobile, on charge in the kitchen, had a message. On checking I found that I'd had a call from PC Blair Wilkie, one of the divisional wildlife crime officers, at 1.30 in the morning. In a way I was quite glad that I missed the call. It was now almost 6.00 a.m. so I phoned back to Brechin Police Station, where Blair works. The story was that Blair and another police officer, PC Kay Stewart, had responded to a call to one of the famous Angus Glens, Glenlethnot. The report had been made by a shepherd and his wife who were out seeing to their dogs about 11.00 p.m. They had seen a lamp operating in the field next to their house, and in the beam of the lamp they saw three men with two large dogs. One of the men, they thought, was carrying a gun or a rifle.

Blair and Kay made for the area and as they approached they saw a vehicle driving along the road with a spotlamp being operated from the car and shining into the roadside fields. They stopped the vehicle and detained the three men, all from Aberdeen. When they later searched the men's car there was nothing to link them to hare coursing; no dead hares or blood, but they did have two lurcher-type dogs and a baseball bat. The officers assumed that this was the 'rifle' that had been seen by the witnesses.

By the time I phoned it was an hour past the maximum time allowed for the detention of a suspect – 6 hours – and the 'Aberdeen Three' had been interviewed and arrested, their excuse for being in Glenlethnot being that they were looking for rabbits. Since they each had a long list of previous convictions the decision had been made to keep them in the cells to appear in court the following morning. But with what would they be charged? Glenlethnot is not an area where there are a lot of hares, but there are a lot of their smaller cousins, bunnies.

I arranged to meet PC Bob Russell, another divisional wildlife crime officer, when he came on shift at 8.00 am, with the intention of having a look at the area and also get statements from the shepherd and his wife. Due to the late hour of the report of the incident, and the logistics of getting three men who had been detained, their two dogs and their vehicle from the middle of nowhere back to a police station, the witnesses had not yet been fully interviewed.

We travelled to Glenlethnot in Bob's 4WD police vehicle. As arable fields gave way gradually to permanent pasture and hill ground my fears were confirmed that hares would *not* have been the target. As we passed one field I saw what looked like a dead rabbit lying about 100 yards from the road in a grass field. Bob stopped and I walked across a rather sodden field to the rabbit. It had been the victim of a stoat or weasel, neither of which I saw as I made my way over the field. It was still alive, though barely. The back of its neck was eaten down to the bone and when I lifted it to put it out of its misery its head wobbled about as if ready to fall off. I've seen this many times. It must be a horrible death for the rabbit, being paralysed with fear by a predator not much more than a quarter of its size, which then begins to eat the rabbit while it is still alive. On nature programmes I've seen footage of a stoat chasing a rabbit, sometimes over hundreds of yards, before catching up with it. The narrator then tells the fireside audience that the stoat will kill the rabbit with a quick bite to the neck. Not my experience at all, and maybe a concession to the more squeamish viewers, while those of us with more knowledge grasp the esoteric and gruesome reality. In any event the rabbit had not been the victim of a dog, which was the reason for our current quest.

Bob and I met the shepherd and his wife in the farm steading near their house. While Bob was noting statements I set off to see what evidence I could find in the fields. These lay on either side of a narrow country road just down from the farm and rose quite steeply from the road. I could already see some huge rabbit warrens, especially on the bank running from the roadside. This was upland permanent pasture, not land that would be favoured by hares at all.

I began to walk along the field beside the witnesses' house, going in the opposite direction that the three men had travelled. It was a lovely sunny winter's day and it was just great to be outside. There was plenty evidence of rabbits, which were big and healthy. Being permanent pasture, there were clear runs used by the rabbits leading from the field to the gaps in the netting fence that allowed them entry to the wood that ran the length of the field. As I walked along the wood side I noticed the rump of a roe deer in the trees not 30 yards away. It was only the back end of the deer that I could see, its white diamond-shaped tail end patch contrasting with the brown/grey of its winter coat, but that was sufficient to know it was a buck. Had it been a female the longer white hairs on the rump, looking almost like a tail, would have given it away. Up to that point the deer hadn't seen or heard me, but a few seconds later, when it looked round from behind the tree, it bounded off, giving its alarm call, somewhere between a cough and a bark, several times as it ran through the trees. I could see the small antlers were in velvet, having been cast after the rut in July/August, and starting to grow again from scratch. I reflected that I much preferred the darker winter colours of its coat to the foxy red animal it becomes in summer.

I continued the length of that field and the next without seeing any traces of where the men had been, or any sign of a rabbit they had caught. There was a small patch of rabbit fur on the ground at one point but there was no way of knowing if this had been the spot a dog had made a kill, whether it had been a rabbit killed by a fox, or whether it had simply been a fight between two buck rabbits – though that's much more common in spring than in November. I made my way down to the gate that led from the second field to the road, and that is where the trail became much more interesting.

From the fresh tyre marks beside the gate this was obviously where the Aberdeen Three had parked their car. I could see two distinct sole impressions in the soft earth, and also dog paw marks, though it wasn't possible to say whether there had been one or more dogs. The tracks led into the field and went to the right. I photographed the marks, then headed in the same direction. The field was almost split in two by a narrow bog, which would have been difficult to cross, even in wellies. When I came to the bog I turned left and followed it back up the field. Though the marks told me a dog had crossed it, none of the men had, so I continued back in the direction I had earlier come, at the roadside edge of the field this time, rather than along the wood at the top.

When I was back almost below the shepherd's house I found a dead rabbit in the field just inside the fence. It had been partly predated by a crow but not too much damage had been done. It is because of predation to rabbits and hares left behind that we should really have been here at daylight, fully an hour earlier. I was aware in the quick resumé given by the shepherd before I left that the men had crossed the fence below his house. I noticed that the top wire of the fence was bent down almost touching its neighbour below, just where the rabbit was lying. This would be where they had crossed. The shepherd had also said that they had to lift one of the dogs over the fence. When I looked at the fence at the opposite side of the road there was a second fence about 12 inches inside the first, with a single strand of barbed wire level with the top wire of the main fence. I doubted they would tackle this in the dark. Much more likely they would make for a gate I could see fifty or so yards further down the road.

My assumption had been correct, and I photographed sole

impressions and paw marks entering this gate. Following the direction of the marks, I climbed to the top of a large rabbit warren, and found a second rabbit, this time with very little predation; only a small hole at the top of one of the back legs where a crow had begun to have breakfast. Since I needed corroboration of these finds I left the rabbits where they were so that I could take Bob to them in due course.

I made my way back through the field in the direction of where the Aberdeen Three had parked their car. I stayed on the flatter ground at the top of the roadside slope, and found a third rabbit. This one had also been partly eaten by a crow but when I picked it up I could feel the broken ribs that were a clear sign that it had been taken by a mammal. Continuing on to the gate at the far end of this field I saw and photographed the sole impressions as the men had left the field. I now had photos of three different sole impressions, hopefully the same pattern as the boots the men had been wearing. I'd now to show Bob all of this, bag and label the rabbits, then head back to Perth to the Scottish Agricultural College vet lab to have post mortem examinations carried out to confirm the cause of death (hopefully) as having been taken by a large dog-sized carnivore.

When I arrived, Graham Baird, the veterinary pathologist, was busy carrying out post mortem examinations of two cattle that had mysteriously died. He was kind enough to stop and divert his attention to the much smaller carcasses that I had brought in, and soon came to the conclusion that the rabbits had been killed by crushing injuries consistent with a bite from a dog. The three men could now be charged with a contravention of the Night Poaching Act 1828, the offence being three persons, one of them armed with a baseball bat, being on land without permission in the unlawful pursuit of game or rabbits.

I was really looking forward to the trial of the Aberdeen Three but I was not to be treated to that privilege. As often happens when there is really strong evidence, an accused person pleads guilty at an early stage. This way a one-third discount on any penalty is assured. In this case two of the three offered a plea of guilty while the other one, with far fewer relevant convictions, maintained his plea of not guilty. This was accepted by the fiscal, who has to balance the public interest of a trial, which in this case had nine witnesses, and with three accused and three defence solicitors would have taken two days.

When this type of plea is entered, it is usually the person with the fewest relevant convictions who puts his neck in the noose. Unusually, the two with the worst records took the rap. I was flabbergasted when I heard the penalties. One of the two was out of work and was fined £750 (and this with a third discount on what it would have been after a trial). The other, who told the court he was in employment, was fined £1,000. I've no doubt that the three would have agreed to split any fines three ways, though with their background I'd not be surprised if the man with no penalty reneged on the deal. Who would trust a pact made by a parcel of rogues?

I reflected on the penalty; nearly £600 per rabbit. The two fall guys of the Aberdeen Three were lucky. In an earlier century they could have been *'transported beyond seas for any term not exceeding fourteen years nor less than seven years, or to be imprisoned and kept to hard labour for any term not exceeding three years'*.

Some readers may think that this is an excessive penalty for this type of offence, when in some cases a person convicted of poisoning birds of prey can be fined considerably less. The first point to consider is that it is unusual for anyone convicted of poisoning birds of prey to have a previous record, so invariably they must be treated by the court as first offenders. The two convicted in this case had horrendous records, plus the crime they committed was an aggravated offence, with three acting together and one having a weapon. I'm glad that after the evidence-gathering and the reporting of the case to the procurator fiscal the police role is completed; prosecution and sentencing are not our business.

CHAPTER 15

Animal Cruelty

POLICE officers deal with many animal welfare-related offences, some against domestic animals, some against wild animals and some against wild animals that are in captivity. However if this number is brought down to individual officers' caseloads they might amount to less than 1% of the thousands of cases they investigate during their careers. For that reason I try to ensure that the officers make contact either with me or one of the Divisional wildlife crime officers early in the investigation so that we can ensure they are on the right track, aware of the legislation involved and aware of their powers of search, detention or arrest of a suspect, or their powers to seize animals, or even to have them destroyed.

I'll kick off (literally) with a hedgehog story in this chapter, but first I'll say a bit about this rather prickly customer which is loved by most of the population but considered a pest by a minority. Because of their habit of eating eggs, hedgehogs had to be cleared off the Uists and Benbecula in recent years. As a consequence of the thoughtless act of someone taking some hedgehogs from the mainland to these outer isles their numbers increased in the absence of natural predators and comparatively few vehicles, and they began to wipe out populations of dunlin, redshank, snipe, lapwing, all ground nesting birds, by devouring their clutches of eggs. There are also stories about hedgehogs eating ground-nesting birds alive while they are sitting on their eggs. I'd be surprised if this were true but, since I've no experience of it, I'll reserve judgement.

Hedgehogs are welcome in my garden any time. I've a big chunk of the garden where I grow vegetables and when they come in there and annihilate some of the army of slugs then I'm most definitely their patron. I see them from time to time on the grass when I put the lights on at the back of the house and sometimes catch them in the headlights if I'm coming in the drive late at night. I probably hear them more than see them, and their snuffling as they root among leaves and undergrowth is a familiar sound when I'm putting my ducks in to their shed last thing at night.

I was pleased to have been consulted in June 2007 by officers who were dealing with a report of a hedgehog having been savagely kicked to death in the Highland Perthshire town of Aberfeldy. The officers had been in their parked police car in the very early hours of a Saturday morning when they saw two men kicking what they initially thought was a ball back and forth across the street. Suddenly realising the 'ball' was a hedgehog, the police drove along to the men, both joiners from the west of Scotland and visiting Aberfeldy. The hedgehog was clearly dead but of course the question was, 'had it been alive at any stage while it was being kicked?'

I got the hedgehog from the officers and arranged to have a post mortem examination carried out to establish whether or not it had been dead when it was being kicked. Though a bizarre pastime, it would not have been an offence to have played football with an already dead hedgehog. However the unfortunate hedgehog was indeed alive while it was the unwilling participant in a midnight football game. There was no visible sign of injury externally, but there was severe bruising under the skin covering the ribcage on both sides of its chest. In addition, several of the ribs were broken at either side of its body and when the chest cavity was opened up these rib fractures were found to be linked to severe haemorrhaging around the lungs. We saw a number of large blood clots in the chest cavity and all in all, the injuries were considered by the veterinary pathologist as traumatic chest injury, causing death, and being consistent with being kicked.

The men pleaded guilty to the offence. One was fined £360 and the other £400. I saw these as significant fines and proportionate to the illegal actions of men aged 37 and 41 who should have known better.

In the month following the Aberfeldy incident, two police officers, one of them a Divisional wildlife crime officer, PC Shaun Lough, were patrolling a Perth housing estate late at night when they saw a youth walking towards them drinking from a bottle of lager. This was enough to focus their attention on the 19 year-old but what followed shocked the officers. As the man got closer, the officers saw a hedgehog leave a garden and walk across the road near to the man. As he came up to it he kicked the poor beast with such force that he propelled it several metres along the road.

The officers stopped the man and saw that one of his trainers still had several of the hedgehogs' spines embedded in it. Naturally this was taken as evidence in the case. The officers saw that the hedgehog was lying motionless at the kerb-side within a small pool of what appeared to be urine. Suspecting that the animal was unwell, the officers asked the Force Control Centre to see if a vet was available to have a look at the animal if the police took it to the surgery, but none could be contacted. While the officers' attention was diverted in dealing with the man, his unfortunate victim appeared to have recovered and the officers saw the tail-end of it disappearing into the garden from which it had come.

In this case the evidence was of a different nature, with the two police officers having seen the animal alive before it was kicked. The man was charged, at which point it was discovered that he had been celebrating his birthday. He explained that he didn't think it was a hedgehog he kicked; just leaves and grass. Tumbleweed blowing down a Perth street on a windless night is stretching the imagination. In addition to a fixed penalty notice for drinking his bottle of lager in a public street, the kick at the hedgehog cost the man £200.

Excess alcohol is the causal factor behind many of the animal welfare incidents. Likewise CCTV is nowadays the means by which many convictions are secured. In a case in July 2007, six days after the second hedgehog incident, another 19 year-old fell foul of the law, this time because of kicking a herring gull. Cameras in a Dundee street picked him up at 3.00 a.m. as he walked along the road eating a pizza out of one of the giant cardboard boxes that are found lying everywhere in our towns and cities; only moderately better than the polystyrene versions that will still be here long after we are gone.

Several gulls were carrying out a night shift, scavenging for the remnants of food discarded by the homeward-bound clubbers and partygoers. Pizza-man kicked out at the gulls and they flew out of his way. One was slightly slower than its fellows and a second kick was aimed at it, this time connecting and propelling the tumbling gull on to the edge of the road. It lay stunned long enough for a running kick by Pizza-man, this time launching the gull up in to the air and right to the other side of the road. Not content at that he crossed the road and kicked the gull back in to the centre of the road.

The advantage of CCTV is that the operators can then follow a suspect and direct police units on to him. Another offence was committed when pizza-man threw his cardboard box on to the street, despite a rubbish bin being yards from him. Just before the police car arrived he was demonstrating to his friends how clever he had been in managing to kick a gull up in to the air. The fate of the gull is not known as the cameras were concentrating on the culprit. Pizza-man's fate was to receive a fiscal's fine, again a result proportionate to the scale of the offence and the fact the man charged had no previous record.

July 2007 seemed to have been a bad month for cruelty. During the early evening of 19th my mobile rang as I was standing on the bridge over one of the two burns that run through our acre and a half of land. I had just frightened a wily carrion crow out of a spruce tree where I knew there was a woodpigeon's nest. Despite the nest being directly above my vegetable garden I don't bother the woodpigeons as most of the vulnerable vegetables are netted. I had heard loud flapping and knew that the bird was defending either eggs or chicks against some sort of predator. A carrion crow was the most likely, though a grey squirrel visits the garden from time to time. The crow cleared out when I clapped my hands, but having found an easy meal I was pretty sure it wouldn't give up.

The phone call took my attention. It was a labourer who had just finished work on some new houses being built beside the prestigious Gleneagles Hotel. He wanted to report cruelty by an Eastern European worker and, unusually, was willing to give a statement to that effect. Not every witness to a crime will stand up and be counted. The labourer's story was that he had taken a particular interest in the nest of a swallow, which he'd watched being built under the porch of one of the partly-built houses. He'd observed the birds flying back and forward with mud, constructing the nest, and later often saw the bird looking down at him from the completed nest as it incubated its clutch of eggs. He'd then seen the Eastern European man, who I'll refer to by his nickname, Zebe, poking at the nest with a long piece of wood. He'd told Zebe to clear off and leave the birds alone, which he did, but that was not the end of the matter.

That was not the end of the matter either with the woodpigeon defending its nest. As I finished my phone call I heard a clattering noise coming from the tree again and knew that the crow was back. I clapped my hands loudly. This time *two* carrion crows flew out of the tree. I could hardly believe that the first crow had got assistance, possibly so that one could nick the eggs while the other distracted the woodpigeon. I was left wondering how one bird could communicate to another the fact that there was a meal to be had if they worked as a team. I had foiled them again, temporarily, but in the morning I saw a half egg shell under the tree. There were none of the tell-tale blood vessels in the inside of the shell that show when a chick has hatched from an egg and I was in no doubt that the contents of the two white eggs made a satisfying supper for two carrion crows.

The Gleneagles labourer phoned me a second time, now to tell me that a joiner and his apprentice had seen Zebe carrying two young chicks on a piece of cardboard. They challenged him about this and Zebe said that they had fallen on his head when he accidentally knocked a nest with a pole. He was told to return the chicks to the nest (something that would not be possible if he had knocked the nest down) but was later seen by these witnesses throwing the chicks into a puddle of water. To help the chain of evidence, the astute Gleneagles labourer had taken one of the now-dead chicks from the puddle and had hidden it so that I or one of my colleagues could see it. He was also able to tell me that the nest had gone but that there was some mud and feathers – the nest lining – on the ground under the porch.

I collected the bird the following day but it was a further week before we managed to catch up with the remaining witnesses and Zebe. I photographed the location of the nest and was surprised that the birds had started to build a new nest in the same spot. With the birds coming back and forward with mud it gave me a chance to positively identify them as swallows, essential for a conviction. In any case their fellow migrants from Africa, house martins, normally nest on the outside of buildings rather than inside, and it would be less common to see a house martin's nest under a porch.

Constable Doug Ogilvie, one of the Divisional wildlife crime officers, and I interviewed Zebe (with some difficulty) through one of his fellow countrymen. Zebe was charged under the Wildlife and Countryside Act 1981, with intentionally or recklessly killing a swallow by throwing it into water, and with intentionally or recklessly destroying the nest of a wild bird: a swallow. He pled guilty to the killing of the chick and was fined £110. His plea of not guilty to destroying the nest was accepted by the Crown. The maximum fine for this offence is £5000. Though £110 might seem a lenient fine, for a person with no convictions and with a rather meagre income, I considered it was proportionate.

I'm distracted again by another bird in the garden as I write this chapter in early December 2009. Not a crow or a woodpigeon this time but a great-spotted woodpecker. When I glanced out the window I thought I saw a small bird falling from a larch tree 20 yards from the window. The 'small bird' turned out to be a blue tit-sized piece of lichen, and when I looked for the cause of it falling from the tree the agent was a black and white barred bird roughly blackbird sized. The woodpecker was male, as evidenced by its red forehead (absent in the female) and it was extremely busy looking for grubs and insects hiding under the bark and lichen. It systematically made its way up the trunk, using its sharp claws and its strong tail feathers, and was dislodging a veritable snowstorm of lichen. I marvelled at its resilience as it hammered the tree trunk with its strong bill. Even when it was out of view behind the trunk I could keep track of its progress by lichen being thrown left and right. When it was three-quarters way up it decided to explore the peanut feeder and made a dive down towards it with only one quick flap of its wing to correct its flight path before landing nicely on this much easier, though maybe not quite so tasty, meal. There are many advantages in having the computer beside the window and a frosty December afternoon is as good a time as any to study the hungry inhabitants of the garden.

When police officers deal with animal welfare cases it is sometimes incidental to another, sometimes more serious, investigation, and very often involving alcohol or drugs. On one occasion, in November 2007, police officers were called to a second floor flat in a housing scheme in Dundee and their investigation led to the unfolding of a weird, and very dangerous, sequence of events. The subject of the investigation – I'll simply call Mark, a chronic alcoholic and heroin user – had two brothers staying with him temporarily, Brother G and Brother J. Brother J came home late in the evening to find brother G drunk in the front bedroom. Worse, Brother J detected a strong smell of petrol coming from the house and noticed that the rug in the hallway was wet. In the room beside him was a can of petrol and a cage with a brown rat. The rat had been left by a friend, naively, for Mark to look after. 'Looking after' did not include what followed.

Enter Mark to the bedroom. He took the rat in the cage onto the balcony. Brother J thought this was to allow the rat some fresh air, as he (Mark) had done before. Not so. Mark threw the caged rat over the balcony to the street below, then picked up the can of petrol and began waving it about the room, spilling much of the contents in the process, some of it over the semi-comatose Brother G, who realised the danger and regained some of his senses pretty quickly. Brother J, sensibly, began to gather up anything that was likely to start a fire – matches and cigarette lighters. The bold Mark then began to wave the can over the balcony, where neighbours were running about trying to recapture the rat, now free from its shattered cage after its freefall adventure. This was too much for the neighbours, who contacted the police.

Mark was arrested and charged with culpable and reckless conduct, a Common Law offence unique to Scotland which encompasses any act not contained within a statute where there is a substantial risk to the life or health of another person. He was also charged under the Animal Health and Welfare (Scotland) Act 2006 in relation to the rat's speedy downward journey, and more importantly, its abrupt stop at the terminus.

Mark pleaded guilty, adding another conviction to his considerable tally. He received 3 months imprisonment for culpable and reckless conduct, held, rightly, to be the more serious charge. He also received 2 months imprisonment for 'chucking the rat,' a sentence that probably prevented this becoming a new competitive event at Highland Games. Happily, the rat was returned to its owner.

There are many animal welfare issues that police officers deal with where there is insufficient evidence for a case to be reported to the procurator fiscal. The use of crossbows feature all to frequently, with one of the worst incidents in neighbouring Northern Constabulary in 2009 when a red deer hind was found, still alive, with a crossbow bolt through its back just under its spine. The poaching of deer is one of our most regular calls, especially from October to March. Most are taken by dogs, shot from the roadside or in snares. A crossbow against deer is a particularly cruel way to take a deer, most likely resulting in an injured deer making off, as indeed was the case here.

Birds are more likely to be the target of crossbow-crazed hooligans, but in two cases we dealt with neither bird was killed by the bolt. The first was a mallard duck on the outskirts of Perth, seen staggering about with a crossbow bolt through its body. Luckily there were no vital organs struck and after the bolt was removed by a vet the duck survived. An oyster catcher with a bolt through it was not so lucky and had to be put down by a spade-wielding shopkeeper. In both cases press appeals were made. There were many responses from people who were sickened by the acts but unfortunately no-one was able to give any clue as to the person responsible.

A call for help came to me from one of the Divisional Inspectors. He was on duty when some of his officers were dealing with a particularly nasty individual who he was sure had thrown cement powder into a pond where there was a valuable koi carp, resulting in its death from suffocation. There was a suspect, who had also put a hose down the chimney of the carp owner's house and turned on the tap. Not the kind of neighbour anyone would want to wish on their worst enemy. I arranged a post-mortem examination of the fish to try to confirm the presence of cement. Various samples were taken for further histo-pathology tests but unfortunately cement couldn't be confirmed.

Farmers are sometimes suspects in relation to mistreatment of their stock. I often have a bit of sympathy for them as effectively their stock is their livelihood. From my background of farming I know that there must be few occasions when a farmer will deliberately starve his animals. There is no money to be made from skeletal stock. There is usually some underlying cause for farm animals not being given sufficient feeding and I like to think that we take this into consideration. This was exactly the case when it was reported that there were 5 dead sheep and several dead lambs on a farm in north Perthshire. The place looked really run down and the farmer appeared to have fallen on hard times. Wives usually pull their weight on a farm, especially a hill sheep farm. In this case the farmer's wife was unwell and in addition to seeing to the stock the farmer was in and out of the hospital to visit her. He was obviously having difficulty coping on his own. The remaining stock seemed well cared for and there was no point in pursuing a case in relation to the dead sheep. We liaised with the Scottish SPCA to give some advice and the matter was left at that.

Two much more serious cases followed, the first being an allegation that two men were throwing a live hen in the air for their peregrine x gyr falcon hybrid to catch. Unfortunately we could not trace the hen, which would have been the source of evidence as to whether it had been gripped by a falcon while alive or while dead. When the men were traced they claimed the hen had been dead, though we were neither able to confirm this nor disprove it.

The other incident was similar, in that we received a report of a man catching jackdaws in a Larsen trap – a legitimate enough practice – but the caller said that he was then tying them on a piece of string and flying his hawk at them. He did have a Larsen trap, unset, in his garden, but there was no evidence to substantiate the claim.

A similar method is used utilising tethered pigeons to decoy peregrines within shooting range. On an Angus grouse moor where we had a number of claims of illegal conduct relating to the gamekeepers we did one time recover a pigeon with about 10 metres of fishing line tied round one of its legs. The pigeon had somehow managed to escape and I have no doubt that this had been its purpose, though there was no means of linking it back to any individual. However we still maintain an interest in this estate and live in hope. Their luck may run out.

Dogs are probably the most frequent recipients of cruel treatment, with a growing trend for Staffordshire terriers to be the breed most regularly abused. Staffordshire terriers are great with people, though some are not quite so gentle with other dogs. In the right hands they are great dogs but unfortunately they are sometimes kept as status symbols by petty criminals, and some who are not so petty. In most towns they can be seen being strutted round the streets, generally not on leads since that may reflect weakness on the part of the owner, rather than the common sense approach of responsible dog owners who don't want to risk their dogs running onto the road. Occasionally it's only the semi-upright gait of the owner that enables passers-by to discern man from beast!

In one incident in Dundee many of these factors were evident. One afternoon two young women were waiting outside a school when they saw a black Staffordshire x labrador puppy, with no collar, in the middle of the road. It seemed to the women to be eating some rubbish. Its owner, a man nearing 40, described by the women as 'appearing to be in a foul mood,' ran on to the road and kicked the puppy in the face. It howled and ran off into nearby bushes. The man called to the unfortunate dog to come to him, but to no avail. Readers who have either dogs or common sense will already have realised what sort of clown this man is. He then ran to the bushes, grabbed the pup by the scruff of the neck and shook it. No doubt the poor pup, even at 4 months old, would have anticipated this, hence its reluctance to come anywhere near its brutish owner. Not un-naturally the two women were extremely upset and contacted the police, who charged the man, resulting in due course in a fine of £175.

In another incident a man was walking his two small dogs when a Staffordshire terrier ran out of a garden and attacked them. The dog walker attempted to separate the dogs but the Staffie was bent on continuing the fight. The man unfortunately fell to the ground and injured his knee, before eventually managing to get a spare lead on the Staffie and tie it to a lamp post. The police and an ambulance were called, and the Staffordshire terrier's owner was traced and charged with failing to keep his dog under proper control. Though the injured man required hospital treatment his dogs were lucky enough not to require veterinary treatment. In a court judgement compensation was required to be paid to him by the owner of the Staffie.

In one of the worst cases of cruelty imaginable, a 17 year-old youth was visiting his friend in a house in Forfar, Angus. At one point the visitor made his way to the kitchen while the friend remained in the sitting room. After a short time he wondered what his visitor was doing and went through to the kitchen to investigate. The 17 year-old was standing beside the microwave oven, which had been switched on. Inside the microwave was one of a litter of 4 week-old kittens that were from the family cat. The son of the household rushed to the microwave and took out the kitten, which he saw was having difficulty breathing. He put it on the floor, where it was shaking uncontrollably, was unable to walk and was clearly in great pain. After a brief argument about what had taken place the unwelcome visitor rushed out of the house.

The police were called and took the kitten to a vet. It was given treatment but after six days had to be euthanased as its internal injuries were so severe. The 17 year-old admitted his actions to the officers and was charged with causing unnecessary suffering to a domestic animal under the Animal Health and Welfare (Scotland) Act 2006.

In due course he pleaded guilty. I wasn't in court but in a news report, the sheriff hearing the case at Forfar, Sheriff Kevin Veal, is reported to have said, 'To put a small, defenceless animal inside a microwave and then activate the oven, with the injuries the animal thereafter sustained is altogether appalling and utterly unacceptable.' I certainly agree with him. He sentenced the youth to 120 hours of community service, ordered him to pay compensation of £150 towards the vet's fees and banned him from keeping animals for 7 years. Sheriff Veal acknowledged that he had considered a custodial sentence to emphasise the disgusting character of the offence but did not believe this would challenge the youth's problems. He added, 'I recognise the appalling actions of the accused, and I also appreciate the necessity that any disposals pronounced today will express the outrage of the wider community.'

This had already turned out to be the case. It is not surprising that when locals learned of what he had done, the youth was a figure of hate in the small market town. There were angry scenes outside the court after he was sentenced. Abuse and eggs were hurled at him and he had to be escorted from the court in a police van.

Police are frequently called after a pet rabbit has been killed, and sometimes this upsets me even more than a crime committed against a person. There really are some very strange people in the world. I am usually involved either in giving advice to the investigating officer or arranging and attending a post mortem examination of poor bunny.

In August 2008 a woman in the city of Dundee had been victimised so much by youngsters in her area that she decided to move house. She got up early on the morning of the flitting and went to the garden where she had two rabbits in a hutch, as she saw one of them had escaped and was running about. She caught it and replaced it in the hutch, at which point she noticed that the padlock had been broken. She then went to what she thought was the second rabbit, to discover it was just the skin set up to look like the rabbit was still alive. The grief-stricken woman phoned the police, to be told, wrongly, that it was not a police matter and that she should contact the SSPCA.

I found out about this later in the day, and realised that I had to re-double my efforts to educate the civilian call-takers (who are often the first point of contact between the public and the police) that crime committed against animals is usually no different to crime committed against people or against property. The rabbit had been taken from the hutch and had been carted off elsewhere to be killed and skinned, before the skin was brought back as part of the sick ploy. Apart from any cruelty committed in the killing of the rabbit, the crimes committed were theft by opening a lockfast place (the hutch) and breach of the peace by placing the remainder of the woman's pet rabbit in a manner that could do nothing else but upset her. This was very much a police investigation.

I made contact with the SSPCA and recovered the rabbit skin. I needed to try to find how the rabbit was killed to establish, in addition to the other offences, an animal welfare offence. My notes at the time were that:

> 'it had been poorly skinned, not by an experienced person such as a gamekeeper, butcher or fishmonger. The head is missing as is part of the skin; in other words the skin has not been taken off cleanly in one piece. Rather it has been pulled off with one large piece first then several smaller pieces. One of the back legs is still attached to the skin. Unlikely that the rabbit was gutted before being skinned since there is an absence of blood on the skin. There are no obvious marks on the skin consistent with subcutaneous ante-mortem bruising. As such it is not possible in my opinion to determine how the rabbit was killed or if suffering had been involved.'

Great effort was put in to this investigation by the police officer whose case it was, and though he had a strong suspect, it could not be proved that he took and killed the rabbit. Whoever it was he is a very sick individual who might well go on to commit crimes of violence against people.

There are very few cases when I have sufficient experience to make this sort of examination myself, and on almost every occasion I rely on Graham Baird or David Gibson for their expertise, the two veterinary pathologists at the SAC vet lab in Perth.

This was the case, in December of 2009, when it was reported that two rabbits, one white and one dark grey, had been taken from their hutch at the edge of a Kinross-shire village and killed, one being beheaded. If a person had been responsible for this we were, as in the Dundee case, looking at a real oddball.

Graham examined the two rabbits for me the following day, but on this occasion the result, though still gruesome, was natural. There was clear evidence once the rabbits had been skinned that they had been taken by either a fox or a small dog. As in the hare coursing post-mortems there were puncture wounds on the body and broken ribs. We both noted that the rabbits had been gripped further back than was normally the case but there was no doubt that it was the work of an animal and not a person.

One mystery remained, however. The head of one of the rabbits was missing and the neck did not look like it had been gnawed, rather cut with a knife. There was very little blood on the white fur round the neck. This would tend to indicate that the head was taken off some time after death. Nothing is ever simple!

CHAPTER 16

Operation Easter and Threats to Nesting Birds

MANY CALLS to the police relate to some criminal conduct towards nesting birds. Thankfully the day of the egg thief is nearly gone, but taking birds' eggs or disturbing rare nesting birds for photography purposes can be a real threat to some already scarce species.

Operation Easter was initiated in 1997 by Tayside Police and RSPB as a co-ordinated response to egg thieves, and has been managed by Tayside Police since that time. Initially it linked the police forces in areas where there were rare birds whose eggs were regularly targeted by this strange breed of men, egg collectors, and those forces where the known egg thieves were housed. In 1997 there were 60 people – all men – in which we took an interest. By about 2003 this number expanded to 130 as more intelligence was gathered, and by that time every UK police force was involved. Since then the operation has been tremendously successful in gaining evidence to convict the egg thieves we targeted, and many of their egg collections have been found and destroyed. The position in 2011, some 14 years on, is that a high proportion of the former egg thieves have either given up egg collecting or now resort to going abroad for eggs, where it may be fair to say that the police seem to have less synchronisation of effort. From a high of 130, less than 25 known egg collectors remain of interest to Operation Easter in 2011. In July 2011 we await the court outcomes of a linked investigation where four men from the north of England, Scotland and Sweden were found with a combined total of 21,000 eggs.

What amazes me is that the media still has an insatiable appetite for articles about egg collecting, the same as they have for freshwater pearl mussels. This is all the more surprising as neither of these, as subjects of journalism, are furry, feathery or cuddly.

Summarising some of the more interesting results since 2005, I'd kick off with the recovery of 3600 eggs from the home of one of our suspects in Norfolk. This man specialised in collecting the eggs of the nightingale, of which he had 166 eggs, and those of the nightjar, with 89 eggs. If these eggs were all collected in the same general area this would have had a serious impact on the numbers of these birds, which are not common in any case. I'd hazard a guess that only a small fraction of the UK population have ever heard the beautiful liquid warbling song of the nightingale (I've only heard it in France), and probably even fewer will have seen the strangely nocturnal nightjar, or have heard its purring call, usually described as a *churr*, which rises and falls in pitch. Yet the activities of this ecological vandal had the effect of making the chance of appreciating these thrilling sights and sounds even more unlikely. Two hundred of the eggs were from the even rarer birds on Schedule 1 of the Wildlife and Countryside Act, with 24 of those being eggs of the little tern, the smallest of the terns, a dainty bird endangered in the UK and unfortunately sometimes the victim of unwitting disturbance during nesting by holidaymakers to shingle and sandy beaches. The man pleaded guilty and was sentenced to ten weeks imprisonment despite having no criminal record. It was a good result.

In the summer of 2005 the home of another egg thief, this time from Northumbria, was searched and over 800 eggs found. These included eggs of the little ringed plover, little tern, red-throated diver and the stone curlew, a primitive-looking sandy-coloured bird with huge yellow eyes, thick yellow legs and a stubby black and yellow bill. These are all Schedule 1 birds, with the stone curlew just beginning to make some progress with breeding in Norfolk, helped by the RSPB and some eco-friendly farmers. The man was sentenced to 280 hours of community service, which is a direct alternative to imprisonment.

In the search of another house in Warwickshire in the autumn, the police were really looking for a weapon after a complaint of assault.

No weapon was found but the second prize was 76 wild birds' eggs. This time the rarer eggs were those of the kingfisher, little ringed plover and tree pipit. The man was sentenced to four months imprisonment, this being his eighth conviction for taking eggs. With the scarcity of some of these birds that are targeted, a jail term is now the most likely sentencing outcome for egg thieves.

In the early spring of 2006 two men from Merseyside were arrested in Wales and charged with intentional or reckless disturbance of a nesting goshawk. One of the men, who had featured in other cases, was sentenced to four months imprisonment, suspended for a year, and had to pay costs of £800. In the summertime 400 eggs were recovered from an address in Middlesbrough, though the man has since disappeared.

In the next of the 2006 cases, two men we had taken an interest in, one from Norfolk and the other from Leicestershire, pleaded guilty to several taxidermy and egg-related offences and after a trial lasting eight days were found guilty of other similar offences to which they had pleaded Not Guilty. The offences included the trade in eggs from Russia and Norway, with further offences being committed during trips to North Rona in the Outer Hebrides where Leach's petrel, storm petrel and arctic skua, all sea birds, nest. Examples of all of these birds were recovered as taxidermy specimens, having been taken from the island as live birds. One of the men, a landowner and businessman with property in London, was jailed for four months and ordered to pay costs of £30,000. The other man, a retired magistrate, was sentenced to two months imprisonment suspended for a year and was ordered to pay costs of £8,300. This case is described in detail in *The Thin Green Line*.

2006 was really a bad year for egg thieves. On 8 November police assisted by RSPB searched a house in Grimsby and recovered a (then) record 7,600 eggs. In due course the householder pleaded guilty to possessing 653 eggs of the rarer Schedule 1 species, possession of 6,477 eggs of other wild birds and taking chough, peregrine and barn owl eggs, all species in Schedule 1 of the Wildlife and Countryside Act. He was sentenced to 23 weeks in jail and ordered to pay costs of £1,500. Another excellent result.

The co-ordinated work of the UK police forces, along with assistance and often advice from RSPB, was paying dividends. Egg thieves were on the back foot and reports of the eggs of rare birds being plundered were reducing. The egg thieves knew they were likely to be jailed if they were caught, and they were much more likely to be caught now that all the forces were pooling intelligence and working together. In the spring of 2007 one of the men we had taken an interest in was found to have peregrine and raven eggs in his house and he was jailed for 26 weeks. A younger *socius criminus* had four skylark eggs when the police came to call, and was sentenced to 50 hours of community service, had to pay costs of £250 and had his equipment, including a valuable camera, forfeit by the court.

Besides reports of suspected egg thieves, many of the calls I get in spring and early summer relate to a variety of threats to the nests of birds. Most of these calls are genuine, but I have to guard against the odd person who wants to capitalise on this to suit his or her own ends. Development projects are not always accepted with glee or even grace. Neighbours to the development site might enjoy their open vista and might not relish a house or factory being built in front of them. This is entirely understandable, but some try to use the police as a means of stopping this, by reporting that trees or bushes about to come down contain nesting birds. This may be true, and of course if that is the case, and can be substantiated, then the bushes and trees must remain until the birds have completed their breeding season. In many cases there are no nesting birds at all and the plot to cause delay is foiled!

As an example it was reported that a pair of barn owls were nesting in an old farm steading and that the buildings were shortly to be demolished to make way for a build of expensive houses. It was late March 2008 and, though it's really not my job, I went one Saturday morning to meet the contractor on site since it was not far from my house. I scoured the farm building with the contractor and saw nothing but feral pigeons. There was absolutely no trace of the large black pellets, full of the bones of small rodents, to demonstrate the presence of barn owls. No doubt there were some suitable nesting places but certainly no presence of *Tyto alba*. The most interesting part of the visit was a dead sparrowhawk that had probably chased a pigeon into the building and most likely crashed into a window when it was trying to get out again. I doubted that this was a genuine call, particularly since it was made anonymously. I rather suspected that it was a caller who didn't want new neighbours.

In a case where there was no doubt that there was mischief afoot, I received a call about a building that was to be taken down in the village of Muthill in the west part of Perthshire. The caller – again anonymous – said that there was a blackbird's nest in the building. The month was June so this was entirely possible. I made contact with the contractor, who said he had been besieged by locals with all manner of excuses that might prevent this development going ahead. It's not my place to judge, and it may be that the reasons the locals didn't want the development were valid. However it is my job to ensure that the law is applied, and if there was an active blackbird's nest and the work would adversely affect it, then the work would need to be delayed. I visited the site to see if this was the case, and saw the most rudimentary and ridiculous man-made structure that was meant to represent the intricate mud and dried grass weavings of the blackbird. The building was demolished the next day.

In one completely genuine case a lady contacted me to say that a roof was just about to be taken off an old farm steading under renovation, and that the building was full of nesting swallows. I was due to be passing the building that afternoon in any case so I said that I would look in and assess the situation.

The building was a long two-storey building. On ground level there were arches, now bricked up, that had at one time been part of a cart shed. There was also an opening halfway along the building that led through to further buildings behind. On the upper level the small windows were long gone, leaving square openings through which I could see the graceful swallows with their long ribbon tails coming and going. There were piles of new wood stacked up in the yard, and a two-storey portakabin office block, beside which I parked. I sought out the site foreman, an affable fellow, and told him why I was there. He agreed that the roof was coming off within the next week and told me about the plans for the old building to be converted to luxury houses at considerable cost. He was aware of birds coming and going from the building, but didn't know what kind they were or why they were entering the building.

The foreman agreed to give me a tour, and the first thing I spotted as we entered the opening that led through to the buildings at the back was a swallow's nest on a ledge, with a semi-circle of fledgling swallows peeping over the edge awaiting the parents' return with a beakful of flies. He'd never noticed this nest, which, for someone not aware of birds, didn't surprise me. We continued through the building and counted twenty swallows' nests, most of which seemed active, on the ground and upper levels. Some nests had well-grown chicks, and at others a swallow that had been brooding eggs or very small chicks flew off with a *tswit, tswit*, as our presence disturbed its routine. In one nest that I could reach there were 5 white eggs with a bit of dark speckling at one end, and in the elongated shape typical of swallows' eggs. The eggs were nestling in a layer of white feathers, gathered by the parent and providing a warm buffer between the brooding bird and the caked mud which was the nest structure. I showed this to the foreman and he seemed sympathetic.

The dialogue relating to this nest went along the following lines:

'So how long will it take for these eggs to hatch and the chicks to leave the nest?'

'Depending on how long the bird has been brooding them, it could be anything between three and maybe five weeks.'

'Well it's near the end of May now. We'll put off taking off the roof until the end of June.'

'No, that won't do. The nests are all at different stages. Some have chicks just about ready to leave, then the swallow will have another clutch in the same nest after that.'

'Well how long will all that take? There's a lot of money tied up in this development. These are going to be very expensive houses.'

'To be safe you'd need to wait till the end of August, maybe even a wee bit into September, till all the nests are clear.'

The earlier sympathetic expression changed to one that seemed to be a mixture of apprehension and determination.

'No. I'm really sorry but we can't wait that long. This is a big job and we need to crack on with it.'

'That's OK, but you need to be aware that the penalty for every egg or chick that is destroyed carries a fine of £5,000 and/or a period in jail of up to six months.'

Silence for a minute while the face changed to consternation.

'Well . . . well, we'll better just wait till September then.'

I thought that was a wise choice. We went through the building again and since there were few nests on the ground level, we agreed a plan that would allow some of the work to be carried out immediately. All the nests on the ground floor were at one end. Swallows are reasonably tolerant of humans so it was agreed that a tarpaulin could be put up separating off the much smaller part of the building with the nests, still with access to the swallows through an open window to the rear, thus allowing work to be done on the rest of the ground level. It was as much of a compromise as could be done within the law.

I visited several times after that, and as other bits of the building became clear of active nests other development work was given the green light. My last visit was in the last week of August, at which time I was able to say that the use of all of the nests had ended for the season. I thanked the foreman for being so accommodating (even though I'd virtually been holding a gun to his head) and arranged for a local newspaper to come in and cover the good-news story. This gave the company, Haddens of Aberuthven, some very good publicity which I've no doubt stood them in good stead for future business as being seen as environmentally friendly. The swallows benefited; the company benefited in the long run, and some swallows still managed to find a suitable nesting place in the by-now completed development the following year. The biological term *symbiosis* almost fits the bill. Even yet I get calls from Haddens asking advice before they embark on any development that might have complications for wildlife.

In another planned demolition of a house and outbuildings near Crook of Devon in Kinross-shire nesting swallows delayed proceedings when they started to nest in the outbuildings. This time it was right at the start of the nesting season, but the owner agreed to wait until the autumn before he went ahead. I can appreciate that in many cases delays because of nesting birds may not be something that the owner of the property would consider. I'm rather surprised that this is not flagged up either by architects or council planning departments, since they must encounter this issue regularly.

The early summer of 2009 must have broken all records for the reporting of house martins' nests being damaged. Most were single nests and were dealt with by a warning, though there comes a time when warnings must be replaced by reporting for prosecution. Invariably they resulted from calls to us by neighbours, disgusted by the extremely un-neighbourly conduct of poking a nest down with a long stick in more accessible places, climbing a ladder and reaching up with a stick in the case of some of the higher nests, or in some cases hosing the nest down with a pressure hose. In two cases neighbours had photographed the culprits up a ladder; in one case with a stick and in one case with a hose. This was great evidence not only of the illegal activity but of the identity of the person involved. That the neighbours were willing to go to court and give evidence surprised me. They had maybe not thought out the consequences of being shunned by some neighbours while being praised by others. This was a factor in our decision to deal with these cases by warning.

There was an example from an earlier case on which we could base our decision-making. A warning had been issued in the same circumstances the previous year in a small rural hamlet of brand new houses. Some advice was given to the householder to glue a CD in the apex of the roof, which would prevent the birds nesting the following year since the mud used for their nest wouldn't stick to the CD. News had obviously spread and when I went round the hamlet the following summer half of the houses had CDs stuck in the apex, while the other half, their occupants more sympathetic to the birds sharing the outside of their house, all had house martin nests with parents busily flying to and fro feeding chicks. What frustrates me somewhat is that I would love to have house martins at my house, of similar structure, and they won't come!

In a more serious set of circumstances we submitted a case to the procurator fiscal. A visitor to a holiday complex at a Perthshire hotel looked out of his window one morning to see a man with a ladder and a long pole going round the hundred or so holiday houses within the hotel grounds. He had obviously been sent to destroy the house martin nests and this seemed like a regular routine. The man called on his wife to watch what was happening and we had our two witnesses.

The couple had gone home to England before reporting the incident to me but only one day had elapsed. I passed the investigation to two of our local officers, PC Greg Samuel, a new divisional wildlife crime officer, and PC Ian Thomson, an experienced officer enthusiastic at investigating any allegation of crime, especially if a bit different from the norm. Their initial investigation suggested that there were three suspects: the person who had carried out the destruction of the nests, a maintenance operative; his boss, the maintenance manager, and, in turn his boss, the general manager of the hotel. They arranged to interview them the following day and I said that I would attend an hour or so earlier, photograph any destroyed nests and meet them at some stage after their interviews of the suspects.

I was quite amazed at the number of nests that appeared to have been destroyed. Just about every house had the remains of a house martin nest either in the apex or somewhere under an overhang of the roof. They were in the form of a horseshoe-shaped series of small mud balls stuck to the building. That the mud was dark and fresh told me that in most of the cases this was a nest from the current year that had been knocked down and was being rebuilt. I photographed about 70 or 80 of these before the memory card in my camera was full, and had only gone round half of the houses. It was late June in 2009 and all of these nests should have been complete and have had young house martin beaks at the entrances waiting to be fed. There was only a handful in that much more satisfying state and it was obvious from their location that they were causing no mess to any of the visitors to the hotel. The remainder were above places where the birds' droppings would be falling on windows or on decking used by the visitors for sitting out if we ever got a dry, sunny day. I could see the hotel's point, but what was happening was illegal. There were hundreds of house martins flying around; most, I imagined, very frustrated at having flown thousands of miles from North Africa and having no progeny to show for their massive expenditure of energy.

When I walked around the hotel complex there was a good selection of wildlife. In some trees at the edge of the grounds there were bat boxes and bird nesting boxes. A smallish pond held two mallard drakes and I hoped that the ducks were nesting nearby or were rearing a brood of ducklings, though for mallard – wildfowl that begin laying in February and March – the season was getting on a bit. If they were on eggs it would be their second, if not their third, attempt to breed. A moorhen, with its red frontal shield above the beak clearly visible, shared the pond and swam towards the far side, constantly flicking its tail in the same manner as the next bird I saw, a grey wagtail, which flitted about above the small stream that ran from the pond. I knew its nest wouldn't be there as I was aware that it prefers to nest above fast flowing water. I also knew there would be good mix of wildlife under the water that I couldn't see. In the trees I saw many of the commoner woodland birds, plus a tree creeper, making its way up the bark of a tree in its quest for insect life, and a red squirrel. The squirrel, on seeing me, made for the higher branches but segments of cones dropping to the ground told me that I hadn't put it off its food. The hotel clearly liked wildlife. Except house martins.

From the interviews of the three suspects it transpired that the destruction of the house martin nests was a twice-weekly event, so that the nests would not be completed and no eggs would be destroyed. One of the suspects said that this had been taking place for at least three years. Another commented that house martin numbers were getting a bit less, which was hardly surprising.

The case was reported to the procurator fiscal, who, I think rightly, did not proceed with the case against the two employees but prosecuted the general manager; the person in overall charge. He pleaded guilty and was fined £300. His defence solicitor had said that 'there are hundreds of nests in the hotel grounds and only specific ones were targeted. The economics of the hotel didn't allow daily cleaning of the bird mess, which would have been needed to keep the matter under control.' He hoped that the birds would move to a more convenient nesting site. I wondered how this might come about? I was also amused at a comment in a local newspaper after the case that the manager 'was working with a police wildlife officer to come up with alternative solutions. This includes putting CDs in the eves to discourage the birds nesting there, building bird boxes in trees and feeding stations on a pond.' CDs have been proved to be a success, but I've yet to hear of a house martin using a nest box or where feeding stations on a pond may prevent a repeat of the 2009 experience!

In another 1999 case, this time in Dundee, a woman was looking out of her window when she saw a man across the street on a flat roof. He had climbed out of the skylight and seemed to be trying to clean out guttering at the edge of the roof. He then made towards the corner, making a shooing motion with his hands. The woman was surprised to see the man, whom she recognised, lift two birds, one in each hand, and throw them off the roof. She saw one of the birds fall on to a car port some two storeys and about 30 feet below. The other fell behind a wall at the back of the car port. The woman thought the birds were young oyster catchers and saw that the one on the car port was lying motionless as if it were dead.

The witness ran down the stairs and across to where the birds hand landed. The man who had thrown them also appeared there and she asked him why he had thrown them. He denied having thrown them and said that they flew off the roof as he had come close to them. She knew exactly what she had seen and contacted the police.

Police officers attended and managed to recover the dead oyster–catcher from the car port roof. They searched for the second one, including in the bins, but couldn't find it. The officer dealing with the case had spoken with the suspect, but he had denied throwing the birds off the roof. He contacted me and I arranged a post mortem examination of the bird that had been recovered. I confirmed it was a young oystercatcher, (an essential element of the likely charge) with wing feathers half grown, and would have been unable to fly. Some birds develop their wing feathers very quickly. Examples are game birds such as pheasants, partridges and grouse. They are able to fly within a few days of hatching and they depend on this ability to keep them safe from predators. Other ground-nesting birds, such as oyster-catchers, curlews and lapwings, develop their wing feathers much more slowly and depend on camouflage to keep safe. A young oystercatcher will freeze when a predator comes close, and many times it will not be seen and will avoid becoming a meal for a fox, crow or gull.

The post mortem examination, carried out by veterinary pathologist David Gibson at the Scottish Agricultural College vet lab in Perth, showed that the bird had died from a cardiac rupture. In fairly straightforward cases I corroborate the post mortem and take photographs for the court. This saves the two veterinary pathologists having to attend court.

Since the officer dealing with the case was not a wildlife crime officer I went back with him to see the man alleged to have carried out the crime. He was a man of 60 years and had never been in trouble with the police before. I am well aware of the noise that oystercatchers can make when they are being protective of their chicks. I've walked over many a field or moor in early summer to be harangued by oyster-catchers, peewits or curlews that have chicks on the ground. Oystercatchers are by far the most vocal and I knew exactly why the man had wanted rid of the chicks. Get rid of the chicks and the noise from the parents will cease. This is why in wildlife crime investigations it is an advantage to have a wildlife crime officer present. We specialise in a particular crime, as do drug squad officers, fraud squad officers, traffic officers and many more specialist branches of the police.

Over the years I have always found it an advantage in any criminal investigation to give the person suspected a lifeline of sorts of which he can grab hold. I told him the result of the post mortem examination, that I appreciated his problem with the noise from the oystercatchers, and suggested that he had probably been at the end of his tether and had reacted stupidly, probably now regretting his actions. He immediately agreed in part, saying that he had caught the birds and had launched them into the air, hoping they would fly. It was not he but his elderly neighbour who had been wakened in the early morning by the loud *peep peep, peep peep, peep peep* of the parent and he was simply trying to help her out. It was an admission of guilt, albeit with a degree of mitigation.

He was charged with intentionally or recklessly killing a wild bird. In a conversation after the charge the man admitted having for some of his life worked on a farm. As a farm worker he would have been well aware of oystercatchers, probably the most common nesting birds in arable fields and permanent pasture. He most likely would have known the wee penguin-type wings the bird had at that stage would not support flight. However this admission was after caution and charge and not admissible in evidence.

The case was reported to the procurator fiscal and I think the decision was fair. The man had attained 60 years of age without having been in trouble with the police or the courts. The offence was at the lower end of the scale, taking the wide range of all crimes into consideration. No proceedings were taken. He got a real fright and I don't think he'll offend again.

The next case was also marked no proceedings, though I'm still not sure why. In any event we as the police did our bit and the prosecution part is the remit of the procurator fiscal. The police are not always given reasons why a case takes a particular direction.

In April 2008 I received a phone call from a man who passed a small piece of woodland on a knoll on route to his work in Forfar. He saw that trees were being felled round the edge of the woodland on the first day but thought little of this. He was aware that there was a large rookery in the centre of the wood but the forestry work was nowhere near it at that stage. When he passed the following day most of the trees had been felled and the machine harvester felling the trees was still busy at work in the centre of the wood. Rooks were flying in panic everywhere since most of their nesting trees were gone.

We lost no time. I was lucky that Constable Doug Ogilvie, one of the divisional wildlife crime officers, was temporarily in an office job in Divisional Police Headquarters in Perth. I grabbed Doug and we set off for Forfar. . . in time to see the very last tree being felled! The machine operator had cut the bottom of the tree and was pulling it up through the claws of the harvester that strip the branches and cut the trunk into specified lengths. We spoke to the operator, who said he was told to do a job and was just getting on with it. He knew there were rooks' nests in the trees, admitting there would have been at least thirty. He gave the name of his employer and left with the harvester to go to another job.

Doug and I rummaged among the brash from the fallen trees.

There were dead young rooks everywhere and we photographed a selection of them. Some of the nests were still attached to the branches that had been cut off by the harvester. What really amazed me was that the nests, instead of being made of twigs and small branches as are most rooks' nests, were made mostly of wire. The rookery was directly opposite a rubbish dump, and the rooks had found a ready supply of rusty wire in the dump to make their nests. I'd never seen this before and thought that they would have lasted for years, giving a much longer life span than twigs that in the course of time would rot. The main risk was likely to have been during a thunder storm; I wouldn't like to have been a rook sitting on a wire nest when the night sky was illuminated by flashes of lightening.

Doug and I then traced the owner of the harvester. He admitted seeing the rooks but said that he had never received any guidance about wildlife and forestry operations. He referred to the rooks as vermin and appeared to disregard their presence in the trees. It was clear from speaking to him that the felling was to take place regardless.

Next we saw the forestry manager. He had seen the rooks, and admitted there were between 30 and 100 nests but didn't think in late April they were on eggs or rearing chicks. He gave the order to fell the trees.

We also obtained statements from staff of the nearby golf course. Their estimate of rooks nesting in the wood was in excess of 100. They were not particularly enamoured by the rooks and the associated noise but knew they were protected and were content to live and let live.

All foresters work in the countryside and probably all class themselves as countrymen. Even a person brought up in the centre of a city cannot fail to see and hear rooks, the most gregarious and noisy of birds, collecting on their communal nesting site from December, by February picking their nest site that they will use for breeding, and during March collecting sticks to either build up a nest from the previous year or build a completely new one. They are raucous birds that draw attention to themselves. The huge nests they build are in trees usually bare of foliage at the time and are easily visible. When the chicks hatch in April they are almost as loud as their parents as they call for food. Living beside a rookery can be a noisy experience.

For a while we had eight nests in our trees at home and the noise was deafening, yet these 'countrymen', in late April, ignored up to 100 rooks, their nests and chicks.

I was disappointed when the case was not proceeded with, but I'm always mindful of the fact that the role of police is the investigation of crime and ends when the case is passed to the procurator fiscal, whose remit is the decision on whether or not to prosecute. However in this case a reason would have been appreciated.

After a case dealing with rooks, which many people consider as pests, it is probably appropriate to conclude with a word on wild birds and their protection. We must begin from the base line that ALL wild birds are protected. Some, at times, can be pests, and indeed rooks can be pests to me when they steal my ducks' eggs. Under one or more of four general licences issued annually by the Scottish Government these pest species can be dealt with by 'authorised persons', generally the owners or tenants of land where the problem is occurring. In certain circumstances this could be you in your garden. Only the birds listed on the general licence can be dealt with and only for the reasons and by the methods given in the general licence. In general terms the licences cover the protection of wild birds, livestock, serious damage to growing or stored crops, protection against disease, for public safety reasons and for air safety.

Putting this in perspective so far as rooks are concerned, the most likely reason for rooks to be controlled is because of damage to growing or stored crops. They do take some wild bird eggs or chicks so these reasons can't be excluded. I've been in regular communication with a man who is acting on behalf of neighbours who allege they have had rubber picked from car windscreen wipers and from double glazing by rooks. This type of damage is not covered by any of the general licences, nor is it a reason for which Scottish Natural Heritage can issue a specific licence. I've sent the man copies of the three main general licences (the air safety one certainly doesn't apply in this case) to ensure that whatever action he takes will be within the terms of the licence. The same rooks feed in nearby fields and he has now engaged the co-operation of a local farmer, who, if they start eating newly sown grain in the springtime, will allow the use of cage traps on his fields to reduce the numbers.

On a more conservational theme, an interesting call came in to me from a raptor worker one day in May 2009. He was in a bit of a panic as a Kinross-shire farmer was about to start work in extending the size of a quarry so that he could build a house. The face of the quarry that had to be scraped back to make more room for the house held a kestrel's nest, and even if the machinery did not destroy the eggs the bird was likely to desert because of the close proximity of the JCB. I visited the farmer and we had a look at the quarry. I climbed up to the nest to verify that indeed there were eggs; sure enough there were six. I explained the legal position to a rather disconsolate farmer, who reluctantly agreed to hold off for a bit. Since the quarry was quite large I gave him a guide as to how close he could come to the nest with his work, provided he started at the end furthest from the bird so that it gradually became used to the noise. That allowed him at least to do some of the work, for which he was grateful. The kestrel was also grateful and fledged five young from the nest.

Lastly, a case that turned out to be somewhat worrying. In the early summer of 2008 I had a call from a detective officer who was dealing with family protection issues at an address in Dundee. She related that in a young child's bedroom a pigeon had for some strange reason decided to set up home under the child's bed, entering and leaving by the window, which I assumed must either be permanently open or broken. It was now incubating two white eggs. For some reason the officer had initially contacted SSPCA, who gave the advice that 'legislation prevented the incubating pigeon being moved'. While it is correct that all wild birds are protected I've already outlined the general licences issued by the Scottish Government that allow derogation from the law. The one that covers protection against disease was more than adequate in this case, with the respiratory disease psittacosis being a very obvious risk. After my advice the pigeon that laid in the oddest of circumstances was evicted and the nest and eggs were binned.

CHAPTER 17

Snaring Creatures and Criminals

THERE ARE several organisations that lobby strongly for snaring to continue, while there are those on the other side of the debate who want it to be completely banned. The Scottish Government has listened closely to both arguments and appears to prefer legislation aimed at much more professional and responsible use of snares. Changes that have since 11 March 2010 been imposed on gamekeepers, farmers and others who use snares is that a stop must be fitted to each snare to prevent the snare becoming too tight on an animal and strangling it. This will also have the effect that if a dog or a deer puts its foot into a snare then the snare will not close sufficiently to trap the animal. This is sensible and, since proprietary snares come fitted with a stop, this was already pretty much in place through voluntary practice. In addition, snares must not be used where they can be dragged, or where they are likely to fully or partially suspend or drown the captive animal.

A further change we still await under the Wildlife and Natural Environment (Scotland) Act is much more fundamental though will not be enforced until 2012. The provision is that all snares be tagged with a code issued by the police to the person using the snare. This may well entail some extra work for each of the eight forces in Scotland, and may well fall to the co-ordinator in each force to prepare a spreadsheet and issue code numbers appropriate to individual snare operators. This has been tried and tested since March 2008 with crow cages and Larsen traps and had made the use of these traps much more professional. The operator telephones the identified source within his or her police force area, gives such details as satisfies the police, then receives a code and a police telephone contact to be displayed on each trap. There is a precondition with the use of cage traps in that the person operating the traps must have read and understood the appropriate general licence that allows them to use it. I was shocked at the number who had not read, or had not even heard of, the general licences. As did most of my colleagues, I emailed or posted out the general licences to the uninitiated. We now have the benefit of many more trap operators being acquainted with the law, which should keep them out of trouble. Since the legal requirement for codes on snares is imminent, hopefully the improved knowledge and professionalism of snare users will follow.

In Tayside it is my mobile telephone number that goes on the tag on the traps. This gave rise to an amusing telephone call one day from a man in Dundee. The conversation went along the following lines:

'Alan Stewart, wildlife crime officer. Can I help you?'

'I passed a trap for crows the other day and it had the telephone number on it that I'm calling now.'

'That's right. This number should be on any trap in Tayside that is being operated to catch crows or other members of the crow family that are allowed to be controlled.'

'That's fine. I have a crow in my garden that is keeping me awake by pecking on the window in the early mornings. It's also robbing the nests of the wee birds in my garden and in my neighbour's.'

'So do you want a code number for your Larsen trap to catch it?'

'I don't have a Larsen trap.'

'So how can I help?'

There was a short pause as the caller at the other end of the line gathered his thoughts.

'I thought you went round catching crows. Have I got this wrong?'

On a later date I had a call from a farmer who coincidentally lived quite near me. This time the conversation went,

'This is Farmer Bloggs from Mains of Muckrie. I see you have a crow cage in the West Muir and I need to put the cattle on the grass there.'

'No I don't have a crow cage there. . .'

'But your name and phone number are on it.'

'It's not mine. I just issued the code number for it to the game-keeper.'

'Are you not Alan Stewart? Your name's on it as well.'

I explained the reason for the code, the police contact telephone number and the fact that Raymond Holt, a friend of mine who was the keeper involved, though not being required to do so, had put my name on the tag as well. I gave Farmer Bloggs Raymond's phone number so that the problem could be resolved, to receive the parting comment, 'Well this is not good enough. I need my cattle on the West Muir this afternoon . . . '

I'm sure that Raymond got hell as well. After all it was *his* trap.

Returning again to the misuse of snares, I was called to a classic example of this at the end of May, 2008, on the Perthshire-Angus boundary. The circumstances as reported to the police via Ian Hutchison of Scottish Badgers, a former Tayside Police officer and one of the earlier wildlife crime officers, was that a badger had been found dead in a snare on a farm. The snare, Ian had been told, was on the fence of a small L-shaped wood which was in the middle of a very large grass field.

I always seemed to be told to be less hands-on with investigations and to delegate more work to the 12 divisional wildlife crime officers. Despite the number, frequently when they were required there were either none on duty, since they work shifts, or they couldn't be freed of their general policing duties. This was yet again the case, though I managed to obtain the services of a young police constable, Neil Hunter, not with any wildlife crime investigation experience but with plenty of enthusiasm to learn.

The three of us, Neil, Ian and I set off, and quickly found the unfortunate badger. From a distance it looked freshly caught but close up we could see that it was completely desiccated and had obviously been caught months earlier. We checked the fence round the small wood and found another seven snares, all of which had been set in exactly the same manner. The problem now was to find evidence that would link the snare that had caught the badger as being set by any suspect that emanated from the investigation.

I have considerable experience of snaring, having in years gone by caught many thousands of rabbits in snares, and having, from time to time if bothered by a fox getting to the captive rabbits before I did, set fox snares to deal with the problem. The first thing that was obvious to me was how unprofessional the setting of the snares had been. Though no doubt grass was much longer at the end of May than when the snares were set I couldn't imagine what marks on the ground or under the fence would indicate to the person setting the snare that a fox would come through the fence at this particular point. Generally a snare would be set where there is a clear path or track that is used by a fox. I could not imagine any fox using this particular spot with any regularity, if at all. The poor badger seemed to have been incredibly unlucky.

Next, the snares had been secured to the fence wire by being knotted. I'd never seen this before. Almost all professional keepers use a small rectangular piece of metal with two holes at either end through which to thread the end of the snare so that it is secure, but can't be tightened beyond the point that would make it easy to remove the snare again, whether or not a fox had been caught.

The snares were bound to the fence by silver duct tape. This would not hold them on the fence after a fox had been caught but would steady the snare in position and would prevent it being blown about by the wind. Lastly, a short length of orange baler twine, as a marker, had been tied to the top wire of the fence above most – but not all – of the snares. This, again, was unusual and I'd never encountered a professional keeper doing this; they would know exactly where the snares had been set without any marker. It would also quickly alert anyone finding one snare as to the location of the remainder and may lay them open to theft or vandalism.

We photographed everything that was thought to be of evidential value, and took possession of all the snares, including the duct tape, and of course the desiccated badger. There was surprisingly little smell from the badger, and despite maintaining its bulk, it was not much more than a fraction of its weight. I didn't want it taking up valuable space in the chest freezer we have for dead animals, so I bagged it and it hung in my garage for the next few months without any of my family being aware. I always expected a nose more finely tuned than mine to seek it out and ask what on earth was in the black bin liner suspended from the rafters. Despite being incongruous among the garden tools, waterproof jackets, bags of layers meal and wheat, the badger in the bin liner remained incognito.

Enquiries with the farmer revealed that he ran a small shoot as part of a syndicate. He had employed a part-time gamekeeper, but after a few months the man was found not just to be inexperienced but completely incompetent and was sacked. He was told to ensure that all his snares, traps and pheasant feeders were brought in to the farm steading before he finally terminated his employment; a sensible instruction since the part-time keeper was the only person who would know where they were.

According to the farmer and other witnesses on the farm he failed to do that, and a number of snares were found, still set, several weeks and months after he had gone. One of these snares, found by the new part-time keeper, a pleasant and keen young man of 19, had caught a calf by the hind leg. The snare had been set on a fence, which was contrary to advice given by a number of shooting and game management organisations, (and illegal now after the changes to the law in March 2010.) From the opposite side of the fence, which gave him a degree of safety from the calf's irate mother, the new keeper managed to cut the snare and release the calf. He hoped that the snare would drop off the calf's leg but to ensure the calf was fine he and the farmer inspected the stock the next day. Their check of the stock – no easy task with cows and calves milling around in a field – did not show any lame calf so they assumed that the snare had fallen off. Unfortunately it hadn't and a later check revealed that the calf had gangrene in its foot and had to be put down. There was now a likely suspect in the form of an ex-part-time gamekeeper.

Further enquiries with the full-time keeper on the neighbouring estate revealed an interesting piece of evidence. He was well aware of badgers in the area and did not use snares close to their sett in case he caught one. He was checking the boundary fence between the neighbouring estates one day in early spring of 2008 and found two snares set at gaps in the netting; ideal places for badgers to come and go from the woodland. He was furious and removed the snares. He told me that he knew that the person who set the snares was the neighbouring part-time keeper, my suspect, but he had not seen him near the snares. He was able to say that the two snares were on the first 100 metres of the fence as it sloped up from a burn, they had been knotted on to the wire of the fence and, crucially, that each had a piece of orange baler twine tied on the top wire of the fence.

A circumstantial case was building up, and was in essence revolving round the un-professionalism of the person setting the snares. If it had been the now sacked part-time keeper then he was not just setting fox snares on a fence but was setting them on a fence that was a boundary fence with the neighbouring land. This fence was also the boundary of the large field containing the small L-shaped wood and the two groups of snares were only about 200 metres apart. I was satisfied that there was evidence that the person who set the snares round the wood where the badger had been caught was the same person who set the snares found by the professional keeper. I still needed evidence that the person setting them had been the previous part-time keeper.

This was obtained in part by the lambing shepherd on the farm, who had seen our suspect checking snares in the vicinity of where the calf had been caught. He had seen the snares on the fence but had not paid any attention as to how they were secured to the fence nor if there was any twine attached to the fence as a marker. Evidentially this did not hep much, but what was really important was that in the early spring of 2008 he had also seen the suspect walking up the first 100 metres of the boundary fence, up from the burn, on almost a daily basis. (This of course was where the neighbouring keeper had found the two snares that were likely to catch badgers.) Though the shepherd had not seen the two snares on the holes in the netting he was of the opinion because of the regularity of the visits to that area that the purpose was to check snares. We were now beginning to link the setting of the snares to the suspect, though with not yet enough for a conviction.

The last links in the chain came when I spoke to the farmer about the snares that were used by the suspect. All were identical, though they were the common type that could be bought from most gun and fishing tackle dealers and hardware shops. This added nothing evidentially. I told the farmer about the silver duct tape used to bind the snares to the fence and he was sure that there was a roll of similar tape still in the 4WD vehicle that had been used by the sacked keeper and now used by his successor. We went to the vehicle and the roll of tape was indeed still there. What was even more important was that the tape had been split by a knife into widths of one-third and two-thirds so that the user could have a choice. There had been far more use of the one-third strip, and when I compared this with the widths that bound the snares to the fence it was an exact match. I was of the view we had now linked our suspect to the setting of the snares.

The difficulty arose that the suspect now resided in the south of England. I contacted the local wildlife crime officers for the area and they agreed to visit him and interview him about the crime. I was pretty sure that we would be able to obtain the suspect's DNA from the duct tape on the snares but there was little point in doing that unless we had something with which to compare it. Had the suspect been in Scotland then he could have been detained, interviewed and a DNA sample taken from him. My colleagues in the south of England told me that they didn't have the power to do that unless they arrested him, and there was insufficient evidence for them to do so. The only evidence that we might obtain was an admission during an interview that he had been responsible for setting the relevant snares and for leaving them behind, still set.

Unfortunately the interview came to nothing. The suspect came in to the police station by appointment, giving him plenty time to think about his strategy. He made 'no comment' answers to the questions put to him. Nevertheless I still thought there was a circumstantial case and it was submitted to the fiscal by Neil Hunter. It is the role of a procurator fiscal to make a decision on whether to prosecute or not based on a number of factors, one being sufficiency of evidence. In this case the decision was to mark the case no proceedings.

We had done our job; the fiscal had done hers. I had no complaints, but I'll always wonder what the outcome might have been had the case gone ahead. . .

The badger in this case would not have been the intended target, nor was that the case in another incident that involved a full-time keeper. We had been told about the badger by a walker who had encountered it. He described it as a 'pile of fur and maggots.' The snare was most certainly not getting checked every day if that was the case.

I visited with PC Graham Jack. In the interval between the walker reporting the snare and us arriving there – probably just over 24 hours – it most definitely had been checked. The snare, which had been set in a hole in a netting fence near to a pheasant release pen, had been cut. A small amount of fur and several thousand fat maggots remained on the ground, but there was no sign of the business end of the snare and the remnants of the badger.

The badger didn't take much finding. A putrid smell wafted to our noses from a pile of nettles and there, in the centre, was the badger – or at least what was left of it. It was the month of August and maggots can turn a corpse into a semi-liquid mush within a few days. We reckoned that, because of the humid weather over the previous week, the badger had been dead no longer than a week and a half. The snare remained round the neck and the end of the snare had been cut, matching the piece left on the fence.

As we left the woodland we met the suspect gamekeeper on the road. He admitted it was his pheasant pen and that he had set snares round it as he knew there was a fox in the area. He initially claimed he checked his snares every day, but when he realised that we had found the 'hidden' badger he admitted that he had been rather busy and hadn't had time to make regular checks. He was on the verge of retiring and already had five charges relating to wildlife crime that were due in court before long. Graham and I didn't see much point in a further charge being added and decided to give him a last chance.

Many of the offenders we dealt with are gamekeepers and it's easy to get the reputation, unjust as it might be, of persecuting gamekeepers. I always tried to be fair (as in the last incident), and the number of keepers who are charged does not reflect the true number of those we found committing wildlife offences. Some at the lower end of the scale were dealt with by a warning. My philosophy was to try to get gamekeepers on side, and by doing so, for them to encourage their errant peers to stop illegal activity.

This incident occurred in 2004. I finally realised through an incident in 2009 that I would get little thanks from the Scottish Gamekeepers' Association for fairness. In 2005 I had produced an hour-long DVD on wildlife crime. Naturally, since it forms a significant proportion of the work of a wildlife crime officer, I had a section on the persecution of birds of prey. When I made the DVD I consciously tried to be fair to the majority of keepers who work within the law and, very often, alongside the police. I was aware of how impressionable young people can be and had determined that, if an incident I was describing had a gamekeeper who was a suspect, there would only be mention in the narrative of a 'person' rather than a person in any particular occupation.

I was shocked to learn in mid-2009 that the SGA chairman had made a complaint about the DVD to the Scottish Government and to DCC Iain Macleod, then ACPOS portfolio-holder for wildlife crime. Not a cheep to me, despite the fact that he was on a group that I chaired. I was furious, and at the same time, hurt, considering he was a man that I had worked closely with and he had stabbed me in the back. The complaint listed what I and many others considered were four extremely petty grievances, the 'worst' of which related to a comment made by a landowner about a golden eagle. I had been noting a statement from a head gamekeeper in 2003 when he told me of an incident the previous year when a golden eagle had flown over a grouse drive and had spoiled it by moving the grouse away from that particular part of the glen. His boss, the landowner, collared him later in the day and told him that he didn't expect to see a golden eagle on his grouse moor and that it better not be there on the next shooting day. I mentioned this in the narrative of the DVD, thinking that this would divert some of the blame for killing birds of prey away from gamekeepers to employers, as there is no doubt that sometimes a gamekeeper can be put under pressure from his employer that is difficult to resist if he wants to retain his job.

My effort to rationalise some of the reasons that birds of prey are killed had backfired spectacularly.

The SGA's campaign to discredit the DVD didn't end there. In the next edition of their magazine someone who appeared to have learned their journalistic skills with whichever tabloid was most likely to win the Gutter Press Award wrote an article criticising me for producing what was headed 'A Scary Movie' which had been 'withdrawn from use' and asking their members to report to them if they had evidence that it continued to be used in schools. Continue it did, and it has now been viewed by 12,000 school pupils and their teachers with nothing but positive comment!

As it turned out the DVD was becoming dated because of a number of legislative changes. The Scottish Government staff, far from being critical of it, gave me funding to bring it into line with current law.

While I'm having a rant, I can see from the Raptor Persecution Scotland blog that I, a senior procurator fiscal and an eminent sheriff are getting no thanks from a now retired employee of RSPB. He has accused me, not for the first time, as being an 'apologist' for the SGA. It's strange that the SGA don't see it that way. It seems that even-handedness incurs wrath from both sides of a debate, whereas by taking sides I would have been the champion of one and the enemy of the other! At a time when police and prosecutors are putting more effort than ever to preventing, detecting and prosecuting wildlife crime he regularly berates them in the Raptor Persecution Scotland blog.

This does not help his cause. Firstly I wonder where he gets his evidence to justify some extremely serious allegations. Secondly his misguided comments are likely to be counterproductive. He has been out of the wildlife crime investigation loop for many years, and, frankly, is now completely out of touch. Whatever frustrations he now has, they should be targeted at those who are committing wildlife crime; not at those working their socks off to improve the situation and enforce the law.

Rant over.

The two badgers to which I referred earlier were snared accidentally (though still criminally), but reminded me of a career housebreaker that I also snared accidentally. The incident took place in the mid-

70s when I was a young constable on a beat in Perth city centre. It was a freezing cold winter's night and after wandering round the streets in the second half of the shift, ensuring that the various properties were secure I decided, about 5.00 am or so, I would be justified in having a cup of tea and a slice of toast in one of the town's hotels.

I knocked on the door and the night porter let me in. The kettle was on the boil and the porter threw a couple of slices of bread into the toaster. We both took our tea and toast and sat in front of the log fire. He was probably relishing some company during the night; I was enjoying the company but certainly relishing the heat from the fire. When I looked at my watch I saw that it was 6.00 am – finishing time, and I was still nearly 10 minutes from the police station. I wasn't worried about the extra 10 minutes' work, but knew that if I wasn't there by 6.00 am the sergeant would be wondering where I was.

I rushed out the door and took as many shortcuts as I knew to get to the office. I cut through a vennel from Perth's High Street to Mill Street, and as I emerged at the opposite end I almost knocked over one of Perth's incorrigible housebreakers. John McIntyre was a bit of a legend. At that time he would be well in to his 50s, yet was an extremely fit man. I had seen him doing somersaults and handstands to entertain us while he was in custody at the police station on past occasions. He looked somewhat less fit that night; in fact positively fat. He wore a long coat that was bulging from his sides. And clinking. I told him I was going to search him, but he said not to bother. He could see the game was up and told me that he had locked himself in the toilet of one of the town centre pubs, the Ship Inn. His latrine hideout went undetected after closing time, and before leaving the pub by the front door just before 6.00 am he filled all of his pockets with the most expensive bottles of whisky in the place. His cunning plan was to head home in relative safety during the changeover of police shifts from night shift to day shift. He was astonished to have found a police officer still on the streets when he thought he would have a clear run. I never let on to him he had been snared by accident or default.

Another housebreaker I 'snared' at night was due to much more diligence. By this time, probably 1970, many of the officers were mobile and I had a blue and white 'Panda' car: a Ford Anglia. I was covering my much larger beat checking property, when I passed a licensed grocer's shop locally known as the Midnight Grocer. It was a forerunner of what is much more common now with corner shops open from 'Eight till Late'. It looked decidedly different as I passed, since the plate glass window had been smashed.

I wheeled round and drew up in front of the shop, noticing quickly that one of the large 'Dalek-type' rubbish bins had been thrown through the window. As I peered through the huge jagged gap in the glass I saw a figure prostrate on the floor at the back of the shop. I recognised the prone figure as one of the regular drunks that seem to feature in just about every town centre. And I could hear him snoring. When I entered the shop he was lying beside the drinks display with two empty whisky bottles beside him. While John McIntyre preferred a take-away, this housebreaker's preference was for a sit-down meal. Despite such a clean capture he had the audacity, at least in the initial stages, to plead not guilty!

The last housebreaker that I'll refer to as being 'snared' on the night shift was an extremely unusual character. While most house-breakers are driven by the need for drink or drugs, this young guy (who I think had the surname Watson) was a student doing a degree course. He came from Glasgow and quite regularly came through to Perth on the last train in the evening. He then broke into a variety of premises, always in the same areas of Perth, and disappeared back to Glasgow on the first train in the morning, usually before 6.00 am. The areas he favoured were St John Street, where there are a number of expensive shops, and the area round the railway station, where there are sufficient licensed grocers to fulfil the needs of many weary travellers. Watson appeared outwardly respectable and I suspect was converting the stolen goods into money to fund his education.

It was round about the same time as the John McIntyre capture and I was walking round my beat, which this time was right at the heart of the city. As I came round the corner from South St John's Place to St John Street and looked to my right I was just in time to see a fleeing figure run from St John Street into South Street. Bobbies patrolling the beat at four in the morning don't see too many fleeing figures and any they do see arouse bucketfuls of suspicion. I naturally took off in pursuit.

When I reached South Street the runner was nowhere to be seen, so I assumed that he had taken a quick left into Princes Street. We were just past the days of having to phone in every hour to the police station to confirm we were still alive, or so that jobs could be allocated, and I had a brand new two-piece radio. I called the officer on the neighbouring beat, Leslie Bright, and asked her to meet me in Princes Street as quickly as she could. She was no time in getting there and we began a search of the street and the closes to find what happened to the runner. Thankfully he had not gone too far and I spied him hiding under a van. He was slim, but underestimated the space that was available under even the largest of vans. When he crawled out it didn't surprise me that it was Mr Watson. He certainly wouldn't have been in Perth window-shopping and, knowing his favourite haunts, the real reason for his visit would soon come to light.

I had him picked up by the beat car and asked Leslie to go with him to the police station. I was joined by the nightshift detective officer, Ian Cantwell, and we quickly found that the glass in the bottom half of a tobacconist shop door in St John Street had been smashed. Large chunks of broken glass at break-ins usually yield good sole impressions of the unwelcome visitor, and this was no exception. Without going into the shop it was obvious that the shelves had been cleared of cigarettes, these being one of his preferred commodities.

Ian and I called back at the police station and persuaded Watson to tell us where the cigarettes were. I was surprised that he had taken them so far; indeed in the opposite direction to his eventual rendezvous at Perth Railway Station. They had been left in a black bin liner up a stair in George Street and would easily have passed, even to the householders, as a bag of rubbish had they been encountered before Watson was ready to collect them.

I've probably snared half a dozen foxes in my time, but I had much more satisfaction in snaring foxes of the human kind. Even if the odd one was an accident.

Chapter 18

Shooting geese in winter

I USED to be very keen on wildfowling, mostly with grey geese as my quarry. The grey geese that visit the UK in winter are the greylag goose and the pink-footed goose. The pinkfoot is slightly smaller, with a chocolate-brown head and much daintier bill than its cousin. One of the main differences between the two is that greylag geese go back to roost in water – either a river or loch – at night and, providing they are not disturbed, will remain there till first light. Pink-footed geese are much more inclined to move about during wet or moonlit nights, continuing feeding on stubble or on the potatoes missed during harvesting. If geese are heard flying around at night there will be a strong chance that they are pink-footed geese.

My goose shooting was very occasionally carried out as greylag geese were coming into the evening roost on the River Earn in Perthshire. This was where a good gundog was essential as often the shot goose fell into the river, or worse, across on the other side of the river. There would have been no point in shooting geese that couldn't be picked: this is just not in the sportsman's code of good practice. Shooting geese coming off the roost in the morning is preferable to shooting them coming into roost at night, as it causes them much less disturbance. With the availability to the geese of the whole of the River Earn to roost and the unlikely chance of coming over where I lay in wait I permitted myself the indulgence of evening shooting on rare occasions, but left early enough to allow the geese plenty time to settle back into the river.

Much more testing was trying to anticipate the flight line of the geese off the river in the morning and lying in wait, sometimes with decoys set out, well away from the river. I never owned a goose call and had to rely on my skill at anticipating the flight line to have any chance of a shot. Many early morning forays were uneventful, though windy mornings when geese are inclined to fly lower were much more successful. Sporting ethics also dictate that the shooter does not remain shooting the geese overlong, so that they can get a chance to settle and begin feeding. In any event, by an hour after sunrise the geese had gone well beyond where I lay in wait.

I reflected back to one trip I made through the fields towards the River Earn to shoot geese one morning. It was a route that always took me past a strip of woodland where there were almost always roe deer grabbing their last sweet morsel of grass before retreating into the solace of the woodland to rest, ruminate and who knows, maybe to reflect on their life thus far. Walking quietly, with the two labradors to heel, I often got within 20 metres of the deer; walking when they had their heads down grazing, and stopping when they lifted their heads to survey the scene and watch for any approaching danger. It sometimes developed into a test of wills: my remaining motionless so that they would be unsure in their monochrome worlds whether I was a dreaded human or not, while they, equally determined, stared and stared, sure that something was just not right and unwilling to take a further mouthful of grass until they were satisfied they were not in danger. The dogs, Moss and Tweed, were not part of this game and it was usually they who ended the stalemate by wagging a tail or some other movement that had the knock-on effect of the deer bounding into the wood.

The route to my goose shooting position also held another surprise one morning. The area was alive with rabbits, and even had a fair stock of unusually coloured ones in their midst. Black rabbits were common, and occasionally I saw sandy-orange coloured ones or silvery-grey ones. On this occasion it was not a rabbit but a hare that took my full attention. This hare was jet black; the first time I had seen a black hare. It was nibbling at winter barley about 100 metres away, hopping a few metres at a time to get another succulent patch. There was no mistaking it as a hare and I watched it for well over half an hour before I walked towards it trying to get a close-up view. Not being as trusting as the roe deer, it took off across the field. The fact that it ran into the centre of the field rather than the wood should put to bed any doubting Thomas that I had been looking at hare rather than a rabbit.

I was late for my goose shooting and the morning was a blank but I had a far better reward with the sighting of a black hare than a couple of geese. To this day I have not met another person who has seen a black hare apart from a friend of mine, Gerry Oliphant, who stayed locally and saw this one from time to time.

Returning briefly to black rabbits, I experimented from time to time with coloured rabbits if I found a young one with myxomatosis. Myxy nowadays kills only a small proportion of the rabbits that fall victim to the disease. It is spread by the female rabbit flea and the seriousness of the epidemic seems to alter from year to year but a high proportion still survive. My experiments entailed taking these coloured versions with the disease home to see if they would recover and how long this would take. This was not a scientific experiment since I did not factor in the stress that may have been caused to the rabbits being taken out of the natural environment, though counter-balancing this was the short time that they may have survived in the wild anyway since they were blind and easy prey to a number of predators. I never lost a single rabbit, in fact one black rabbit became so tame that I kept it for a while in the house once it had fully recovered, before giving it its liberty.

It was hopping freely about the house one day when the doctor called about some malady or other that one of my daughters had contracted. Jan was dealing with the doctor in the sitting room when suddenly the rabbit hopped out from behind the settee. It caught the doctor's eye and he suddenly exclaimed, 'There's a wee rabbit!' as if it had just hopped in from the field. My wife was in stitches as she tried to explain to the doctor the reason for the rabbit's freedom of the house. Traditionally black rabbits in the wild are referred to as 'the minister'. I've never before had a minister and a doctor in the house at the same time!

Getting back again to goose shooting, the Montrose Basin in north Angus, at the mouth of the River South Esk and just upstream of the town of Montrose, is a wildlife reserve run by the Scottish Wildlife Trust. It is a mecca for grey geese, holding from September through to late April many thousands of pinkfeet though much lower numbers of greylag geese. Shooting on the Basin – a roughly circular salt marsh completely covered at high tide but with only a ribbon of water flowing through the centre at low tide – is limited to certain areas only and is controlled by Angus Council. Shooting permits from the Council are required and the area is extremely well supervised, not only by the Council's seasonal wildfowling officer but by staff of the Scottish Wildlife Trust and the Council's Countryside Rangers.

Because of the level of supervision, shooting practices are of the highest standard and any malpractice that takes place is quickly nipped in the bud. In most cases malpractice is of a minor nature and dealt with by the staff of the Basin. On the few occasions this amounts to *illegal* practice the matter is reported to the police and generally relates to the shooting of the third variety of geese present on the Basin in very small numbers, the Barnacle goose. These geese are protected and are completely different from the grey geese, being black and white rather than grey, and even smaller than the pink-footed geese. They are easily recognisable in daylight, and during an evening flight it is incumbent on a shooter to identify the species before he pulls the trigger. Thankfully wrong identification is rare and only two cases have been reported in recent times.

The most recent case of illegal practice reported to the police by the Basin staff was something entirely different: the offence of shooting two pink-footed geese during the closed season. For those who are not wildfowlers, greylag and pink-footed geese can be shot from 1 September until 31 January, though the shooting season is extended until 20 February provided the shooting is carried out below the normal high water mark. This allows a short extension for shooting on the foreshore, though once geese leave the foreshore for their daily inland feeding grounds they are protected.

In 2007, ten days after the close of the inland shooting period, a wildfowler and his son were on the foreshore for an evening's goose flighting. They left just as it was getting dark and began to walk back to their car. Conditions of being granted a licence by Angus Council to shoot geese include the rule that guns must be in gunslips between the marsh and the car park. As the two walked back along the path to their car a skein of pink-footed geese was seen by two other wildfowlers who were leaving the marsh to fly low just ahead of them. Two shots rang out and two geese fell dead from the skein. The two witnesses, a man and a woman, caught up with the errant wildfowlers, the elder of whom apparently blurted out that he couldn't resist the temptation. He compounded the annoyance of the witnesses by asking if the witnesses' dog could retrieve the geese for him.

Though the geese were shot only 400 metres or so above the high water mark – the area limit between 1 and 20 February – it was a matter that would have to be reported to the police. As well as having broken the law, the shooting of the geese in these circumstances was a clear breach of the code of conduct observed by the majority of wildfowlers. It seemed entirely reasonable for the man to have been satisfied with two ducks he shot legitimately below the high water mark, a reasonable bag by wildfowling standards. He appeared to have been tempted by the opportunity of an out-of-season shot and had been caught out.

The witnesses reported the matter to Angus Council, who then contacted me about the breach of the law. The suspect was later traced and disputed that he had taken the shots from above the high water mark, yet his admissions of being 'at the edge of the reeds', 'standing behind trees' and the admission that one bird fell at the side of a track and the other in a ploughed field are all indicative – apart from anything that the witnesses said about being 400 yards above the high water mark – of being out of bounds. The man was charged and the case was adjourned several times at court before being abandoned. I never did find out the reason for this. I suppose on the scale of wildlife crimes it was quite low down and may have been better dealt with, in any event, by a warning or a fiscal's fine.

Responsible goose shooters observe a bag limit which is recommended by the British Association for Shooting and Conservation, an extremely responsible and professional organisation that works closely with police wildlife crime officers the length and breadth of the UK. Generally the bag limit per gun is 5 pinkfeet or 2 greylags, though this recommendation could be altered if there is a major fluctuation in goose numbers. It is not a legal limit, though we are often contacted where there is suspicion that these bag limits are not being observed. If we can, we attend and speak with the goose shooters since if they do happen to be rascals they might also be shooting protected species.

2007 was a year when we had more than the normal number of such calls. The first alleged that four men from the north of England had shot 96 pinkfooted geese on a morning flight in Kinross-shire. We made contact with the men about 5.00 a.m. the following day, and they admitted having shot 27 pinkfeet on their previous morning flight. Their shotgun certificates were checked and found to be in order and they were left to their shooting. I felt that it did no harm to remind shooters of codes of conduct: allowing bad practice brings shooting into disrepute and does the sport harm in the long term.

Within days we had another report of four guns having shot over 100 pinkfeet on a morning flight, this time in Angus. This time the visit to the shooters revealed that there were in fact six men and their bag was 35 geese, not as serious a breach of the code as was reported but still slightly over the bag limit.

CHAPTER 19

Deer, Dogs and Sheep

UNFORTUNATELY, deer poaching is still rife in Scotland. Since the deer are invariably taken in the middle of the night off minor country roads where there's a sparse population, (most of whom will be asleep), the poachers have the clear advantage. Like most types of wildlife crime, detection rates are disappointingly low.

Poaching of all kinds forms a high proportion of wildlife crime investigations nationally so it's no surprise that tackling poaching crime is seen UK-wide as one of the wildlife policing priorities. Wildlife policing priorities have been set for a number of years by the National Wildlife Crime Unit, working together with the Joint Nature Conservancy Council, and a number of other statutory and non-statutory agencies. Priorities are set either according to the conservation status of the species against which crime is being committed, or, in the case of poaching, the volume of incidents. The priorities are agreed by the Association of Chief Police Officers (ACPOS) in England, Wales and Northern Ireland, and the Association of Chief Police Officers (Scotland) and are reviewed annually.

Usually the only evidence that someone has been poaching deer are the grallochs left at the roadside, or an injured beast that has died and been found by a stalker or gamekeeper. One such deer, a roe doe, was reported to me in mid-January 2007 after having been found in the middle of a field by a Perthshire keeper. He had found the deer just after midnight and it was still warm. It had been shot in the neck with a .22 rifle and had managed to struggle two field widths from the road before expiring. The bullet had passed right through the neck so was not able to be recovered for any ballistics examination. How on earth do you detect a crime like that?

Similar circumstances were evident in a crime at the end of 2008, though this time it was a white fallow buck that was found by the stalker on Atholl Estates in Highland Perthshire. This buck, the only white one in the herd, was well known on the estate and had probably been shot from the roadside for its head as much as for the venison. Like the roe doe, it had been shot by a .22 and had run off to die, probably many hours later and a good half mile from the road. It was a complete waste of a lovely buck. Its shooting may have been connected to another incident a month earlier when a dead fallow buck was found about ten miles further south at the side of the former A9 just north of Dunkeld. This buck was shot by a centre-fire rifle, probably a .22 hornet. The shot must have killed the deer, though the fact that it was not picked up, and had been newly shot when it was found by a party heading home after a pheasant shoot, suggests that the poacher had been disturbed.

About the same time, December 2008, in a large area of forestry in Angus, poachers were also at work. I'd a call from the Forestry Commission stalker that he had been told by people who lived within the forest that the gralloch of a roe deer had appeared overnight at the side of one of the forest tracks. Importantly there was a pair of blue plastic gloves left behind, so there was a good chance of obtaining DNA. Though I had directions to the house of the woman who had found the gralloch, I didn't know her name or what the address was, but I passed details to one of two officers on duty in the small town of Brechin, who covered the area, to recover the gloves for DNA testing. This was a simple task, but none of us had counted on two separate sudden deaths occurring almost simultaneously in Brechin that naturally had much more priority over the officers' time than a deer poaching incident. (The unexpected death of any person is investigated by the police and a report compiled and sent to the procurator fiscal.)

Next morning, with the gloves still not picked up, I went up to the forest and knocked on the lady's door, looking for directions to the gralloch and the gloves. 'I've put all of that in the bin,' she said, 'as the dogs were sniffing it and I was worried that they might eat some of it.' 'That's OK,' I said, 'where is the bin?' Her reply floored me. 'It's just been emptied. You've just missed the lorry.'

Significantly, far more poaching incidents were now being reported. There had been a press launch of the poaching wildlife policing priority by the then Minister for Environment, Mike Russell MSP, in October of 2008. This had made people realise that police were taking poaching seriously and that it was worth reporting incidents that they encountered. I suspect that deer poaching had in any case increased in the autumn of 2008. There were two reasons for this: firstly the economic downturn was starting to kick in and more people were being tempted to make a quick buck; secondly the price of venison escalated, making even the smaller roe deer a valuable commodity. There were definitely more deer poachers becoming active.

The recovery in February 2009 of roe deer remains near Sheriffmuir, some twenty miles west of Perth, was particularly worrying. On this occasion the remains of two roe deer, a doe and a fawn of the previous year, were found dumped in a roadside ditch. The remains were in a strong plastic bag and were found by an estate head gamekeeper. I was returning from a conference when I got the call and coincidentally was passing the estate at the time. I looked in and together the headkeeper and I removed the contents from the bag, being careful not to contaminate any DNA that may have been recoverable. The deer had been expertly butchered, with only the valuable venison, the haunch and the saddle, having been removed. There was not a speck of dirt, a blade of grass or a leaf of bracken sticking to the carcasses; they had been taken to a clean environment, probably the poacher's home, to be butchered. In this case the deer had been shot with the proper calibre of rifle, and that was what worried me. It was almost certain they had been shot at night time and it would be highly unlikely that the poacher would be aware of what the backdrop was if his shot missed the deer. The remains were also recovered in an area with numerous road signs peppered by bullet holes. Is this sheer vandalism or is the poacher zeroing his rifle?

So far these have been deer poached by men with weapons, but many are also taken by men with dogs. (Note that I am saying 'men' rather than the politically correct 'people.' I would bet that there are no women out there poaching deer at night or taking them with lurchers). In April 2008 I had a call from a farmer to the west of Kinross to say that he'd found a roe buck in a wood up against a deer fence. The buck was, in the farmer's words, 'torn to bits by dogs.' He was sure that dogs had been put on to it from the roadside and they'd chased it into a wood, where they'd killed it. Exactly a year later I'd a call from the stalker on Scone Estates near Perth reporting three roe deer he'd found dead within a field-width of the narrow country road through the estate. He skinned one of these deer, a doe, and saw the tell-tale teeth marks on the neck and knew that at least this one had been killed by dogs. Thankfully the two almost fully-formed fawns in the doe had not been born, nevertheless they were still victims.

A week or so after this incident a doctor living on the outskirts of Dundee was out for an early morning walk with his dogs when he found the grallochs of two roe deer. Both again must have been does as there were four foetuses among the gralloch. On 5 May they must have been days from being born. The doctor was able to tell me that he had later spoken to his neighbour who had heard the sound of dogs excitedly barking just at daylight, which at that time of the year would be about 5.00 a.m. There have been similar incidents since. We did have two particular suspects, residents of Dundee, but so far to my knowledge they remained uncaught.

We were very close to catching two other men in Perthshire that we suspected were poaching deer. I'd a call from Les Fernie, the animal health officer for Perth and Kinross Council who had, the previous afternoon, been called out to examine a bag of deer remains. They had been found inside a wood, just beside the road, near the town of Blairgowrie. He'd left the bag where he found it, knowing it was the remit of the police rather than his, and emailed photographs he had taken. The bag was large and of clear polythene tied with a cable tie. Heads, legs and skins of roe deer could be seen through the polythene, and I could also see that rats had been having a chew through the bag at the tempting contents. By coincidence, a reporter from GMTV was coming to interview me about deer poaching so I thought the recovery of this evidence would provide a good story.

I arranged for the TV interviewer and a police officer from Blairgowrie to meet me on site just before lunch time. We all arrived simultaneously . . . to find that the bag had gone. I had been really hopeful of getting the DNA of one or even both of our suspects from the bag or the cable tie, which would be a good start to an investigation. The chance of that was lost, and whether it was spirited away by environmental health staff or the person who dumped the bag and thought better of it, I'll never know. Frustrations abound in this job.

I was sure that other known suspects, referred to in earlier chapters, were responsible for a horrific attack on a deer near Muthill in Perthshire in early July 2008. A farmer had watched what he thought was a fight between two large dogs in a field late one evening. He suddenly realised it was two lurchers attacking a deer and that there was a man in the field along with them. He called the keeper, Jock McDonald, who is well acquainted with the mix of worthies who regularly poach in west Perthshire, and who quickly joined the farmer. Unfortunately the man in the field realised that the farmer was onto him and ran towards the road, where a yellow van was parked. The farmer later related that there was much yelling and screaming from the direction of the van as the runner high-tailed it from the field. He interpreted this as the van occupant being the owner of the dogs and lambasting the runner for trying to clear out without first recovering the lurchers. The runner had almost reached the van when he about turned, ran back to the dogs then back to the van again, hounds this time in tow. The van with its cargo of murderous conspirators made off at speed, no doubt destined either for Greenock or Port Glasgow.

The registered number of the van was well known to me, and its owner was a friend of the man, John, that I surprised by referring to him by name when he previously visited me at our stand at the Game Fair. He certainly wasn't operating with a single dog, as he claimed he always did, and his manner of taking deer was hardly sporting. A later interview of the van's owner by Strathclyde Police took us no closer to being able to put a case to the fiscal. As with most criminals, unless there is evidence, they remain silent or deny any involvement. Thumbscrews are not permitted.

In the cases I've discussed, the dogs were deliberately set on the deer. There are many more incidents where dogs have simply not been under the control of their owners and have taken off after deer. There were two incidents in quick succession, possibly by the same dog, on Taymouth Castle Golf Course, Aberfeldy, during April of 2007. In the second incident the deer had been mauled but managed to drag itself off with its innards hanging out. In a much more recent incident (April 2011) a distraught man watched a deerhound at the other side of the River Braan in Perthshire near to the Hermitage chase a young roe deer down to the edge of the river. The dog then began to savage the deer and, in the manner of African hunting dogs, ripped through the belly of the deer and started to eat it alive. With the river between them the man could do nothing to scare off the dog, but took a series of photographs that bore witness to the grisly event. Despite a press release, the owner of the dog was never traced. Our fears were what the dog might have done had a child ran from it.

These cases are difficult to deal with since the dog has not been *deliberately* set on the deer. What had taken place is therefore not an offence under the Deer (Scotland) Act 1996. In a similar vein, a wild deer is not 'livestock,' that definition being reserved for farmed animals. There is consequently no offence under the Dogs (Protection of Livestock) Act 1953. We are pretty much left with an offence of failing to keep a dog under proper control under the Control of Dogs (Scotland) Order 2010 which is enforced by local authorities.

Though wildlife crime officers don't specifically investigate dog-related offences I'm usually told about sheep-worrying cases, and very often asked for advice by the officer dealing with the investigation. Many are run of the mill, with a sheep being killed or injured and the dog being caught at the time. Some are more difficult and often need much time and effort to get a result. We try to be innovative and use all possible methods in our attempt to prove that a particular dog was involved, none more so that during a case in 2007 when several sheep were killed by a dog near Carnoustie in Angus. PC John Robertson, a divisional wildlife crime officer who is now retired, was dealing with the case and had a suspect dog, but nothing to link it to the sheep that had been killed. John had possession of the dog, knew whose dog it was, but couldn't contact the owner. I suggested to John that he take the dog to a vet and ask that he make the dog sick. This he did, and was not surprised by the wool and mutton that was vomited up. Good evidence; evidence that in 2011, if required, we could take further by obtaining the DNA profile of the vomited mutton and comparing it to the DNA of the dead sheep. We didn't have to go as far as that in this case and faced with this evidence the dog owner pleaded guilty to allowing his dog to attack sheep.

In a case that started in mid December 2008, one sheep was killed and eleven others injured by a dog near the hamlet of Butterstone, Perthshire. The injured sheep were treated but all later died of septicaemia setting in on the wounds to their neck caused by the dog. The farmer and the landowner suspected a dog kept by a man who lived nearby, but there was no direct evidence at that time to connect it. The farmer shifted the sheep to another field but a couple of weeks later they were attacked again. This time four were killed and several more were injured and had to be put down. The same dog was suspected. The dog was a breed called a Tamaskan, and looked extremely wolf-like. Part of the description of the breed reads:

> The breed is highly intelligent and takes well to any kind
> of training. The breed need lots of exercise and are often
> used for sled racing. They should be kept mentally busy
> because they are smart and can become easily bored. When
> they become bored they will often be destructive.'

In the meantime I learned from a neighbouring landowner that he had seen this Tamaskan dog chasing sheep two years earlier, though this was not reported to the police at the time. He had also seen the dog chasing deer both during the day and at night. I passed this information to the investigating officer, who had difficulty in locating the dog owner since he had another house elsewhere. When he did find him, the suspect denied that his dog had been responsible.

At the time of the second incident I was contacted by the farmer and the person who owned the land. The sheep had been moved well away from the area for safety but would have to come back within a few weeks for lambing. Both were very keen that this case be solved before the sheep were brought back. I'm always keen on the use of DNA and wondered if it would help in this case. I contacted Dr Ross McEwing, an expert in animal DNA, and asked that if we got a sample of DNA from the suspect dog, and managed to get some samples from the throats of the sheep where they were gripped by the dog, could dog DNA be isolated and if so could a comparison be made with the sample from the suspect dog.

The answer was interesting. And expensive. If we took a swab from the throats of the sheep and there was dog DNA there it could easily be isolated. It would not matter if the swab was covered in sheep blood, as was inevitable, since it was easy to separate the two different types of DNA. If the dog DNA was isolated it would be easy to say whether or not it was from the suspect dog. Cost for the isolating the dog DNA from the samples would be £600, though Ross agreed to do it for half of that sum. Cost for the comparison would take the total bill over £1000. It was a lot of money but I thought we would get the samples first and worry about the cost if and when we had reached that stage.

I went later that day with one of the scene of crime officers to take the samples and to photograph the dead sheep. I've been involved with many sheep worrying cases but this was by far the worst. There was little or no damage to the back end of the sheep, which is usually present and is caused when the dogs are gripping the sheep and trying to get them on to the ground. There was a huge amount of damage to the necks of the sheep; in fact the heads were just about torn off them. This indicated to me that the dog had got the sheep on the ground easily and had gone for the throat immediately, causing massive damage. It had to be a big dog: probably a very big dog. We took the throat swabs, and a few days later the officer dealing with the case took a saliva swab from the suspect dog.

I spoke with senior police officers about the cost of comparison of the DNA samples. Not surprising, because of the cost, they were reluctant to go ahead. In the meantime the landowner had offered to pay part of the initial cost to establish if there was dog DNA in the samples we had taken. This was agreed with the senior officers, though we were not sure where the funding would come from if there was a positive result in the first tests. I spoke again with Ross McEwing, who was keen that this type of work be trialled and become more commonplace in police investigations. He very kindly agreed to carry out the complete examination free of charge, and I set off with the samples to his office, then in Livingston.

Up to this point the investigation had dragged on and by the time I got the samples to Ross it was March of 2008. The investigation took an unusual turn, and on the evening of 30 March I got a phone call at home from the neighbouring landowner, a good friend of mine, David Hendry. David told me that he and his keeper, George Simmons, had just shot the Tamaskan as it had been chasing after their small herd of Highland cattle and was very likely to chase them into an extremely boggy area of the field where they could become stuck or injured. The keeper had hit the dog three times with his high calibre rifle, to little effect, and in fact it was only finally knocked over and killed – to the astonishment of both men – by a shot from David's .22 rifle.

I asked David to make contact with the investigating officer, and in due course the Tamaskan's owner was charged with a number of offences relating to the worrying of the sheep and the cattle. In October 2009 the dog's owner pleaded guilty to the charge that related to the cattle. He was fined £200. There were no further incidents after the date the dog was shot. It was claimed by its owner as being worth £800.

In a completely different but equally horrific sheep-worrying incident in November 2009 on the edge of Abernethy in Perthshire a farmer found four of his sheep still alive but with their faces almost torn off. He called the police and a vet and the sheep were put down. The sheep were examined, even to extent of shearing the fleece off one of them, but they had no other marks or injuries whatsoever. As I explained earlier, sheep are usually gripped from the rear first, but not in this case. There was much speculation about what creature had been responsible. This ranged from 'big cats' through to badgers or even the white-tailed eagles that had been released over the past three years not many miles, as the eagle flies, from the farm. I was shown the photographs of the sheep, and I found it hard to believe that they had still been alive with the injuries I saw. The flesh had been ripped from half-way down their faces right to their muzzle, with bone and teeth exposed. It must have been terrifying and excruciatingly painful for the poor beasts. I knew it was none of the predators that had been mentioned, but could not put my finger on what beast had carried out these terrible injuries, then left the sheep without eating any part of them.

One of the advantages of having been a wildlife crime officer for so long was the number and range of experts in their own fields that I know. I copied the photos to a CD and sent it to Dr Hal Thompson, senior pathologist at Glasgow University Vet School. I then sent Hal an email explaining what was coming. Hal had seen this before and was able to identify the mystery beast that had attacked the sheep as a Staffordshire or pitbull terrier-type dog. These dogs apparently go right for the face and hold on. I suppose this has been evidenced already in the attacks on humans, usually youngsters, by pit bull terriers. In a way I wasn't surprised, but I was left wondering if there might have been human assistance. Knowing the type of people that are involved in dog fighting with pit bulls, and their training methods with the dogs, it would not be a surprise if they had held the sheep and encouraged their dog to attack it. I considered DNA again, but unfortunately by the time I was told about the incident the sheep had been incinerated.

There was a further incident on the same farm a few weeks later, this time with just one victim. I suggested swabs from the face of the sheep for DNA but the scene of crime officer went a stage further and took the head off the sheep. I now have a sheep's head in my freezer awaiting comparison with the DNA from any suspect dog that emerges.

A case some months later vindicated Hal's identification of a Staffordshire or pitbull terrier-type dog. Two old donkeys grazing peacefully in a field not too far from where I live were attacked by a dog that appeared to have all the physical characteristics of a pitbull terrier. Witnesses had to beat the dog off one of the donkeys, which it was holding by the nose and literally dragging along the ground. The dog did not *quite* have all the characteristics of pitbull terrier; (a pitbull is a *type* of dog, not a breed) had it done so there would have been even more charges against its owner.

CHAPTER 20

A Spate of Poisonings

THERE IS no question that the poisoning of wildlife is one of the most despicable wildlife crimes dealt with by police. The criminals – and that is the true representation of these people – who lay out poisoned baits have little or no control over which unsuspecting victim may take the bait, and over the years there has been a wide range of wildlife losing their life to this horrific and outdated illegal practice. Many of the pesticides involved cause muscle spasms and it is obvious from the position in which birds are sometimes found that they have suffered terribly. Generally their legs are stretched forward, their feet are clenched and the head is often arched back. On one occasion I found a dead raven that had stretched its legs so far forward and its head so far back that it finished up going over on its tail, which ended up bent backwards underneath it. The pesticide was carbufuran, a dark blue granular substance that was usually sold under the trade name Yaltox. It is one of the carbamate compound pesticides and is still the most frequently encountered after almost a decade after being banned. Medically, the symptoms of carbofuran poisoning include nausea, vomiting, abdominal cramps, sweating, diarrhoea, excessive salivation, weakness, imbalance, blurring of vision, breathing difficulty, increased blood pressure or 'hypertension', and incontinence. Death may result from respiratory system failure. Clearly not a nice way to die.

With these symptoms, of which the onset is rapid, it is logical that victims generally do not travel far from their 'last supper'. Most victims I have found are either lying beside (even over) the bait, or up to 100 metres away. It stands to reason that if a bird feels unwell it is not going to have either the energy or the will to fly. It may glide, in which case it will most likely go downhill for a short distance, but it will be unable to flap its wings for long, which takes considerable energy. Birds such as golden eagles, white-tailed eagles and buzzards are likely to gorge themselves if food is available. In the early morning when roads are quiet I've seen buzzards so full after eating a road casualty rabbit or pheasant that it can hardly flap up off the road ahead of traffic. Many are struck by vehicles and are obvious on roadside verges as casualties themselves. In the short time taken to have a fill from a poisoned bait, these birds are likely to feel extremely unwell even before they satisfy their hunger. The feeding habits of red kites are different, and I'll return to them later.

In Tayside we had been trying to work with landowners and gamekeepers for many years in an effort to reduce the incidence of poisoning. After high numbers in the late 1990s, from 2002 poisoning incidents were becoming less frequent. There were three reports in 2002, with two containers of pesticide and four baits being recovered, along with two crows, a sparrowhawk and a buzzard as victims. The majority of these baits and victims were found on Edradynate Estate, Aberfeldy. Note that I am sticking to facts *and only stating where the birds and baits were found.* In policing, officers must stick to facts and cannot make assumptions of guilt until there is sufficient evidence to report a case to the procurator fiscal and a court has subsequently found the suspect guilty.

In 2003 there were only two buzzard victims and a container of pesticide recovered. In 2004 three incidents saw the recovery of a container of pesticide, four baits and eight buzzards as victims. There is much more detail on these in *Wildlife Detective* with one of the cases resulting in a pigeon fancier being convicted. In 2005 no incidents were reported, and, even assuming that only a proportion of the illegal activity that takes place is either discovered or reported, I thought we were making progress. Alas, no.

In 2006 we really were back to the start again. A poisoned pheasant bait was discovered on Scone Estates, north of Perth, and a buzzard was discovered on farmland on the opposite side of the River Tay. No connection could be made between the two since different pesticides were involved. As it turned out the pheasant bait was not too far from a dead buzzard and a dead hooded crow that I picked up on the same estate back in 1996. The buzzard indeed turned out to be dead but the hooded crow, when I was about to pick it up and put it in a polythene bag, moved ever so slightly. I studied it for a couple of minutes and realised that it was still alive, as the sun had come out and the day was warming up. I suspected the buzzard had eaten a bait laced with alpha-chloralose, died, and was partly eaten by the crow. The crow had almost succumbed to the hypothermic effects of this pesticide but had been saved by the weather. It fully recovered in the police car and I later released it. I was amazed not only by the bird's recovery but also that it was a hooded crow, not the usual pure black carrion crows we get in the east of Scotland. Liver and gullet samples from the dead buzzard, and faecal samples from the rejuvenated crow confirmed my suspicions about the pesticide involved.

Still in 2006, a tawny owl and a buzzard were found on a horse and donkey sanctuary in Angus. The sanctuary owner is a very caring individual who was devastated when he found them; more so when he realised they had been poisoned. I was certain their deaths could not be connected to the farm on which they were found, and though we suspected they were linked to certain individuals elsewhere, we were unable to establish any evidence to confirm this. A shepherd's collie on Millden Estate, Glenesk, also fell victim to a most unusual pesticide: Gamma HCH, though we were unable to establish the origin of this pesticide. A poisoned rabbit bait found on Glenogil Estate, also Angus, led to a major police operation, and this in turn led to the recovery of another poisoned bait, this time a pigeon, and the discovery of traces of two different pesticides in five estate Land Rovers, two game bags and on four knives. Despite a thorough investigation, no person was able to be charged.

2007 was no better, though the circumstances were completely different. All five incidents were in Perthshire and, unusually, all involved red kites. These birds feed differently to other species. If anyone has ever seen red kites at one of the several feeding stations in the UK – a diversification from farming carried out by entrepreneurial farmers to augment their income and to provide a huge amount of pleasure to the public – they would see that the kite swoops down and picks up a morsel of food, without even landing in some cases. The bird then eats the morsel in the air or flies off to a nearby tree to eat the food at leisure. This different feeding strategy means that a kite that is poisoned may not be found so near the bait as may a buzzard. This demands a different investigation strategy by the police.

We had a suspect in the first of these cases, a kite that was picked up on Invercauld Estate at the Spittal of Glenshee in January 2007. Because it had rotted away almost into the ground, it had probably been dead since the spring of 2006. Search warrants are difficult to obtain and, contrary to the impression some folks have, the police can't just run out and get a warrant to search someone's premises or house on a whim. When we have a suspect we keep an eye on that person and very often they feature in other wildlife crimes. Evidence can build up and in time *may* become sufficient for a warrant to be granted.

With the death of the second red kite, found north of Perth in June, this would probably have been poisoned in springtime, but this time there was no suspect. Four years later I still have no idea who may have killed this bird.

In July a red kite was found on Glenturret Estate in west Perthshire, this time fairly fresh, maybe dead a month or so. We had no real suspect but made a search in an area about a mile or so radius from where the bird was found. This was much wider than we might search if the bird had been a buzzard, golden eagle or white-tailed eagle. After the search we were no further forward and the investigation was put on hold, though an interesting aspect of the investigation was the proprietary mix of pesticides, carbofuran and isofenphos, traced by Science and Advice for Scottish Agriculture when the bird was examined. The period of inactivity didn't last long, and in September another dead red kite was found on the boundary of the same estate but more than a mile from the first. It was beginning to decompose and could well have been killed around the same time as the first bird. This second incident tended to narrow the field down for suspects, and this was narrowed down further when a third kite was found in October in the very same area. All three birds had died of the same mix of pesticides, it was likely that all had been killed about the same time, and it was extremely likely that the same person had been responsible.

Finding the criminal and establishing sufficient evidence to convict him was always going to be difficult. If a gamekeeper was involved, as statistics show is very often the case, it is hard to prove a case even when there is only one gamekeeper responsible for that area. Some large estates, particularly intensively managed grouse moors, now have seven or eight gamekeepers plus a sporting manager, which, if they are thought to be involved, complicates the enquiry considerably. However prosecution doesn't always have to be the route that the police go down. A person being charged is one option, but if it looks like evidence is going to be impossible to obtain, stopping the criminal activity is as important, especially where rare and reintroduced birds are concerned.

On the estate on which I thought the answer lay I knew the owner, factor and head keeper well. I knew that the estate policy was to work within the law, yet no matter how often this is reinforced with employees, not all take heed. I spoke to the head keeper, and discussed my suspicions with him. He agreed to make his own enquiries and get back to me. He knew his employees better than I did and may well have had his own thoughts on the matter. The deal was that if he got the matter sorted it would end there. He worked quickly, and I had a call from the factor that evening stating that the head keeper had found out who had been responsible: one of the under keepers. I confirmed my deal with the factor and we agreed to meet the next day with the 'suspect,' since the factor wanted to speak with him and wanted me to do likewise.

It is important to have mutual trust and this is what made this route possible. The outcome was that an underkeeper was sacked and there has been no more poisoning in that part of Perthshire. I considered that a second prize, but a success nevertheless. The public seldom know of this work that goes on behind the scenes to try to safeguard wildlife, which is why I get so annoyed at blogs and other negative comments by people who don't realise the difficulties of getting convictions and the work police wildlife crime officers and others put in to try not only to enforce the law but to prevent people breaking wildlife laws in the first place.

May 2008 saw the recovery of a poisoned white-tailed eagle in Angus, just downhill from and just over half a mile from the boundary of Glenogil estate where we had the operation in 2006. The bird had not been dead long, perhaps a week. The bird had been found by the landowner and when the distraught man took me to the bird I knew from the typical pose of the bird in death that it had been poisoned. Though this was early in year two of the East of Scotland white-tailed eagle release and fifteen had been released in 2007, this was not one of them: it was a bird that had fledged on the Island of Mull in 2007. This demonstrates the distance that these magnificent birds travel. It would be true to say that the whole of Scotland is their territory.

Even before we had a result from SASA I organised a search uphill from where the bird was found. Halfway between where the eagle died and the boundary fence of Glenogil Estate a dead buzzard was found. The searchers – a police wildlife crime officer, PC Colin Proudfoot, and two members of RSPB Scotland investigations, Bob Elliot and Ian Thomson – continued uphill a few hundred yards from the buzzard to the boundary fence. The boundary actually took the form of three fences running parallel. The outer one, an old broken fence, appeared to be the original boundary, with a double electrified deer fence inside. The outer part of this double fence was the height of a normal stock fence, while the inner part was much higher, with the tops of the posts being six feet from the ground. Bob Elliot is 6'4", and his height was an obvious advantage when he spotted something. This turned out to be the first of 32 cubes of venison that they discovered on top of the posts, with half of a white hare lying between the double electric fence and the old march fence.

In due course, the analysis of the baits and white-tailed eagle confirmed the presence of pesticides, in this case a mix of three poisons. This made it reasonable to assume that the white-tailed eagle had been killed by eating either the venison cubes, part of the white hare or another bait laced with the same mix of pesticides. The analysis of the buzzard showed only two pesticides. From decomposition it had clearly been dead longer than the eagle and traces of the pesticide that was absent does tend to dissipate more quickly than the other two.

There was public revulsion when the death of the eagle, (named White G because of the letter G on the white wing tags), hit the press. Unfortunately no matter how sympathetic the public are to an investigation, and how desperately they want the person responsible caught, if there is no direct evidence linking the deaths to an individual then there is no case that the police can put to the procurator fiscal.

There was no improvement in 2009, which kicked off with a dead tawny owl found on the boundaries of two estates near Aberfeldy in Perthshire. Edradynate estate, on one side of the boundary, had a horrendous history going back more than a decade, of poisoned baits and victims being found on its lands. The owl was confirmed as having been poisoned, and led to a search on Edradynate Estate, where two poisoned buzzards were picked up by two police wildlife crime officers. The same month, March, took us back to Glenogil Estate after a report was received of a dead buzzard being seen, suspected of having been poisoned. Police wildlife crime officer Harvey Birse, and Ian Thomson of RSPB, went on to the estate and returned with not one but two poisoned buzzards.

There was no let-up, and during a further search of Edradynate Estate in April, we found a further three buzzards that were confirmed as being victims of poisoning. April also saw the recovery of a poisoned buzzard on Millden Estate, and in June the recovery a poisoned red kite on farmland near Tannadice in Angus. The red kite was still alive but died shortly after it was picked up. Kites may travel further before eventually succumbing to the fatal effects of their last meal and this distance may even be extended if they happen to be feeding chicks in a nest some distance from the bait.

In July a poisoned golden eagle was found on Millden Estate. This later hit the headlines with even more public fury than the killing of the earlier white-tailed eagle. The golden eagle had been named Alma by Roy Dennis, one of Scotland's top naturalists. In July 2007 Roy had fitted an expensive solar-powered GPS radio transmitter to Alma as a chick on an eyrie on Glenfeshie Estate near Kingussie in Inverness-shire. This was part of an exciting project to monitor the life of a young golden eagle, try to determine how they travel around Scotland (and indeed the north of England) and unravel the mystery of why many of them seem to disappear before coming to breeding age at about five years old. Alma's progress was not just monitored but was displayed regularly on Roy's website so that the world could watch her movements.

Roy was with PC Bob Russell and I when we picked up Alma's body. He was completely devastated, not only at the frustration of his ground-breaking work coming to a premature end but at the waste of the life of a healthy young golden eagle; a charismatic and emblematic bird that draws tourists to Scotland and a bird that hill walkers love to see on their days out in remote countryside. The GPS signal given by the radio transmitter at Alma's death gave a reading so accurate that it was less than 10 metres from where she lay in the heather. The long-time suspicion that many young eagles were being poisoned had, at least in Alma's case, been vindicated. Roy was equally distraught at seeing the few native trees that were growing up the sides of some of the burns on the estate had been cut down. These trees would have made ideal roosting places for birds such as a golden eagle. Was this why they were removed?

At the time we were investigating the death of Alma, another white-tailed eagle was found on the Glenogil Estate, later confirmed as having been poisoned. This bird had been dead for some months and despite a signal being transmitted by its radio tag, took a great deal of finding. This and other unavoidable delays due to crucial players necessary for the sequential progress of the investigation being on leave severely limited any chance of finding the person responsible.

A poisoned red kite was found in central Perthshire, almost on the boundary of three different estates. With no clear suspect (even yet) this made tracing the culprit extremely difficult. This was the last poisoned bird found in 2009, and including an incident with a poisoned buzzard I relate towards the end of this chapter, brought the total of poisoned birds to fourteen. If fourteen had been found, I wonder how many were poisoned and not made known to the police? Double that number? Ten times that number? Fifty times that number? Unfortunately we'll never really know the proportion.

It clearly illustrates how difficult it is to catch the person responsible for the poisoning of wildlife if I say that in only one of these fourteen instances discussed was there sufficient evidence to enable anyone to be charged. 2010 was little better, with three poisoned red kites, four poisoned buzzards and two pigeon baits recovered. By late April 2011 we already have recovered two poisoned buzzards, two poisoned crows and two pheasant baits. All of these recent investigations are still live so to avoid the risk of jeopardising any chance of a conviction I can give no more detail.

Though we had strong suspicions in some of the cases, none resulted in cases being submitted for prosecution. If, as the reader of this chronology of crime, you are frustrated, imagine how we as wildlife crime officers felt. However the luck of the wildlife criminal can't last for ever, as is demonstrated in the next case.

In September 2008 I was contacted by a couple of people who will always remain anonymous, concerned about the bragging of a gamekeeper who had recently moved from Invercauld Estate, Glenshee, to be a keeper on a low ground shoot near Longforgan, Perthshire (which I am not going to name as in due course the evidence showed that the shooting tenants did all they could to ensure that their employee worked within the law.) It appeared from my informants that the nickname already given to this man was 'The Terminator'; a man who allegedly wouldn't put up with any bird or mammal that posed a threat to the rearing of his pheasants. Since locals to his area had given him this dubious title, I'll stick with it. From my local knowledge, I knew the ground on which The Terminator worked to be rich in a wide variety of wildlife, including badgers. The specific information was that he was using the pesticide alpha-chloralose to 'control' birds of prey.

I have known for many years one of the shooting syndicate who employed him and my impression is that he would neither encourage nor condone the use of pesticides or any other illegal activity. More and more landowners are now in this mould, though it's unfortunate that a few remain who despise biodiversity and want little else on their land except a monoculture of grouse or pheasants.

When illegal practices are taking place, be it wildlife crime or any other aspect of criminality, it is usually not long before the police know about it. My information began to build up and within a few days I had another phone call about two dead buzzards that had been seen on one of the farms keepered by The Terminator. It was Sunday lunchtime and I was unable to get a wildlife crime officer either to make enquiries or to go with me. Since it was a time when the keeper was less likely to be about I had a quick look myself.

I had been directed to the birds, one of which lay about 200 yards from a wood on top of a hill. I found it easily enough: it was below a telephone pole in the middle of a steep field running down from the wood. It had probably been there for several weeks and had been partly predated by a fox or some other creature. My experience told me that it was most likely that it had picked up a poisoned bait in the wood and glided down to the pole. It had probably perched there and when it had become too ill, had toppled off on to the ground. This was a scene I had encountered many times.

I walked up to the wood and found a brand new pheasant release pen just inside the woodland edge. Fox snares were set round the pen and there was obviously a legal pest control programme in place. I had a walk through the wood, since the second buzzard was meant to be at the far end. A jay flew ahead of me screeching at my intrusion into its sanctuary and my disrespect at disturbing its life. I caught an occasional glimpse of its white rump as it kept a safe distance ahead of me. Jays are the wariest of birds, and are especially beautiful considering most of their corvid cousins are black. Jays seem almost pink in colour and have the most vivid blue feathers on their wings; feathers that are often used by fishermen in the creation of flies to tempt a trout or salmon. It is these special moments that bring some joy into what might otherwise be a negative reason for being in the countryside.

The second buzzard seemed to have disappeared, and the one that I had picked up proved negative for either shotgun pellets or pesticides. Nevertheless my informants were adamant they were correct in their assessment of what was taking place so I arranged a low-key search of the wood in a bit more detail than my earlier quick walk through in the company of *Garrulus glandarius,* an appropriate name for the jay as a bird that always has plenty to say for itself.

In this isolated countryside, a car lying at the roadside would be noticed by anyone with a suspicious – or guilty – mind. I therefore dropped off one of the wildlife crime officers, PC Shaun Lough, along with Ian Thomson of RSPB, for a search and I made a patrol of the roads in an unmarked car to see if I could see anything of interest that might further the investigation.

After a couple of hours I met up with Shaun and Ian. They had been searching in the area of the pen when they saw a small square of disturbed ground. They gently excavated the earth, to reveal a recently dead buzzard. Not far away they excavated another square of earth, to discover the remains of a buzzard on which a myriad of subterranean beasties had feasted, almost reducing the carcass to a skeleton. This was handy, since a small, perfectly circular, hole from a shotgun pellet was easily seen in the skull.

While the two searched another wood I nipped down to Dundee Airport with the freshly-killed buzzard and, courtesy of the security staff, ran it through an x-ray machine that was more used for looking for weapons or explosives than a few pellets in a bird carcass. Pellets there were, and not a few; the bird had been at fairly close range and had upwards of thirty pellets in it. These showed as small white dots on the black and white image, and small black dots on the coloured (brown) image, an image that made the buzzard look as if it had been in the oven for an hour and was ready to serve at the table.

So what could we do with this evidence? We could approach the suspect and reveal the strange burials beside the pheasant release pen that was operated by him. He was unlikely to make any admission, and we would have shown our hand. I trusted my informants, yet there was still no evidence of the abuse of pesticides to kill wildlife. A much better plan was to wait. This is a strategy that is in force in relation to a few shooting estates where we have strong suspicions of illegal activity but not enough to approach any suspect with any prospect of a prosecution or a conviction. It is a strategy that is used UK-wide, including in all of the incidents earlier related in this chapter. Aged 63 as I write, I might not have time to wait 5 years, but hopefully there will be a successor who will have that time and more.

Patience is a virtue, no more than in the investigation of wildlife crime.

Patience paid off.

In this case, the following August 2009, a Saturday this time, I had a call at home from a couple who had been walking in the wood round the new pheasant pen earlier described and had found a distinctly unwell buzzard inside the pen. They'd taken the bird home and I advised them to contact Shanwell Animal Rescue Centre in Dundee to collect it, but they phoned back a short time later to tell me the bird had died, and had vomited before eventually keeling over. I already had some suspicion that the bird had been poisoned; the vomiting confirmed it in my mind.

I collected the dead buzzard (and the vomit) and arranged a search for the next day. If it is possible to act quickly in a pesticide abuse case this has a better chance of success. I dropped off the searchers again, this time PC Charlie Everitt of the National Wildlife Crime Unit and Ian Thomson. The result was the recovery of a well-predated pheasant poult from the pen that I was sure would be the bait.

Buzzard and pheasant poult were examined and very quickly Elizabeth Sharp at SASA was able to tell me that both had traces of carbofuran. I was a bit surprised that this didn't tally with my information, as the pesticide should have been alpha-chloralose, but it was a positive result and we needed to keep up the momentum. In this case there was sufficient evidence for a warrant to be granted to search a shed I was told was used by The Terminator, where I suspected the pesticide may be kept.

A week later a plan was about to be put in place, and PCs Shaun Lough and Colin Proudfoot were in situ before daylight beside the pheasant pen awaiting the arrival of the suspect. I met another police officer, Peter Lorrain-Smith, not a wildlife crime officer but co-opted for the job in hand, Ian Thomson of RSPB and Willie Milne of Scottish Government Rural Payment and Inspections Directorate (SGRPID), both partner agencies in the investigation of pesticide abuse, outside the Perth police station. Daylight was breaking and as I was just about to get in to my car a peregrine shot over my head, not 30 yards above me. I just had time to gather my senses when a second peregrine followed the first. Unusual in a city environment, I suspected they were a parent and a chick from a nest site on the edge of Perth and were on patrol for early morning town pigeons that might do for a breakfast snack. The four of us left the office and waited in a car park a mile away from the pheasant pen. We were able to view the wood and the pen with binoculars and awaited the arrival of the key player in the drama that we hoped would unfold.

By 9.00 a.m, two hours after we had parked, there was no movement of our suspect. My information was that he fed the pheasants – still in the pen on 9 September, this rather late time of the year – just after daylight. Not today he didn't. I decided to send out two scouts, Jim and Willie, who wouldn't be known to the suspect, to see if there was any sight of him. In half an hour the two returned, saying that his Landrover was parked at the roadside at the other end of the estate, and that he was probably in the wood adjacent to the vehicle, though they had never seen him. In policing always expect the unexpected.

The unexpected happened. A quad bike suddenly appeared heading for the wood that held the pheasant pen, and I alerted Colin and Shaun, who I thought might be pretty cold by that time and would welcome some movement to warm them up. They phoned me a minute or two later to say that it was not our suspect on the quad bike, but a person who apparently fed the birds in that pen on a Wednesday. Bloody Hell.

We left Shaun and Colin with the 'temp' and the rest of us drove round to where the landrover had earlier been seen. No Landrover. We went to the shed that was covered by the warrant for a search to take place, but no sign of anyone there. It was an open shed and not the place I would have thought that game rearing equipment would have been stored in any case. We continued on up a dirt track and found a brand new shed that was much more like a safe place to keep equipment. Better still, there was a Landrover in the process of parking near the shed.

Peter and I drove across to the Landrover and I introduced myself to its occupant. This was our suspect. I told him why we were there and asked Peter to caution him. When I made him aware of the recovery of the buzzard and the bait from his pheasant pen he admitted that he had put the poisoned poult in the pen as he was 'getting hammered with buzzards'. I asked what he had put on the poult, and he said it was a mix of alpha (alpha-chloralose) and Yaltox (carbofuran). Next I asked him where his supply of the pesticide was and he took his jacket from the Landrover and produced a small tub from one of the pockets, handing this to me. I carefully opened it and saw half an inch or so of dark blue granules at the bottom. I suppose at that point our suspect realised that there was no going back.

The warrant we had did not cover a search of the unlocked Landrover, but in the circumstances we were entitled to search it using powers that Peter, as a police officer, had under the Wildlife and Countryside Act. In any event there was no need to use these powers. The Terminator anticipated what was about to happen and said, 'Well you'll find this anyway.' He went to the back door of the vehicle and in the manner of a magician producing a rabbit from a hat took out a dead buzzard. 'I shot this earlier with the .243,' he admitted. This was the .243 which was propped against the passenger seat of the Landrover, along with its smaller cousin, a .22.

We now had a clue to the use of two pesticides, though the contents of the tub were yet to be tested. If indeed the tub contained alpha-chloralose and carbofuran we would need to get the buzzard and the bait found the previous week re-tested to see if there was evidence of both pesticides in them. This turned out to be the case.

We also had to confirm, so far as was possible, that the buzzard had been shot with a high-powered rifle. I took the bird to Perth Prison, where the staff kindly allowed the use of their scanner. An x-ray confirmed that there was some serious damage to the buzzard; much more than would be the case if it had been shot with a .22. Since I've shot plenty of rabbits with a .22 I was happy that I knew the difference. If the case went to trial and the fiscal wanted a more detailed examination of the bird this could always be done by a veterinary pathologist at a later date. My preliminary examination, which cost the public purse nothing, would suffice meantime.

As it happened no further evidence was required. The gamekeeper – or by now the ex-gamekeeper – appeared in Perth Sheriff Court on 15 February 2010 and pleaded guilty through his defence solicitor to intentionally shooting a buzzard and to possessing a quantity of two pesticides with which he could commit an offence. His pleas of not guilty to a charge of intentionally or recklessly poisoning a buzzard and to possessing two rifles with which he could commit an offence were accepted by the Crown. I was not in court, but according to a newspaper report, the sheriff told the defence solicitor that, 'Anyone employed as a gamekeeper would be aware of very considerable restrictions there now are on the damage to and destruction of wild birds. Anyone in that position would be expected to know it was illegal.' He was not prepared to sentence that day and wanted the ex-gamekeeper to appear before him for sentence. Could this mean jail?

There are regular calls from a variety of organisations for a person convicted of killing birds of prey, by poisons or otherwise, to be jailed. There is absolutely no doubt that some deserve this fate, though getting the evidence to have them standing in a dock is fraught with a whole range of difficulties, as readers who have come this far in the book will understand. Statistics kept by RSPB over many years show that the occupation of the majority of people convicted of bird of prey persecution is that of gamekeeper. Most gamekeepers don't have previous convictions, and most people with a clean record, as it were, don't get jailed the first time they are found guilty of a crime or offence, unless for a crime at the top end of the scale such as murder, robbery, rape or maybe the poisoning of an extremely rare bird such as a golden eagle. There is no doubt that if a gamekeeper were to be jailed for killing birds of prey that would send out a very strong message and would act as a deterrent to others. But for a gamekeeper to be imprisoned it needs to be either for a series of wildlife crimes of the worst type or, as I have said, the person having a previous record.

The man dubbed by his neighbours as The Terminator appeared for sentence in due course. I was not in court to hear any pleas in mitigation put forward by his defence, though I knew the defence would major on this being the first time the ex-keeper had found himself on the wrong side of the law. On the first charge, that of shooting the buzzard, he was fined £400. He was admonished on the charge of possessing the two pesticides. An earlier motion by the prosecution for the forfeiture of his .243 rifle and telescopic sight, claimed to be worth £1,000, was withdrawn. A newspaper reported the presiding sheriff in the case to have told The Terminator just before sentencing, 'You may not have appreciated how serious the courts take the illegal destruction of wildlife. I think you will be aware of that now.'

Not everyone will agree.

CHAPTER 21

Crime against Bats

THOUGH bats are as furry as rabbits and guinea pigs, they don't muster up anything like the human enthusiasm and excitement that other wee beasties that can be handled, stroked and cuddled do. In their own right they are lovely creatures that deserve support and respect from us, but because there are fears that they might get entangled in ladies' hair or they might carry rabies they are at best avoided and at worst, neglected as protected mammals. Indeed their protection is extremely high. If the nest of a white-tailed eagle, one of our rarest birds of prey, is damaged, for this to be an offence it has to be shown that the act causing the damage was committed intentionally or recklessly. If a bat roost is damaged the offence is technically complete, whether or not the person causing the damage knew of the presence of the roost in the first place. A roost has further protection in that bats don't even need to be occupying it at the time of the damage.

So pay attention to bats!

Despite the law, some might consider the presence of bats a real inconvenience. This was exemplified in the summer of 2008, when I received a call from Scottish Natural Heritage to the effect that a building in Angus with a bat roost had been demolished contrary to planning permission. I allocated the investigation to Constable Kenny Linton, one of the divisional wildlife crime officers, but since he was exceptionally busy at the time and was about to go on leave, I agreed to kick off the enquiry. I wanted to establish if indeed there had been an offence committed, if so what were the circumstances and, more importantly, what was the evidence available.

I spoke with SNH staff first of all, and learned from them that a property developer in Angus had bought a house which he apparently stated he wanted to substantially alter for his own use. Planning permission had been sought by the man, who I'll call Dev the Developer for the purposes of the tale. Dev's plans were submitted to Angus Council and, as is the norm for council planning departments, were remitted to SNH for comment. SNH knew from records of bat workers that there was – or was likely to be – a bat roost in the property, and instructed that a bat survey be carried out before planning permission was granted.

The bat survey was carried out by a long-time friend of mine, Brian Boag, an expert in many aspects of wildlife, and bats in particular. Brian identified, through watching the house for bats emerging at dusk, that there were brown long-eared bats bats in the attic of the building. He produced a report in June 2006 – two years before the complaint was made to the police – that recommended mitigation measures to ensure the bats were not affected by the alterations to the building. In particular he instructed that the access points were not closed off, the work was not to be started before September of that year as there may still be bats roosting in the building, and that the alterations to the part the bats were living in were to be completed by 1 April 2007, before the bats returned to the property from their winter roosts and re-commenced breeding. Approval was granted on condition that a written plan to accommodate these mitigation measures was submitted. Dev the Developer could now go ahead.

It appeared that unforeseen problems were encountered and SNH staff were informed that due to these problems the work would only be partly completed by the deadline of 1 April 2007. This meant another visit from Brian and another report, which was virtually about how to make the best of a bad job. The bats, when they returned in April, were going to find the house partly demolished and that they had no summer roost in which each of the females could have their single baby bat.

A wee bit on the lifestyle of bats might be useful here for some readers. Long-eared bats hibernate for the winter, probably starting around late October or early November and continuing through till early April. The bats will probably hibernate in trees or places cooler than a house might be, and most will vacate their summer roosts in houses by September.

Having slept through the cold winters that we have to endure, bats come out of hibernation hungry, and on warmer April evenings, they are actively moving between several options of breeding sites. They become fully active in May and give birth to their single pup in late June, mostly in loft spaces where there is some scope to fly about. Numbers in the roost are generally low, and they tend to make little noise and if possible avoid areas above ceilings of occupied rooms. By July the pups are learning to fly and by the end of August the maternity colonies begin to disperse. September and October is the mating season, and once this exhausting period is completed the annual cycle is complete and the bats are ready to hibernate again.

But as I said, in April, the breeding site was gone.

Brian's second report recommended that the attic quickly be re-instated to accommodate the bats and that if possible it be done by the end of June. This was apparently ignored; in fact sometime in the last few days of June the whole house was demolished.

During the summer of 2008, once we had notification of the alleged offence, I started gathering evidence for Kenny Linton. I noted numerous statements from Angus Planning Department officers and took possession of a large number of documents that would be of value for a prosecution. I noted statements from the SNH staff involved and learned from them and from Brian that the bats had a maternity roost in the property since at least 2000 and would otherwise still have been there. I interviewed the previous owners of the property, who were incensed at the destruction of the bat roost. In their six years of residence they had been well aware of the bats and hated the thought that the bats had been made homeless.

In due course Kenny interviewed the property owner and charged him with destroying the roost, which is in contravention of the Conservation (Natural Habitats etc) Regulations 1994. This carries a maximum penalty of 6 months imprisonment and/or a fine of up to £5000. If a court considers that a person committed any crime for commercial gain then it is likely to impose a penalty at the higher end of the range. The case seemed sound and we had certainly put in a lot of work to get the necessary evidence. Kenny and I considered that we had done our work well and we and the various witnesses awaited the court case.

I try to monitor what is happening with wildlife crime cases submitted to the fiscal and I was concerned that I was never seeing a court date for this case. I knew the case was unusual and complex, and assumed that the preparation of the case by the fiscal was taking longer than usual. The Regulations state that a case must be called in court within six months of the prosecutor receiving sufficient evidence. This period was slipping away and I had visions of our work going down the tubes. I voiced my concerns to the detective chief inspector about this and another couple of cases nearly reaching their time-bar and he passed my report to the fiscal. I was shortly after contacted by a senior fiscal – not the original one to whom the case was sent – who thought it was a strong case and would progress it immediately. But the reminder, if fiscals should need a reminder, was too late and the case had run out of time.

I hate complaining about fiscals since police officers (and support staff wildlife crime officers) can get things wrong as well, but this was not the only wildlife case that failed to make it to court. I accept valid criticism and expect others to do likewise. I appreciate that fiscals have a heavy case load and their day is completely full; but then so is mine. I regularly take work home; but maybe they do as well. Where the difference lay was that I got it in the neck from the witnesses from Angus Council, from SNH, from Brian Boag, from the Bat Conservation Trust and many others. They had been expecting a court case and whatever outcome may have resulted from that. The fiscals were blissfully unaware of this fall out.

It was dusk on 3 May 2011 as I was typing this chapter and since it was about bats I went outside to see how many were flying around. Between the conservatory at the back door and the larch woodland 20 metres away is a place that the bats seem to favour. Bats need trees both for winter roosts and for the production of insects, and our garden with the woodland and the burns seems to give them decent foraging. The bats, which are pipistrelles, the most common bat in this area, wheel in figures of eight above the trees gorging on the myriad of midges and other insects that are equally enjoying a balmy late evening. On this occasion I could only see three, though it *was* still quite early. Eight is the most I have managed to count, but counting bats flitting over and through trees leaves plenty room for error. Counting them is even more difficult in summer, as there are packs of swifts darting and screaming through the evening sky, and if they're high in the sky they become bat-sized and confusing and make any effort to record numbers of bats over the garden almost impossible.

It is my own view, but I think that swifts are the real avian symbol of summer time, even more than their cousins, the swallow and the house martin. I can remember in my youth looking up at – and more importantly, listening to – vast numbers of swifts in what I assumed were family packs circling the houses and occasionally darting up under the gutter of an old tenement to a nest site. Having the advantage of all four toes pointing forward makes this scramble into the nest much easier. Conversely the disadvantage is that the swifts cannot walk on the flat and, apart from nesting, spend the remainder of their time – including sleeping – on the wing. They really are remarkable birds. Most of the old tenements are now demolished and with this reduction in nesting sites the reduction in swift numbers has unfortunately followed in parallel. Somehow I've digressed on to swifts, but I'll come back to bats.

I mentioned rabies earlier, and there can be no doubting that in relatively recent times the death of an Angus man from rabies was the result of a bite from a bat. In this case it was a Daubenton's bat, which I understand are the most likely to carry rabies. Even though the chance of contracting rabies from bats is extremely slight, I would never advocate the handling of bats without gloves. This was never a consideration in the 1970s when a bat somehow managed to enter the police station at Perth and was spotted hanging from the wall of the gents' toilet. I was notified (this was long before I became the force wildlife crime officer but most jobs relating to animals still seemed to come my way) and gently took hold of the bat to put it on the wall outside. I was not in the least surprised that it bit me, since that is a common self-defence reaction in frightened animals, but I never thought for a minute those tiny wee teeth would draw blood. Indeed they did, and, had this happened now I would have taken medical advice on whether I might need an anti-rabies injection. The chances are that I would not, but it was a lesson well learned.

Bat cases in Tayside are uncommon, and the next alleged offence was not reported until 2009. The report was made in late December that year by the licensing section of the Scottish Government, who had been asked by Dundee City Council to grant a licence to demolish the entrance building at the Camperdown Wildlife Park and to disturb the bats that were within the building. Initial enquiry was made by the Scottish Government staff, who realised that the application was retrospective, as the building had already started to be demolished and bats had been discovered. It was a highly unusual situation and one which the Scottish Government had no option but to refuse the licence and report the matter to the police.

I received the complaint, and passed it to Sgt Andy Carroll, divisional wildlife crime officer for Dundee, to investigate. His enquiries showed that Dundee City Council had granted itself permission in 2009 to demolish the entrance building at the Camperdown Wildlife Park in order to build a new visitor centre. Work had started on the demolition in November, but sub-contractors taking down a false ceiling had awakened two hitherto hibernating brown long-eared bats. The contractors stopped immediately and took the bats to the staff of the wildlife centre to look after. They are to be commended for this and I would hope that in other cases where bats are disturbed in situations like this, work stops until the situation can be better assessed.

During Andy's investigation it was clear from the staff at the wildlife centre that many of them were aware of a high number of bats living in the park. The countryside rangers were also aware of bats, but none was found who had been asked by Dundee Council if bats might be present. It was this lack of research, and of course the absence of a report by an ecologist or bat expert, that vindicated Andy's investigation. If an expert had been called in and carried out an inspection of the partly demolished building, as Andy did along with bat expert Dr Sue Swift, they would have found evidence in the form of droppings and wood stains of probably a dozen or so brown long-eared bats having lived there over a long period of time. All had been disturbed and had been forced to move elsewhere. Being partly-demolished, the building was now in a dangerous state and Scottish Government staff granted an emergency licence to allow the building to be demolished under the supervision of Dr Swift.

Unlike the last case, there was a meeting between Andy, I and the procurator fiscal. In due course a member of the council staff, as a responsible agent of Dundee City Council, was interviewed and charged with damaging or destroying the breeding or resting place of a wild animal of a European Protected Species, namely long-eared bats, which was in contravention of the Conservation (Natural Habitats etc) Regulations 1994.

In this case I think all of us agreed that the procedure undertaken by Dundee Council was sloppy rather than intentionally criminal. The matter was dealt with by a written warning by the fiscal, which I think was the appropriate outcome. We are lucky in Scotland that the range of options for breaches of the law is so diverse as to allow appropriate penalties ranging from police warnings, anti-social behaviour orders, fixed penalty tickets, warnings from procurators fiscal and fiscal fines before ever a person might land up in court and have a conviction which might severely limit his or her future job prospects. If an investigation is professionally dealt with from start to finish that is all anyone can ask for and no-one should have any complaint.

'A PIG in the close' was how I was described in a tale I related in *Wildlife Detective*; that situation I described is much rarer than being piggy in the middle. I finally retired on 6 May 2011 but felt throughout all of my time as the Tayside Police wildlife crime officer that I was stuck in the middle of a debate about birds of prey and game management.

In simple terms, most game managers and many of their representative organisations are of the view there are too many birds of prey, especially buzzards. On the other hand those who have a particular interest in birds of prey, such as raptor study group members, and some conservation organisations, particularly the RSPB, are of the view that birds of prey are just returning to the level at which they should be, and that in no way should any action be countenanced that might artificially control their numbers.

There is no question that the bird of prey interests have the legal high ground. All birds of prey are protected. End of story. So far as the police are concerned it is the end of any argument about killing or trans-locating birds of prey and it is not the business of the police to argue for anything different since the law currently states that neither option is legal. The argument, and any associated lobbying, is for those who would wish the legal position altered.

Gaining convictions in complex wildlife crime cases has always been a major difficulty. We see the same few solicitors defending these cases, or even assisting a QC to carry out the defence. They build up a level of knowledge and expertise that individual prosecutors couldn't hope to gain. This has been partially addressed by the appointment of regional wildlife specialist prosecutors, but even this had shortcomings. In February 2011 the Crown Office and Procurator Fiscal Service made the decision to reduce the current specialist prosecutors from fifteen to three. These three, in a full-time capacity, will mark all Scottish wildlife and animal welfare cases and prosecute these cases in court. This should be a much more effective strategy and I look forward to seeing the outcomes.

Legislation is continually improving and routes by which a guilty person may escape justice are being identified and, where possible, remedied. In addition, responsible organisations are trying to use peer pressure to try to reduce wildlife crime. Some say that peer pressure is not working, and for those who expect an overnight change to a problem that has been with us for more than a century, this is correct. However I was particularly pleased to read a quote dated 5 May 2011 from Scottish Gemekeepers Association committee member Bert Burnett in the news section of the SGA website. The quote referred to the investigation by Grampian Police into the poisoning of a young golden eagle. Bert said:

> 'The person responsible for the death of the young golden
> eagle found poisoned in Strathdon must be caught and
> punished for a crime which is an affront to nature. . . we
> need urgently to deal with the criminals who carry out
> these acts. They do not belong in twenty-first century
> Scotland and everyone who lives and works in the
> countryside needs to do everything in their power to put
> an end to these attacks. There is no place for anyone who
> believes this type of criminal activity will be tolerated.'

While many media comments from SGA over the years have been very defensive of their members and have even alleged planting of evidence, Bert's statement is a welcome change in attitude made *publicly*, (though I'm well aware that these have been Bert's views for some time). We might be making some progress and I'll watch with interest from the sidelines.

Of the wildlife crimes related to game management, without question the most difficult either to prevent or on which to achieve a conviction are those committed on large commercial upland shooting estates. Some of the landowners are in receipt of huge sums from the public purse by way of single farm payments. In some circumstances, where the Scottish Government is satisfied that an estate has been involved in certain aspects of wildlife crime, under cross-compliance where an estate receiving money from the public purse is obliged to comply with wildlife law, all or some of this payment can be withheld. An example was the withholding of £107,000 as part of the annual single farm payment made to Glenogil Estate after the recovery of poisoned baits from the estate in 2006. (The *Guardian* and *Scotsman* at the time reported that Glenogil had received public payments of £829,000 in the three years prior to these incidents.) This financial penalty, plus the new offence of vicarious liability in the Wildlife and Natural Environment (Scotland) Act 2011 may help to reduce wildlife crime, though I won't hold my breath.

The Scottish Government has been very proactive in relation to wildlife crime. £240,000 was set aside in late 2008 to cover the remainder of the 2008/9 financial year and the two years beyond that. This was a sum well in excess of what we might have expected, though when the coffers were empty at the end of the 2009/10 financial year the effects of the recession are still much in evidence and further funding on anything like this scale is unlikely. Crucially, some of this funding was channelled towards innovative methods of enforcement, as well as a range of awareness-raising and preventative initiatives.

One of the considerations of the Thematic Review of Wildlife Crime Prevention, Enforcement and Prosecution carried out on behalf of the Scottish Government in 2007 was that every force should have a nominated senior officer appointed as force lead on wildlife crime. Tayside took this on board but for a number of reasons the position always seemed to be transient. In my experience, unless a person knows that he or she will be in a post or have a responsibility on a long-term basis, changes and improvements tend either to be superficial or not made at all.

In early 2010 Superintendent Ewen West, deputy divisional commander at Forfar, volunteered for and was given the role of force lead. In my CID days I had worked regularly in incident rooms on serious crime with Ewen and was pleased at the appointment. Almost immediately he ensured that this aspect of policing was given higher priority. He increased the number of divisional wildlife crime officers, took great interest in the progress of investigations, supported ongoing operations and awareness-raising initiatives and formed a Tayside PAW group, the single recommendation of the Thematic Review we had not implemented.

Simultaneously Ewen changed my line management from Operational Support to Crime Management. This was role reversal as my new line manager was Detective Inspector Jim Smith, an officer of whom I had been in charge when he was a young police officer and I was his inspector. Being under Crime Management was another major step forward, even when Jim was later moved to a different role and replaced by Detective Inspector Caroline Lindsay. Wildlife crime was completely new to Caroline but her professionalism ensured she incorporated it seamlessly into her other crime management responsibilities.

In the autumn of 2011 all but three of the eight regional police forces in Scotland have a full-time wildlife crime officer. When the Tayside force knew I was to be retiring I was pleased when they confirmed that I was to be replaced, in a full-time capacity, by a serving officer, PC Blair Wilkie. This shows the importance the force place on dealing with this aspect of criminality, and the Force Executive is to be commended for this decision in what are pretty austere times.

Wildlife crime investigation is now on a much better footing in Tayside Police. Unfortunately I did not have long to savour this sea change before retiring, but at least I knew I had left the responsibility in safe hands. This was reinforced when I received a telephone call from the chief constable, Justine Curran, just before I walked out the door for the last time. Though we had never met, she said she was aware of and valued the work I had carried out in relation to wildlife crime over the (18) years. I knew it was ultimately her decision to support the continuation of a full-time post. I am glad of her stance and I appreciated her phone call. I have long said that the appointment of a dedicated senior officer as force lead is at least as important as a good full-time wildlife crime officer. My view had been vindicated.

Making a Difference is the current guiding maxim of Tayside Police. As I leave the service, after ploughing a lone furrow for so many years, I believe the correct management system is in place to make a difference.

Other wildlife crime books from Argyll Publishing

The Thin Green Line
wildlife crime investigation in Britain and Ireland
Alan Stewart
ISBN 9781906134372
312pp paperback £11.99
illustrated
A unique book that presents a wide-ranging survey of the scale of wildlife crime in Great Britain and Ireland today – and how the forces of law and order attempt to combat it. Full of fascinating case studies, this informative book appeals across the spectrum of police, prosecutors, the animal cruelty lobby, conservationists and lovers of wildlife and the countryside.

Wildlife Detective
a life fighting wildlife crime
Alan Stewart
ISBN 9781906134259
384pp paperback £9.99
illustrated
An insightful, informative and humorous account of over forty years policing a sector of criminal activity about which much of the public and even some police officers are unaware. Salmon, deer and game poachers are the stuff of folklore and *Wildlife Detective* explores the sinsiter and seriously criminal side of the business.

www.argyllpublishing.co.uk